TQM for Sales and Marketing Management

Other McGraw-Hill Books on Quality

TQM for Sales and Marketing Management

James W. Cortada

McGraw-Hill, Inc.

New York   San Francisco   Washington, D.C.   Auckland   Bogotá
Caracas   Lisbon   London   Madrid   Mexico City   Milan
Montreal   New Delhi   San Juan   Singapore
Sydney   Tokyo   Toronto

Library of Congress Cataloging-in-Publication Data

Cortada, James W.
    TQM for sales and marketing management / James W. Cortada.
        p.   cm.
    Includes index
    ISBN 0-07-023752-2
    1. Sales Management. 2. Marketing—Management. 3. Total Quality
management. I. Title.
    HF5438.4.C67   1993
    658. 8—dc20   93-37
                                                              CIP

1 2 3 4 5 6 7 8 9 0   DOC/DOC   9 9 8 7 6 5 4 3

ISBN 0-07-023752-2

The sponsoring editor for this book was James H. Bessent, Jr., the editing
supervisor was Marion B. Castellucci, and the production supervisor was
Donald Schmidt. This book was set in Palatino by McGraw-Hill's
Professional Book Group composition unit.

Printed and bound by R. R. Donnelley & Sons Company.

To my two daughters, Beth and Julia, who taught me the same lessons all parents learn: change is normal and it only gets better.

Contents

Preface

This is a book written by a sales and marketing manager for other sales and marketing managers who, like me, are struggling with some very substantial changes in our profession and our companies. The changes are profound, redefining our roles and our jobs in terms that we are not necessarily comfortable with. The good news is that enough is known about these changes to predict they will make it possible for us to thrive in a global economy with more customers who have rising standards of living, creating more demand for goods and services. But to get to these growing markets successfully we must discipline our actions in a more organized manner than ever before. How we do this is the subject of this book. The collection of activities and perspectives involved make up the concept of Total Quality Management, or TQM.

What I want you to buy are the underlying management principles of quality. Not only are they applicable in marketing and sales organizations, but they also are essential for your survival in the next several years. Change and competition are coming so fast that if there is a loud message in this book it is to hurry up and apply quality principles now. I promise not to present any harebrained ideas; everything you will read has been applied successfully in marketing and sales. What I will do, however, is avoid long strings of war stories; all they would do is make this a fat book which you probably would not have time to read anyway. But I will point you to other sources for detailed case studies if these are what you want.

The second commitment I will deliver on is to keep this book short because it is not intended to be a user's manual for corporate cultural transformation. All organizations transform and improve themselves differently from each other; there is no one right prescription. There are some basic principles on what is important and what gets done first, and some obvious errors to avoid. I fully expect that during your transformation to total quality you will make as many mistakes as have others, but in the end the benefits will outweigh the mistakes.

But why quality for sales and marketing? Isn't quality something of interest only to engineers and manufacturing types worried about how many well-made widgets they can produce more cheaply than the Japanese? What we are learning is that an effective corporation, which is light on its feet and can move rapidly in and out of markets with different goods and services, has to apply the same continuous improvement methods across the entire enterprise that were originally used only in manufacturing. All departments, divisions, and employees have to participate. The ideal is a seamless marketing focus from mailroom to boardroom with the same level of intensity that a salesperson exhibits on the last day of the month but with the discipline that auditors and engineers so prize. It is nothing less than a profound transformation of all that we do. To help you step up to that challenge—maybe the biggest one of your professional life—is our object.

Sales and marketing have to be part of that movement because they are the advocates of the people who really make us successful—our customers. We can do this by applying the principles advocated by quality gurus such as W. Edwards Deming, Joseph Juran, and Philip Crosby, and in a structured mode as suggested, for example, by the Malcolm Baldrige National Quality Award.

So much progress has been made in applying quality management principles in nonsales parts of companies that marketing and sales are next on the list for renovation. Already firms like Xerox, IBM, Motorola, and others have seen that improvements in manufacturing are not enough; the total job must be done across all sectors of their companies. At the moment Federal Express is the classic case of a service organization that has become another example of doing the total job and also buying in on a market-driven, customer-focused view of their business. This book is based on the proven methods currently applied in many such organizations so that you do not have to reinvent the wheel completely, just modify and apply it rapidly.

This book is not a primer on salesmanship or on basic customer-oriented marketing. I assume you understand those subjects and share my belief that good marketeers are close to their customers, always try to exceed their expectations and protect their interests within the corporation. I also assume you appreciate that the greatest assets you have in a world that values services more than merely a well-made product are your people. We share a common heritage of business beliefs that we will test, and in some instances, modify given the new realities. One quick example: Should salespeople be on quota? If not, why not? In a world moving to teams and experts, do individual quotas fit, and if so, how?

Sales and marketing organizations vary in their commitment to and involvement with quality. Thus to serve a wide range of readers, this book offers basic, even elementary, information as well as detailed tactical advice. If you are familiar with the basic concepts of quality management and the current interest in the subject, there is no need to read Chapter 1. If you are already comfortable with the concepts but not sure how to think of them in a sales organization or even whether they are cost-justified, then read Chapter 2. With Chapter 3 I begin the discussion of implementation—the focus of the rest of the book. If you are a practitioner of quality management today, you can begin reading this book with Chapter 3. The third chapter approaches the issues as corporatewide marketing strategy, while subsequent chapters take the process down to the sales district and branch office levels.

Thus this book reflects a desire to offer a balance between the theory of how to run marketing organizations in the TQM mold and the need to get tactical about how to bring it alive "on the street" with sales personnel in direct contact with customers. I end this book with specific suggestions for how to "jump start" or extend your journey to a quality-oriented, market-driven sales environment. I identify some obvious phases companies go through in case you have already started or need to know where you are on this path of continuous improvement, and along the way I point out pitfalls and opportunities. A short review of publications on related topics, with advice on where to get additional information, is offered at the back of the book. Each chapter also lists publications that deal in more detail with topics just discussed.

This book succeeds or fails depending on whether or not it is practical, realistic, and wise. Changing any organization is plain hard work. Most people will resist it, yet leaders of change will find going to work the most exciting aspect of their lives. There are no road maps, yet we know results can be spectacular. Market share expands, profits grow, revenues rise, employee satisfaction improves, and you win more customers. But nothing is free; there is a cost for change. I will point that out, too.

I came to the topic of quality in marketing and sales from personal experience. With nearly two decades of marketing and sales at IBM behind me, I thought I believed in quality—one of IBM's three basic beliefs is excellence in all that you do—and have been enjoying a thriving career. But I found that quality is a discipline of its own. In January 1990 I was asked to participate in the conversion of a marketing organization within IBM into a largely Deming-based one. I thought having run a $100-million-plus organization had been challenging, but this new assignment matched that one.

While for years a great deal of work on quality had been going on inside IBM, with corporate strategies and the nucleus of a marketing quality staff at headquarters for IBM U.S., most progress had been made in manufacturing—as in most major corporations. In fact, Deming had learned a great deal about his principles as applied in business by watching IBM early in life. IBM service organizations responsible for maintaining and repairing products had also applied many of his principles effectively. And while much was going in sales and marketing, it was embryonic in comparison with manufacturing. So I was exposed, in effect, to almost a complete cycle of startup-to-functioning of quality in a sales and marketing organization. As one of the first managers for quality in marketing, I had only the rudiments of a road map to follow, despite several years of previous corporate instructions and publications on what IBM called Market Driven Quality (MDQ) practices. Those early models were heavily influenced by manufacturing practices, while what we learned and what you will read about below is expanded toward a more service-oriented approach.

As this book appears in print the number of IBM employees dedicated to improving quality within marketing is extraordinarily high, while staffs with *Quality* printed on their foreheads are also substantial—and a true testimonial to IBM's historic commitment to quality and excellence. The company invested in these resources and processes at a time when it was attempting to reduce the size of its work force, lower expenses, and succeed in tough years for the information processing industry. Recall that it was also a period of war, a long recession, and the most intense international competition that the information processing industry had ever experienced.

What we learned about quality in sales and marketing, both in IBM Wisconsin where I cut my eyeteeth on quality and across the company, made me realize that organizations could be transformed. The topic was so important that it deserved its own book. I found that many corporations have shown a profound interest in applying quality to all facets of their enterprise, including marketing and sales. In short, what you will read about below is a report on some of the most wonderful and creative innovations underway in the economy of the western world.

This book would not have been possible to write without the help of many marketeers. A wonderful group of individuals at IBM, who have spent their entire careers in sales and marketing and who also are experts on quality, generously and bluntly critiqued the book and advised me on how to improve it. I have benefited enormously from their suggestions, although any failings in the book are my responsibility. My special thanks go out to this team: Marjorie Alhgren, Kris Hafner, Sharon Remer, and Sandy Illies. Others with equally strong practical marketing and quality backgrounds in other organizations were equally supportive: Steve Marlier, senior vice president of the Santa Fe Railroad; Chet Grimsley, director of quality for Industrial Automation Products at Allen-Bradley Company; Dr. Valorie E. Zeithaml of the Fuqua School of Business at Duke University; Linda Legband, a marketing director at ValCom; John Woods, president of CWL Publishing Enterprises; Mardi Coers at the American Productivity and Quality Center; and the staff at the American Society for Quality Control.

The team at McGraw-Hill worked smoothly to bring the book to light. Jim Bessent, my sponsoring editor, understands the importance of the quality movement sweeping the western world and is doing something to help—he is bringing books to market that support the effort. I am delighted he had the faith in my work to include this book in his strategy. Marion B. Castellucci is a wonderful copy editor who worked quickly and effectively. The production team pulled this book through the manufacturing process as fast and as efficiently as any "world-class" publisher could do.

My special thanks go to my family. There were many weekends and late evenings when I sat in front of my personal computer working on this book instead of being with them. They were patient and let me do "my thing!"

James W. Cortada

1

A Quality Revolution?

*I define quality as conformance to
requirements. Period. We should perform
the job or produce the product as we agreed
to do it.*   PHILIP B. CROSBY, 1979

> This chapter describes the quality revolution in the global economy,
> introduces the ideas of the important quality gurus, and concludes
> with the business justification for Total Quality Management in a
> sales organization.

Television stations run programs on the quality movement; our mail is
filled with brochures for expensive seminars on empowerment, Total
Quality Management (TQM), and Baldrige assessments; and we hear
about the American Society for Quality Control (ASQC). Customers ask
about our commitment to quality, surveys show people are willing to
spend more money for a quality product, while automobile dealers pay
attention to their rest rooms, survey customers, and avoid gouging
them on deals. Even organizations notorious for bureaucracy, such as
governments, have caught the quality "bug." Service is the byword,
used as if it had never existed before. We are told competition is global,
and that the Japanese make better products and are taking over the
world's economy. While evidence is mounting that this view is not quite

correct, nonetheless something different, not evident in the 1960s or 1970s, is clearly going on now.

What is happening is nothing less than the ground shifting underneath our feet. As the economies of the western world have shifted increasingly from manufacturing to service industries, new attitudes and requirements surfaced. Products are made all over the world and move rapidly from market to market. An American automobile fabricated in Detroit contains parts from Japan, Korea, Germany, and elsewhere. German automobiles also have parts from all over the world. Chances are the clothes you are wearing today came from various countries: your shoes possibly from Spain, your shirt or blouse from Israel or Asia, and your watch from Japan.

The ground is shifting in other ways as we change how we structure and manage our organizations. Tens of thousands of jobs are being eliminated in large corporations as downsizing becomes routine. Specifically, layers of management and staff are being eliminated, responsibilities are being delegated further down the organization, and manufacturing and sales organizations are being linked more closely together within one structure, as they had been more often than not prior to World War II. For example, at IBM several layers of management were eliminated in the late 1980s, while at AT&T and other large enterprises, divisional headquarters staffs were obliterated or transferred to field and factory.

The rapid changes in the world's economy are reflected in our daily lives through loss of jobs, gaining of jobs, the international configuration of our wardrobes, fabrication of the goods in our homes, and our tastes in music, literature, and other fine arts. The effects on manufacturing methods are increasingly understood, but the "quality revolution" has only just started to touch the lives of marketing and salespeople.

The purpose of this chapter is briefly to define the quality movement and explain some terms and concepts. Chapter 2 provides the formal case in favor of the new paradigm and then asks you to start the journey to quality in marketing and sales.

Shift to a Quality Emphasis

What has happened to cause this ill-defined quality movement to occur? To summarize a complicated topic, since the end of World War II traditional sources of wealth generation—natural resources, healthy national economies, and consumers and cheap labor—no longer are the basis of economic development. Technological innovations, inexpensive and reliable transportation, and communication have made it possible to design better quality products faster, manufacture them in countries where labor is cheapest or tax laws are most advantageous, and then to get them fast to consumers around the world. Manufacturing and distribution have become faster.

Companies began focusing on improving the quality of products for an increasingly global market not protected effectively by national economic policies.

What Companies Are Learning About Quality

One way to gain and sustain competitive advantage was to shorten the amount of time it took to design, build, and deliver a product. Known as *cycle time reduction,* this concept became a fundamental pillar of the quality movement. Automobiles that took seven years to design now take less than four; "high-tech" devices such as computers that were changed every five years now are replaced with new products in less than two years. One conclusion many companies are reaching is that the largest number of opportunities to improve cycle time lie outside manufacturing, which represents from 60 to 90 percent of the cases in which cycle time reduction has already occurred.

The second observation manufacturers made was that sustainable competitive advantage could not be achieved by having better quality products. Everyone was now using robots and computers, for example, to ensure products were consistently made to higher standards. They had to add value to what they made, and that meant enveloping products with services customers found attractive. Services differentiated one vendor's fine products from another. Having warranty and service agreements with automobiles, washing machines, computers, even credit cards rapidly became the norm in the late 1980s. Services often turned out to be more profitable than the actual products.

As it became increasingly obvious that more technology had to be applied and that services had to be wrapped around products, companies drew a third conclusion: that the only difference maker was people. How companies capitalized on their human resources differentiated them from competitors. American, German, Japanese, and other national economies all had access to cheap labor, technology, and fabrication plants. But the work forces varied widely from country to country, industry to industry. Robert Reich, professor at Harvard University, argues that as economic activity becomes globalized, a country's "most important competitive asset becomes the skills and cumulative learning of its work force" because it represents the one asset that has not been duplicated worldwide with the same consistency as technology.

That realization led corporations to focus more on the quality of the work force: its skills, efficiency, and attitudes. They made greater investments in training, showed increased concern in many nations about the quality of children's technical and scientific education, and moved decision making and responsibility for improvements to those most knowledgeable about problems to be solved. In most cases that meant empowering employees with the responsibility and authority to make changes on the plant floor. Applying human resources most efficiently did not mean working them harder, just differently. At the end of the 1980s, William Byham's book, ZAPP! The Lightning of Empowerment, in which a fable about empowerment is told, became a best-seller, "must reading" among managers working on the cutting edge of people empowerment. How the process of encouraging, delegating, teaching, and managing people changed is the subject of most discussions about the quality movement. Subsequent chapters will describe how to make the human resource asset in marketing and sales more efficient.

The New Role of Managers

No longer could managers just tell employees what to do and when. Life had become too complicated; managers could not be expected to keep up with so many changes so quickly. Their role began shifting from a traditional "command and control" approach to a new model in which they created environments in which workers could take the lead in setting targets, determining tasks to be done, and measuring results. In this new world managers spend more time facilitating by knocking down barriers that get in the way of employees doing what they need to and by training and coaching, and they spend less time inspecting or ordering.

This has not been a smooth process. In the past, individuals became managers because of their ability to control, inspect, command, and make decisions, and now they were being asked to push aside those patterns of behavior in favor of a more participatory style in which consensus among employees is strived for, in a world where making mistakes is allowed as improvements are attempted. They must reward people for quality improvements, skills development, and a more intense effort to service customers.

Many organizations realized that their structures had to change, moving from many layers of employees, in a classic pyramid design, to fewer layers in a more horizontal structure, with more cells of organizations operating increasingly on their own in a matrix formation. Instead of an executive "seeing the whole picture" and thus being able to direct and coordinate activities of various groups (e.g., manufacturing, distribution, sales, and administration), we increasingly see organizations that have reduced layers of management by more than half.

These organizations focus instead on creating a corporate culture that encourages independent leadership and ownership of tasks and processes at much lower levels. The role of "seeing the whole picture" is pushed down the organization. In practice that means employees need to know more about what the entire enterprise does and hence must see their tasks as part of larger, interconnected processes—just as senior managers instinctively did before.

The Value of Processes and Flattening Organizations

In this environment, it becomes crucial to create a system or set of processes that allows traditional functions to support each other efficiently. Design has to work with and feed output to manufacturing, manufacturing has to talk with distribution and sales, sales has to link back to both manufacturing and design with customer preferences. All have to work efficiently and quickly at peer levels without having to go to higher-level managers for coordination. That can only be accomplished by looking at all the activities of a company as processes or even as one seamless process. Much of what I talk about in the chapters that follow addresses this issue because in the world of TQM it is imperative that a system of matrix-based processes exist from one end of the enterprise to the other for this kind of organization to succeed.

Why go through all this effort? Aren't the risks of failure enormous? Tinkering with the culture of an organization is dangerous, particularly with that of a successful company. It is difficult to do, yet it is being done successfully. The benefits outweigh risks and costs. It turns out that traditional management overhead drove operating costs up since at least one-third, and up to two-thirds, of a manager's time was spent inspecting employees' work, hence, the rising tide of complaints in the 1980s about companies becoming bureaucracies that were too inwardly focused. The new idea is to eliminate managers, which eradicates overhead expense and shortens decision lines since there are fewer people from whom to get permission. You drive down costs, offer products less expensively yet still profitably and more quickly. Better-skilled employees work more efficiently, thus the results are better and quicker. Technology gets applied to support processes rather than to perpetuate existing structures and practices. Organizations get lighter on their feet and can become more outwardly focused toward customers.

Companies in the 1970s and increasingly in the 1980s found that as they moved into new structures and better applied different technologies in an increasingly competitive world, they had to become more market-driven. For large organizations that was a different realization than they had experienced before. They had to become less inwardly focused and had to respond to market changes faster and with products customers wanted. Survey after survey in the 1980s and 1990s indicated customers were less brand-loyal than before and made more decisions based on quality and functionality. Product introductions increased quickly as competitors leapfrogged each other with new wares and services. The speed with which money traveled through the world economy increased, and markets got "hot" and "cold" quickly and globally.

The Need for Shared Corporate Values

In a matrix-management world few people were available to espouse the culture and mission of the organization. A common set of values had to be developed against which empowered employees could frame decisions. The answer was an obvious one: what the customer wanted. By the end of the 1980s being "customer driven," "delighting the customer," "exceeding customer expectations," and so forth was raised to a fever pitch of almost religious intensity. Corporations changed their measurement and reward systems to ensure increased attention to customer requirements. They developed new processes that interlocked customer feedback on goods and services through sales organizations, service, manufacturing, and design so that they could deliver increasingly what customers wanted, when they wanted it, and at a competitive price.

The greatest progress in building this ideal, seamless organization came only on the manufacturing side of the house. There processes for total quality are frequently in place, employees are most empowered, and product design is tightly linked through culture, technology, and processes to fabrication. Yet if you go to companies experienced in revolutionizing their manufacturing, they will acknowledge that the quality movement has only just begun to permeate their office populations and has hardly appeared in marketing or sales. Influential American companies, such as Ford, Xerox, Harley-Davidson, and Allen Bradley, are now moving into the white-collar sectors of their enterprises, applying the lessons learned on the shop floor. Some point with pride to service organizations that have begun to implement quality processes, such as the repair of industrial equipment or the serving of hamburgers at fast food restaurants, but even in these instances efforts are still tentative.

Only organizations with no manufacturing have taken significant steps in applying quality principles in warehouses and offices. Federal Express and UPS are obvious examples, but so too are the more progressive insurance companies and even some government agencies (e.g., the U.S. Internal Revenue Service).

Yet marketing and sales remain a new frontier for the quality movement. Increasingly it is becoming obvious that marketing and sales are the eyes and ears closest to the customer and thus a vital link in any organization that aspires to respond quickly to rapidly changing market conditions with the right products and services.

Definitions of Quality

There are many definitions of quality; however, they all share the common assumption that quality is defined by the customer. Quality is identified with a body of practices emerging in business and government as defined by various quality gurus, whose disagreements sometimes border on religious wars and turf battles. The term *quality* increasingly requires a comprehensive, organizationwide embrace of a definition or set of processes for implementation. That is why you will hear phrases such as *Total Quality Management, Total Quality Control,* and so forth.

W. Edwards Deming, a leading quality guru, calls it "continuous improvement," while many executives say that they know quality when they see it. Another quality guru, Joseph M. Juran, speaks of "fit for use," while another authority, Philip Crosby, uses the phrase "conformance to requirements." Americans often speak of value received for dollars spent, while Europeans emphasize quality engineered into their goods. A Japanese quality expert, Kaoru Ishikawa, thought in terms of a product that is "most economical, most useful, and always satisfactory to the consumer."

Corporations have struggled with definitions too, because it is important to settle on one that can serve as the inspiration for quality values and practices. Although products have functional characteristics that define quality, there are also process-related aspects. Take the process-related aspect, often called "the moment of truth," when an employee deals with a customer. How that interaction takes place will define quality in the mind of the customer. A rude clerk renting a customer an automobile will leave an impression of poor quality in that client's mind, as will a hotel room not cleaned up. Neither situation is product-based but rather both are service-based. Quality is created at the moment of performance, not in a factory designing in functional quality.

What is received is often the focus of quality, but so too is *how* a customer receives quality—a crucial distinction for service organizations. IBM defines quality as a "delighted customer." Xerox focuses on delivering "innovative products and services that fully satisfy their requirements." Increasingly corporations are crafting their definitions around what customers perceive to be quality rather than the older rallying flag of performing to a set of standards. You see this in such phrases as *market-driven* or *voice of the customer.* Yet many of the engineering paradigms remain and arguably help quantify improvements: *zero defects, six sigma, defect-free, conformance to requirements,* and so forth. They apply squarely to marketing and sales organizations.

The need for definitions of quality that fit into service environments has led to a great deal of research on the nature of service work. We know that service work involves performance more than products and has a very large labor component. In addition, since consumption of a service occurs as it is performed (produced), consumption and production are inseparable and perishable—they occur once, such as an airplane flight or a restaurant meal. Customer-oriented definitions therefore call for focus on the reliability of services provided, willingness or responsiveness of a vendor to service a customer quickly, ability of employees to offer trust and confidence, empathy (we used to call this "customer rapport"), and a good business environment (clean store, well-groomed employees, working equipment).

How to Develop Your Definition of Quality

Developing a good definition of quality as it applies to your organization and customers is an early and crucial exercise. If yours is a firm long in business it has probably developed a reservoir of culture relating to ill-defined notions of excellence that can be sharpened. If your company is relatively new, quality principles can become your management system. The definition of quality becomes part of the cultural baggage you acquire while developing a believable working vision of your company's future. I will have more to say about vision in later chapters since it defines the focus and culture of your organization.

If you do not have a definition of quality, begin formulating one. Three basic steps are effective:

- Ask your customers or clients what they think quality should be.

- Solicit ideas from your employees, particularly those on the sales and marketing side of the house.

- Determine what your competitors worldwide use as a definition.

There are several good rules of thumb to follow while you are formulating your definition of quality.

First, think of two types of customer-focused quality or satisfaction: The "big C" customer, who is the individual who selects and pays for your goods and services, and the "little c" customer, who is every employee whose work you depend upon or who depends on the output of your efforts.

Second, make your definition general enough so that it fits your entire enterprise and is consistent with your vision. It is imperative that your employees "buy in" on the definition because they have to develop strategies for implementing it and measurement systems for determining success. It is often difficult to separate your definitions of quality from a vision statement. This is not a perfect world, so the confusion is tolerable because definitions of quality and vision both speak to what an organization should do and to what level of performance—they are mutually inclusive ideas. The effective definition will ultimately be developed in the measurement systems of success and will be documented by how customers vote with their money on your goods and services.

Visioning is a complex subject about which whole books have been written. However, a good vision statement speaks to an ideal state that an enterprise wishes to achieve. For example, one marketing organization visualizes a world in which its customers always turn to it when there is any kind of a problem to solve. An accounting department envisions a world in which bills routinely go out without errors. The information processing department at Land's End speaks of providing world-class service to the rest of the corporation. IBM says its end state vision is "to be the best at creating value for our customers and all those with a stake in our success."

Visions, like definitions, must be plausible, generate confidence that they are attainable, and be important enough to be worth all the hard work necessary to attain them. They are statements about the future and provide a focus for all activities.

Your Definition Must Be Communicated and Applied

Once armed with a definition, you must communicate and apply it. These actions are as important as the definition itself. First, each employee must understand the definition. That can be done through traditional communication and with executives constantly discussing it.

Second, the definition must be applied to strategic planning and measurements. Effective strategic planning today embodies the creation of a vision and an end state of what the business would like to be in some period of time (say in three to five years). That vision is often a value statement that can incorporate a quality aspect (such as best customer service, quality products, and so forth). When armed with a statement, you can ask, How are we going to apply quality to our daily activities? Building strategies and tactics that address how you are going to implement your quality definition and corporate vision is integral to making quality management part of the fabric of your business.

The Quality Gurus

Whenever we have had a fundamental change in the way organizations operate, individuals have stepped forward to describe the new paradigms, and invariably they each have had a slight twist on the subject. That is clearly the case with the quality movement. It is important to understand the basic tenets of each of the major proponents of quality because the views of a particular expert influence profoundly the application of quality in an organization. Those who follow Deming do things differently than those who follow Juran or Crosby, and so forth. Consultants who work on quality programs also are of one school of thought or another and that too affects their performance.

There is nothing wrong with mixing and matching. However, it is a central concept of this book that just as you want good marketing plans for getting your products to market and supporting customers, and just as a good salesperson plans each sales call and knows how he or she will "sell," so too you need a quality game plan that is comprehensive. And just as in sales, your results will be measured largely by how much business customers do with you. The fact is, quality can and should be measured essentially the same way in any business: by profit margins, productivity, market share, revenue growth, customer satisfaction (loyalty), productivity, return on assets, and so forth.

As in any profession, there are superstars in the quality world and an army of experts behind them, either espousing one of their views or trying to create their own. They affect the quality movement profoundly. Some of the experts will be introduced in references at the end of each chapter or in Appendix C. At this point you need to know the superstars of the basic quality landscape; later you can focus on some aspect of this new topography.

W. Edwards Deming

W. Edwards Deming is the man the Japanese say taught them how to get on the quality path in manufacturing in the 1950s and for whom they named their national quality award, similar in purpose to the U.S. Baldrige National Quality Award. He is also probably the biggest superstar of quality. Lloyd Dobyns, in a television program on quality in the fall of 1991, called him the philosopher of the movement. Deming argues in favor of continuous improvements in all that we do, based on deep and profound knowledge of our tasks, jobs, professions, industries, education, society, and ourselves.

Deming believes in the joy of work. He has argued since the 1930s that activities should be measured by using statistical analysis so that progress can be understood. Continuous improvement is a never-ending cycle of events. Decisions should be based on facts (data), not on gut instinct or mere experience. Nothing is constant, and relationships with customers and employees are ever-changing, ever-improving. Deming's philosophy has a trinity of beliefs: constancy of purpose, continuous improvement, and profound knowledge. These are reflected in a 14-point program. Some of his 14 points are considered more important than others, although he urges people to embrace all. For our purposes, several are crucial.

Constancy of purpose—his first point—calls for appreciating what business you are in and how to stay in that business. It implies that the definition is not one that changes frequently but it is one that you have to get right. Being in the computer business is a bad definition if what you are really in is the information processing business. Being in the car business is not the same as being in the transportation business. There are traps in all definitions of your business; he argues that you must be careful and pick the right one.

Continuous improvement—his fifth point—means that everything constantly changes and therefore you must develop processes that lead you to improve everything. Nothing ever reaches perfection; customers and suppliers change needs and services and so must you; the economy and technology change and so too must you. You develop a plan for moving the ball forward toward better quality goods, services, and so forth.

Profound knowledge is the means by which Deming's fourteen points are applied. Profound knowledge involves understanding systems, a theory of variation, psychology, and knowledge. Systems are collections "of functions or activities" that are clearly understood within an organization. People working within a system work as a team on common goals; Deming cites a well-run orchestra as an example: people, management, equipment, facilities, mission, customers, and services, all of which are continuously changing and improving.

The study of variation is simply the application of statistical analysis to understand what is going on and why, so that corrective actions can be taken when appropriate to improve performance. Workers with less than a high school education are applying basic statistical processes relatively easily, although so far we do not see this activity as prevalent in sales organizations.

Deming's theory of knowledge is that no insight or fact is absolute or definitive. If you change the way you count something, the results will change too. There are no right answers, just answers generated by the methods used to generate them: "Change the procedure, get a new number." Knowledge is good for predicting outcomes based on measuring data. That means you do not just copy someone else's approach to solving, for example, a business problem without appreciating what effects it might have on your unique situation.

Deming believes all people have an innate desire to achieve and to be esteemed by others. That is how he gets to the idea that there should be joy in work. You and I are familiar with this concept in another way: we know people who succeed in part because they like their jobs. A crucial consequence of his idea, however, is that many of our measurement systems are extrinsic in that they reward and punish, knocking out the intrinsic desire for success with rankings, appraisals, merit pay, and punishments. If you are responsible for the performance of a sales force, for example, Deming would criticize you for having quotas and bonuses. He would argue that quotas lead to measurements of success and failure based on whether or not someone achieves his or her imposed targets. Variable bonuses, he would argue, reward and punish people; instead, he would have you strive for a culture that compensates but does not punish. I will deal with these highly emotional issues later.

Deming Challenges Our Practices. Deming challenges many basic tenets that made managers successful. His ideas call for a great deal of hard work and new attitudes toward jobs. He insists on a transformation of how we manage organizations away from a hundred-plus-year tradition to a new one that affects all aspects of an enterprise. His prescription has been called holistic because of its comprehensive nature. Deming would not believe that your company could attempt to improve products continuously without also insuring that marketing and sales were just as intimately involved in the restructuring of services, manner of performance, measurements, and philosophy of operation.

While Deming has been criticized by some for not understanding sales and marketing (he never was in sales), his ideas nonetheless are very applicable. For one thing, he too subscribes to the idea that you serve others, specifically customers. That service, however, is not limited to simply doing what customers want. You have to also figure out what customers need and persuade them. He frequently argues that no customer ever asked for the light bulb; it was invented and then sold. Deming believes that all parts of an organization must work in a coordinated fashion. Sales must tell product development what is needed, manufacturing must communicate and train sales on its products, and both must find common, sensible ways to measure performance effectiveness. Both must work on improving the skills of employees and implementing a common vision.

In the past several years, Deming has increasingly begun focusing his attention on the role of services. In his seminars, speeches, and publications, he is spending more time articulating how his 14 points apply in nonmanufacturing environments. As this book goes to press, he is completing yet another volume describing how to apply his ideas. The bottom line is that his ideas are applicable to sales as much as they are to manufacturing.

Philip Crosby

You probably remember Philip Crosby from a best-selling book he published in 1979 called *Quality Is Free*. It became a best-seller because it was clear and blunt and more prescriptive than Deming. Crosby is most associated with the concept of *zero defects,* or the "do it right the first time" approach to quality improvement. Rather than have managers simply accept the statistical notion that some things will always go wrong, he settled on the notion that you should design and build in prevention of defects. Management's role is to study the process by which things get done in organizations so that one can build in preventive measures to ensure things get done correctly the first time. In turn that reduces costs of operation and manufacture, hence quality is free.

Crosby has a list of four "absolutes of quality management."

First, "conformance to requirements," not specifications, ensures that you are performing to what customers want and not necessarily to what engineers desire.

Second, his management system for quality is prevention. The idea is simply that if you can design out defects you save the cost of fixing problems later. A great deal of work has been done to document the wisdom of this approach in manufacturing where, for example, an additional expenditure of $40 for an automobile part can prevent a more expensive one from failing, requiring a recall valued at millions of dollars.

Third, the idea he is best known for is the concept of zero defects. Unlike other gurus who have a statistical view of the world in which some errors are accepted as inevitable, he argues that goods and services should be produced without fault. This is a concept that is heavily debated and is now being restudied in light of service industry activities in which the product is the performance done in front of the customer (e.g., booking a reservation on an airplane).

Fourth, measure quality with the price of nonconformance, which is an elegant way of saying that you can quantify your failures (defects) in hard numbers. Nonconformance to zero defects is more expensive than conformance.

Joseph M. Juran

Closer to Deming's views than Crosby's, Joseph M. Juran espouses three ideas and treats statistics merely as a tool, whereas Deming uses statistics almost as a management process. Juran believes in understanding what customers want and who they are, and in responding to their needs by applying the correct technology. The three most important components in a quality program are:

- senior management
- the training of all employees to improve quality
- the rapid improvement of quality, even in a revolutionary manner

More than the others, Juran urges speed in improvement as a way to remain competitive. Breakthrough thinking that overturns old processes plays a more important role in his world. He places more emphasis on the role of senior management in leading the charge for change. But, like Deming, he believes that considerable investments should be made in teaching employees how to make changes. These range from using statistical analysis to measure performance all the way to such difficult topics as strategic and tactical planning. We will see again the need for urgency when we look at the Baldrige Award, in which the points you can get have been shifting increasingly to results achieved rather than plans created.

"Fitness for use" is a Juran pearl—his way of saying what the customer wants. Begin with that concept and then build quality programs around it. In short, his gospel is that of the market-driven organization.

Armand V. Feigenbaum

Less known than Deming or Crosby, Armand V. Feigenbaum is nonetheless an expert. An engineer, he first learned about quality at General Electric during World War II, and eventually he became that company's head of manufacturing quality. He is important because, like Deming, Feigenbaum has had a following, particularly in manufacturing companies that today are taking his ideas and exporting them to nonmanufacturing parts of their organizations. He has published less than the other gurus, which is probably why Feigenbaum is a less familiar name than Deming and Crosby.

Feigenbaum has a simple definition of quality: "what the buyer says it is." Other gurus disagree since customers may not always know what you can offer and thus you have to stay ahead of your customers and competition. But customers still vote with their purchases, and perception of quality is increasingly a factor, not just price. Feigenbaum argues that the idea of quality is a process for managing how you achieve customer satisfaction, more competitive pricing, and greater employee satisfaction. He too argues that looking at facts about performance (using statistics) is critical to the successful improvement of any process or task.

Kaoru Ishikawa

The gurus discussed above are all Americans, have for the most part worked on quality since the 1920s and 1930s, and today are celebrities in the business communities of the western world. Japan also has quality experts, some of whom are known in the United States and in Europe. Perhaps the best known is the late Kaoru Ishikawa, father of the quality control circles first developed in the early 1960s.

In the United States these were called quality circles in the 1970s and 1980s. They were groups of knowledgeable employees who made suggestions for improvements. These circles worked only if management took the ideas for improvement and facilitated their implementation. Ishikawa argued in favor of total quality control (TQC), in which all members of an organization have to participate in quality improvements—not just management, not just workers. Quality standards have to be set, while management owns the primary responsibility for improvements. There has to be continuous education on quality and never-ending improvements, all of which lead to reduced costs and better sales. Ishikawa puts the customer in the center of his vision of quality improvement, not the corporation nor any group within the enterprise. Customers are defined as anybody receiving the output of any work done by an employee (the concept of big C, little c customers).

What Quality Experts Have Learned

While all of these gurus had variations of ideas and often debated the merits of each other's concepts, several messages come out loud and clear from them and from those who have implemented their notions:

- You must approach quality specifically and systematically.
- It takes time to implement quality; quick fixes do not work.
- All employees must be involved and be empowered at all levels to make decisions regarding quality.
- Quality requires focus and concentration (e.g., Deming's notion of constancy of purpose).
- Quality is a management process and a business strategy that leads to competitive advantage and less expensive products of superior quality.

- Customers are the central focus of all improvement processes.

- Managers often get in the way of an organization's transformation and are at fault if the workers do not produce quality in all that they do.

In subsequent chapters, we will apply the ideas of these quality experts to a sales organization.

References

Crosby, Philip B. *Quality Is Free: The Art of Making Quality Certain.* New York: McGraw-Hill, 1979.

Deming, W. Edwards. *Out of the Crisis,* 2d Ed. Cambridge, Mass.: MIT Center for Advanced Engineering Study, 1986.

Dobyns, Lloyd, and Crawford-Mason, Clare. *Quality or Else: Revolution in World Business.* Boston: Houghton Mifflin, 1991.

Ishikawa, Kaoru. *What Is Total Quality Control? The Japanese Way,* translated by David J. Lu. Englewood Cliffs, N.J.: Prentice-Hall, 1985.

Juran, J. M. *Juran on Leadership for Quality: An Executive Handbook.* New York: Free Press, 1989.

Nanus, Burt. *Visionary Leadership.* San Francisco: Jossey-Bass, 1992.

2
The Concept of Total Quality Management

The increase in productivity has been caused primarily by the replacement of labor by planning, brawn by brain, sweat by knowledge. PETER DRUCKER, 1973

This chapter focuses on defining Total Quality Management in a sales organization. I introduce the application of the Baldrige management model to sales and provide cost justification for quality in business.

In its simplest form TQM is the notion that there should be a comprehensive master plan for continuously improving quality in an organization. Hundreds of books and thousands of consultants are now available, each with their own system or approach to TQM. Regardless of which one you settle on, the key is a *comprehensive* approach to quality that cuts across all functions and levels of an organization. Anything less does not work well. That is why manufacturing companies, for example, are expanding their quality programs into sales and service departments and why service industries are pushing quality into the backroom or directly out onto the floor where customers are serviced.

Using Quality as a Strategic Weapon

TQM is strategic; it is a broad set of processes that enhances your competitive advantages, leads to continuously improving products and services, and results in loyal customers who come back for more goods and services. It is design talking to marketing and sales, secretaries meeting the needs of principals promptly and efficiently, telephone operators responding to customer calls in a friendly and prompt manner. It is executives investing in their staffs' education on quality and skills needed to perform their work, in an atmosphere in which mistakes are tolerated if lessons are learned from them and applied to making things better. It is a basic belief of the enterprise that each day it can become better and that all employees are infected with the enthusiasm and "religion" of improvement.

Order and common sense are applied systematically to all activities. Heroes are not just those who sell more but those who exceed customer expectations—a true hallmark of service. Failures are turned into opportunities for demonstrating concern for customers' well-being and for compensating them for the firm's failing. Quality becomes a higher purpose: are you building a wall or a cathedral? A small company called C-T-R changed its name to International Business Machines, an obscure automobile company to General Motors, a local telephone company became the American Telephone and Telegraph Company.

Key Concepts in Quality Strategies

Built into the notion of TQM are various ideas presented by the quality gurus:

- continuous improvements
- zero defects
- do it right the first time
- employees closest to the situation know best how to improve it

The center of all discussions is the customer; everyone inside and outside the organization is a customer. Competitive advantage can be gained by reducing the cycle time required to design, develop, and sell products before starting the process again. Product offerings increasingly require services and quality in all that happens.

Measurements of performance track quality indicators and not just financial numbers. Measurements are used to indicate how quality is improving but also to suggest areas for enhancement.

Heroes are people who practice the new thinking and achieve improvements, often working in teams, today called *natural work teams*. These are virtually self-governing groups of employees who look at what is possible and set their own goals, measure their own performance, and define their own activities. They call on managers to facilitate change and knock down barriers. Natural work teams allow supervisors to spend less time inspecting and more time coaching.

Three Basic Quality Concepts in Sales

There are some central concepts of TQM, characteristic of effective quality initiatives, that apply directly to sales and marketing functions.

1. *Information.* A basic tenet of quality programs is that decisions are based on facts. Knowing what your competition actually does and not what you think it does, for example, has been with us a long time. Comparing your processes, tasks, or results (known as benchmarking), however, is relatively new. *Benchmarking* is the act of taking an existing process (for example, billing) and comparing it to the best same process in other companies (e.g., American Express's billing system) to find ways to improve yours and to set goals. The act of benchmarking can cause an organization to set more aggressive goals, for example, for profit attainment, levels of customer satisfaction, or service quality in order to keep up with or exceed the results of competitors. Benchmarking also can lead you quickly to better ways of doing things without having to "reinvent the wheel," which takes time and may not lead to the best improvements.

In a quality-driven environment, information that can be acted upon, not just data (i.e., numbers), is crucial. One form of information comes from executives and managers. They communicate corporate philosophy, what is going on the firm, what the game plan is, and their expectations. In a quality-driven organization it is not uncommon to see senior executives continuously preach the gospel of quality rather than simply focus on last month's sales revenues.

Another form of information is all the data required to perform a service. For example, a quality-driven organization builds customer data bases that provide salespeople information on all kinds of transactions with customers (e.g., billing, what is on order, contacts, previous revenues, annual report data, names, titles, telephone numbers, and so forth). At both IBM and Westinghouse, for instance, salespeople are responsible for gathering increasing amounts of such information while their firms are working to integrate various older files to provide more composite views of customers.

Accurate orders, delivery date information, specifications, and other data make service to customers faster and of better quality.

Information on patterns of performance is increasingly evident closer to those who perform the tasks measured. For example, more often today we see organizations capturing data on accounts receivable trends by customer, sales office, and product or service type. Others collect information on sales opportunities and leads identified by salespeople, who load the data into computer systems. The information is then tracked over time, becoming input for manufacturing and for developing educational programs to build employee skills.

But what specifically is different about the information gathered in a quality-driven world? For one thing, more information is collected about how well things are being done, not just about what gets done. For example, the speed with which telephone calls are answered is measured daily in a quality world, not just how many calls were answered this month. Providing information more frequently, in trend format, is characteristic of quality organizations. Knowing what your expenses were for a month 45 days later does not make you as quick on your feet as knowing 2 days after the close of last month. A quality-focused organization would know exactly how long it took to get expense data to you, would have measurable goals for reducing that time, and would track progress toward that end. Finally, quality-driven organizations make a concerted effort to improve the accuracy and relevance of the information provided. Billing errors are tracked, their causes are studied scientifically, and the effectiveness of their elimination is measured and studied for continuous improvement.

2. *Cycle time reduction.*   Getting to market with a new product or service before your competitors has long been understood by both manufacturing and sales organizations. What is relatively new, however, is looking at all activities as processes that can be improved. Part of the definition of improvement is the reduction in the amount of time required to perform a process. The *rate* of improvement and the *amount* of reduced time are important. They are tracked while targets for further cycle time reduction are set. Cycle time reduction can be as simple as putting customer files on-line so that when they call to find out the status of an order, the answers can be called up on a screen quickly rather than sought out in a file cabinet. It can be reducing the time between shipping and billing a customer, or finding ways to reduce the "sell cycle" from three months to one. Faxing orders to suppliers instead of mailing them is an example of cycle time reduction in the order entry process that can have significant impact on the speed of delivery of information and products to customers.

Cycle time reduction is one of the most important ways to achieve sustainable competitive advantage. In fact, a growing number of executives, particularly in marketing, argue that cycle time reduction is the single biggest benefit of quality improvement efforts because it contributes directly to elimination of errors, delays, and bottlenecks, while improving the ability to do things right the first time and increasing the delivery of new products and services to the right customers before competitors. Linking technology (e.g., computers and fax machines) is a useful way to reduce cycle time. But more important is looking at all customer-related activities as processes (collections of tasks) and finding ways to reduce the time from one end of the process to the other. The act of redesigning processes is called *reengineering* today.

3. *Tasks and processes.* Important in improving quality in any function is the notion that tasks should be looked at as processes, as families of activities. Documenting all the steps required, for example, from taking an order from a customer to delivering it means you have to understand how orders are taken, entered into an order processing system at the office, communicated to a plant, scheduled for delivery, communicated to the customer, and then ultimately shipped, and if need be, installed. Quality experts argue that by documenting the tasks as a process in a flowchart such as Figure 2-1, you can then look for ways to reduce the time from order receipt to fulfillment.

When you look at such a process you will find that you can improve it. This concept is called *entitlement;* that is, all existing processes have built into them room for improvement that you are "entitled" to because you have the process in place. You can measure the cycle time as it is today, make improvements, measure the effect of your changes on cycle time reduction, make more improvements, measure those, and so forth.

But at some point you cannot improve the process any further. It is as "tuned" as it can be, and your statistical survey of cycle time reduction will show a stable condition in which month in and month out orders are processed more or less in the same amount of time. To improve beyond that point requires a radically new order entry process (e.g., the customer orders directly from the plant, not from your salespeople).

New order entry processes can only be achieved if you set goals for cycle time reduction that cannot be reached by improving a well-understood existing one. Looking at what other firms have done (benchmarking) can get you to a new process, but so too can your employees brainstorming ideas and applying their knowledge of what customers want, how manufacturing and administration operate, and what the costs of developing new processes would be. If your competitors can satisfy an order in 30 days and your "tuned" system takes 45, you know that you have to beat

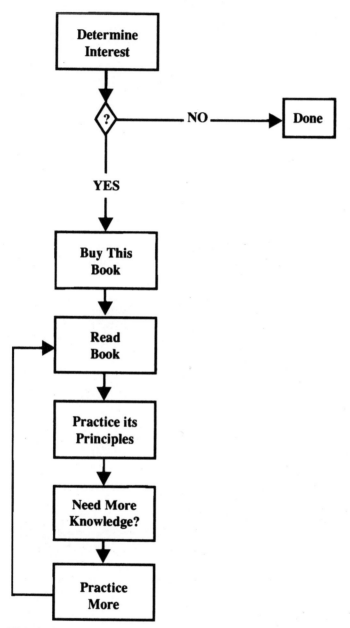

Figure 2-1 Learning about quality: an example of a process flowchart.

30 days. If you decide on 15 days to really nail the competition, you design a new system to do that, but first you must understand your existing system and how it compares to the competition's.

By looking at tasks in groups (processes) you can gain profound knowledge of a function (Deming's idea), design out defects in tasks and not just products (Crosby's suggestion), while creating an atmosphere of constant improvement and customer focus. Sharing ideas with customers to validate that they are worth implementing, and doing your sharing in an organized manner, in itself is a process.

Figure 2-2 (Deming's concept) illustrates continuous process improvement as it might appear to a natural work team. Figure 2-3 shows the interaction of customer focus with an enterprise's activities in more marketing terms. Note that it begins and ends with the customer. Marketing and sales are at the point in the figure closest to the customer and hence are at least as important to the improvement process as manufacturing.

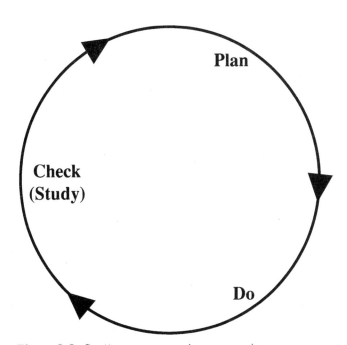

Figure 2-2 Continuous process improvements.

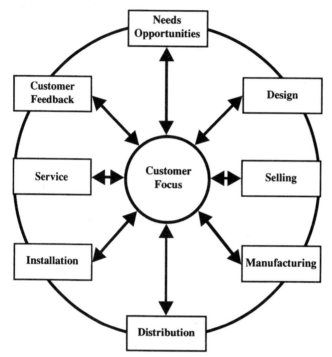

Figure 2-3 Interaction of customer focus with an enterprise's
activities.

The Baldrige Approach to Quality

There are many models of how quality should be implemented. An increasing body of empirical data suggests how quality implementation should look in service organizations, including marketing and sales. The model that is becoming the standard choice in the United States and that will serve as the model for subsequent chapters of this book is the Baldrige approach.

There is a debate about the pros and cons of the Baldrige criteria for quality. However, each year hundreds of thousands of managers, executives, and employees study the Baldrige paradigm and implement it. Increasingly customers want to know what a firm's commitment to quality is; the Baldrige criteria offer a measurement of that commitment and a framework for discussion and improvement. The award associated with the Baldrige approach is also prized as the most prestigious award in American industry, perceived to be worth a fortune in free advertising. In Japan there is the Deming Prize and in Europe there also is a similar award—all three are intended to encourage and recognize achievements in quality improvements.

The Malcolm Baldrige National Quality Award was established in honor of the secretary of commerce in the Reagan administration who espoused the need for quality improvement in business to enhance U.S. competitiveness. Established by the U.S. Congress in 1987, it is administered by the National Institute of Standards and Technology and the American Society for Quality Control, and it is awarded annually to up to six firms: two in manufacturing, two in services, and two small firms. Selection is based on a rigorous measurement of quality achievements in seven categories worth varying points not exceeding a total of 1000. Its underlying assumption is that quality is defined by the customer; thus category 7 (customer satisfaction) is worth several times more in points than, for example, category 3 (planning). Figure 2-4 is a flowchart of the Baldrige framework.

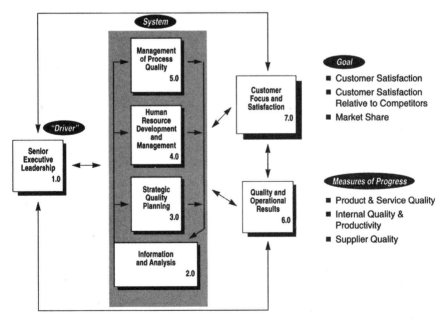

Figure 2-4 The Baldrige model: dynamic relationships in the award criteria framework. (*The 1993 Award Criteria: The Malcolm Baldrige Quality Award.* Milwaukee, Wis.: American Society for Quality Control, 1993, p. 5.)

Key Elements of Baldrige

Senior executives are charged with creating the values and goals of the enterprise and the environment that makes possible sustained pursuit of quality improvement. They drive the organization toward TQM. What the enterprise does to fulfill the vision of quality improvement is gather and analyze information to judge performance, plan the implementation of improvements and quality, deploy and improve employees, and manage the quality process, which constitutes the system or activities of the organization. Two sets of results are looked for: operational results and customer focus and satisfaction. The Baldrige award examiners look for a system of well-defined and well-designed processes that actualize the quality vision. The success of the system is what they look for in quantifiable terms in categories 6 and 7.

The model calls for continuous improvements in results over time with "ever-improving value to customers." The Baldrige model will not tell you how to improve but rather how well you are doing on your journey toward continuous improvement. Those familiar with the process argue that the greatest benefit is that it provides a structured view of your strengths and weaknesses in your terms. Thus it can lead directly with confidence to an agenda for improvements. It prizes fact-based decision making, measurement of process improvements and results, a customer focus, cycle time reduction, better products, more skilled employees, and a long-term view of the business.

Because the Baldrige criteria are so widely accepted and serve as a useful way of measuring progress, a more detailed description of the categories can be found in Appendix A.

Why Baldrige Is Valuable

Not all the quality gurus like the Baldrige Award. They think too many people are focusing on the award rather than on improvements in quality. However, acceptance has been so overwhelming that such criticisms are being brushed aside. The same is true in Japan with the Deming Prize because these awards offer a structured agenda that creates a bridge from the theory of quality to what we have to do on a daily basis in factories and offices.

The emphasis of the Baldrige award has also changed over the years to reflect the increased urgency of competition on a global basis. The premium is for faster improvement and more results sooner. Figure 2-5 shows how the points for each category have changed over the past several years. If you did not modify anything or change results since last

Baldrige Evaluation

Examination Categories	1990 Maximum Points	Δ	1991 Maximum Points	Δ	1992 Maximum Points	Δ	1993 Maximum Points
1.0 Leadership	100	+10	100	− 10	90	+5	95
2.0 Information and Analysis	60	− 30	70	+10	80	− 5	75
3.0 Strategic Quality Planning	90		60		60		60
4.0 Human Resource Utilization	150		150		150		150
5.0 Quality Assurance of Products and Services	150	− 10	140		140		140
6.0 Quality Results	150	+30	180		180		180
7.0 Customer Satisfaction	300		300		300		300
Total Points	1000		1000		1000		1000

Figure 2-5 Point breakdown of Baldrige assessment, 1990 to 1993.

year, and last year you did a Baldrige assessment, this year you would get fewer points. If you or your customers expect improvements, as measured by the Baldrige criteria, you would have a problem that could cost you business. At a minimum the dynamic characteristic of the Baldrige criteria is a reflection of the quickened pace of competition and the need for extensive commitment to a quality process. The bottom line is that even in an award, competition forces everyone to raise the bar. President George Bush, commenting on the essence of the Baldrige effect, stated the case well:

> Quality management is not just a strategy. It must be a new style of working, even a new style of thinking. A dedication to quality and excellence is more than good business. It is a way of life, giving something back to society, offering your best to others.

One final question about Baldrige is who should do an assessment. Is it just the IBMs of the world or small enterprises? Can one part of a business participate but not another? The answers are relatively simple: any size organization or part of an organization can conduct a Baldrige assessment. The process is the same. In fact, doing an assessment today of just the sales side of the house gives you a laundry list of problems to address with other parts of the enterprise. In Chapter 4 I offer a tactical approach to conducting a Baldrige assessment.

Why Quality Is Justified

What is the cost justification of quality? Many readers have enjoyed successful careers not doing any of the things spoken about in this chapter, so why change? The objective of this chapter is get your commitment to implement quality improvements in your marketing and sales organizations immediately. So you need to know if it is worth it. We understand the global nature of quality competition and how it can appear from out of nowhere, even from countries we never heard of before. But even if you only compete with a small business within one state, you need quality in sales and marketing.

Consumers Want Quality

In 1991 the American Society for Quality Control (ASQC) published results of a Gallup survey of consumers in the United States, Japan, and Germany. This was the latest of several surveys by the ASQC, which had learned from previous surveys that quality was a significant determinant of what customers buy. In all three countries, consumers were willing to pay substan-

Which Country Has the Best Quality Reputation? (Consumer Responses by %)			
Product	U.S.	Japan	Germany
Automobiles			
United States	41	1	2
Japan	36	71	18
Germany	18	23	78
Don't Know			
Personal Computers			
United States	48	12	14
Japan	39	80	45
Germany	1	1	33
Don't Know	12	7	8
TVs and VCRs			
United States	28	2	2
Japan	66	91	59
Germany	1	1	37
Don't Know	5	6	2
Clothing			
United States	89	17	7
Japan	3	75	3
Germany	2	2	87
Don't Know	6	6	3
Cosmetics			
United States	81	21	23
Japan	2	68	4
Germany	2	3	67
Don't Know	11	12	6
Health Care Services			
United States	75	23	8
Japan	6	52	4
Germany	9	12	84
Don't Know	10	13	4

Figure 2-6 Global quality reputations. (Adapted from American Society for Quality Control, *Looking for Quality in a World Marketplace*. Milwaukee, Wis.: ASQC, 1991.)

tially more for a product if they perceived it to have outstanding quality. For example, 80 percent of Americans were willing to pay more for quality shoes; 44 percent of the Germans and 41 percent of the Japanese said the same. Looking at automobiles, 29 percent of the Americans, 9 percent of the Germans, and 15 percent of the Japanese polled were willing to pay more; for washing machines, 52 percent of the Americans, 32 percent of the Germans, and 21 percent of the Japanese would pay more.

Americans believe the quality of the products they buy has actually improved worldwide over the past five years. American manufacturers'

Consumers Rate Services in Their Country (Percentage Rating High Service Quality)			
Service	U.S.	Japan	Germany
Banks	48	26	55
Hospitals	46	18	48
Hotels	43	37	40
Airlines	37	32	42
Insurance Companies	32	17	38
Auto Repair	28	21	40

Figure 2-7 Consumer service ratings. (Adapted from American Society for Quality Control, *Looking for Quality in a World Marketplace.* Milwaukee, Wis.: ASQC, 1991.)

recent emphasis on improving quality is now appearing in survey data, which indicate the American public's growing confidence in local products and services. In 1988 only 48 percent of Americans thought American products were improving; in 1991, 55 percent. In ranking quality by nation, Japanese goods were rated first, U.S. goods second, and German goods third. American consumers viewed U.S. products as having more quality than German or Japanese consumers thought. Figure 2-6 provides additional statistical data on perceptions. Only 3 percent of Japanese consumers and 21 percent of German consumers think U.S. workers are committed to quality, although 61 percent of American workers think so. In the global market U.S. hard goods do not enjoy as good a reputation as do its services and soft goods. In the U.S. word-of-mouth advice on quality is crucial to the success of a product or service; in Japan it is function, while in Germany it is price.

In the United States quality is determined in priority sequence first by brand name, then by word of mouth, next by past experience, and finally by performance. Out of eight categories, price was seventh. The top four categories of quality determinants for the Germans were price, well-known name, appearance, and durability, while for the Japanese they were well-known name, performance, ease of use and price. When asked what criteria helped determine the buying decisions, both Americans and Germans cited price first followed by quality; third for the United States was performance and for the Germans, appearance. The Japanese responded by citing performance first, price second, and ease of use third.

Only 66 percent of Americans believe there are enough products made in the United States to meet their quality expectations without having to buy imported goods. In Japan the number was 56 percent and in Germany, 58 percent. U.S. vendors are still seen as style leaders, not quality leaders. Figure 2-7 shows ratings for how various consumers felt about the quality of services in their countries.

Companies Find Quality Profitable

What is a company's perspective? In May 1990 the General Accounting Office (GAO) published the results of a survey of the 20 high scorers of the 1988 and 1989 Baldrige Award in an attempt to answer the question, Does the Baldrige Award contribute to the improvement of corporate performance? It concluded that there was a direct cause-and-effect relationship between the kind of quality practices supported by the Baldrige criteria and actual performance of corporations. Results were measured in the areas of employee relations, company productivity, customer satisfaction, and profitability. The common elements among all were a definitive focus on:

- customer satisfaction
- leadership from senior management
- empowering and training employees
- fact-based decision-making processes for continuous improvement
- the Baldrige management model

GAO also found that individual TQM practices varied widely and that there was no "right" approach. The overwhelming majority reported increased profits, along with improved customer satisfaction and employee morale. Market share had grown, while expenses were dropping. While the study was a limited one, the data clearly suggested the correlation between quality improvements and traditional corporate measurements—most of which related to marketing and sales results, because the successful firms had lower operating costs, higher customer satisfaction levels, and superior and timely goods and services.

Responding companies reported a 13.7 percent average annual improvement in market share, an 8.6 percent improvement in sales per employee, and a 1.3 percent growth in return on assets. Overall customer satisfaction grew annually by 2.5 percent, customer retention by 1 percent, and complaints by 11.6 percent (probably sought after to find opportunities for improving products and services). Significant gains in process improvements were reported: reliability up 11.3 percent, order processing time cut by 12 percent, errors or defects down 10.3 percent, cost savings of 9 percent. Employee satisfaction grew at an annual rate of 1.4 percent while the number of suggestions for improvements received (indicator of employee ownership of company problems) rose 16.6 percent.

Harvard Business School professor David A. Garvin observed that the award has had a positive effect on the bottom line while improving awareness and acceptance of the quality movement. "The award has created a common vocabulary and philosophy bridging companies and industries." The spirit of borrowing good ideas and sharing is also a direct legacy, he argues, of the Baldrige Award: "To become more competitive, American companies have discovered cooperation."

IBM, for example, has come to the same set of conclusions: organizations within the company that are advanced users of quality management principles outperform peers within the company. Some country organizations, for example, outperform peer IBM enterprises and outside competitors by 30 or more percent. Their market shares are always higher, productivity greater, customer satisfaction higher, and expenses lower per capita and by transaction. These observations apply to both manufacturing and sales organizations and across the world, regardless of country or culture. Cost justification no longer is debated seriously within the firm.

Best Practices Are Valued by Corporations

If learning from others is also part of the quality movement, what are some of the best practices most valued by corporations today? A 1991 study by Ernst & Young and the American Quality Foundation began to report the answer. It begins with a quotation from Robert C. Stempel, former chief executive officer (CEO) of General Motors: "The worldwide quality revolution has permanently changed the way we all do business." He called it a "perpetual improvement process involving people in all aspects of the business." The study indicated that success increasingly calls for market segmentation so that the right products of the right quality and price can be offered in a timely fashion. To accomplish that, processes have to be improved and applied effectively. Five hundred firms were surveyed in ten categories. Briefly here are some of the findings:

- *Quality is a critical factor in strategic performance.* Quality is not universally measured, however. Worldwide more than 50 percent measure the effects of quality monthly; 18 percent of U.S. firms, 9 percent of German companies, and 2 percent of Japanese companies measure it approximately once a year. The trend was toward more quality measurements, especially for senior executive performance bonuses.

- *Quality is in the eye of the customer.* German and Japanese firms do a better job than American companies in getting customer feedback at product and service design phases. Approximately 40 percent of all firms consider customer satisfaction critical in strategic planning; only 22 percent of Germans concur. The Japanese also invest twice as much in technology to fulfill customer expectations as do Americans.

- *Competitive awareness is critical.* There is growing interest in understanding what the pace of competitive activity is, benchmarking world-class processes, and analyzing the nature of competition. One-third of U.S. and Japanese companies factor competitive activity into strategic planning; only 25 percent of Canadian firms and less than 10 percent of German companies do.

- *Process improvements are a strategic imperative.* Reengineering processes was most emphasized as part of routine business practice in Japan (more than 50 percent of firms apply process improvements over 90 percent of the time). Less than 25 percent of firms in Germany, Canada, and the United States regularly apply process simplification or cycle time analysis.

- *Employee involvement is on the rise.* The Japanese lead in employee empowerment and participation in decision making, but firms in all other countries expect a sharp rise in the practice in their own organizations. The bottom-line conclusions were that quality:

  - was a movement.
  - was evident in most corporations.
  - affected all segments of a firm.
  - is viewed as a competitive marketing initiative.

Quality Improves Competitiveness

If the positive selling arguments above still need bolstering there is the issue of where your competitors are on quality. Michael Porter, in a series of books on competition, has offered us much insight on the nature of rivals. One of his important points is that not all competitors use technology the same way or as efficiently as others and yet technology can provide sustainable competitive advantages. If you are on a technology curve that is less efficient or more backward, it is harder to catch up and beyond a certain point, you cannot.

The same logic applies to quality because, like technology, it is implemented if it adds value to the organization either in the form of efficiency or effectiveness. So you would expect that if competitors are already ahead of you in quality, your firm runs the same risk as when a competitor is ahead of you on the technology curve.

In fact, that is exactly what happens. Because quality is so fashionable today, you can quickly find out through conferences and publications a great deal about what your competitors are doing in the area of quality. They are also articulating the benefits they are discovering as selling arguments. These are benefits not available to you and thus are competitive leverages against your organization.

Be Patient for Quality Results but Push Hard for Action

We know from various empirical studies, including the recent U.S. government survey of Baldrige winners, that it takes over two years, and often more than three years, before a firm sees a return on its investment in quality. The hardest period to work with quality is the first three years as people learn and apply its principles, which yield less at first. The skeptics and cynics enjoy a field day because all the available data suggests that there are no benefits "so far." In addition costs may actually go up if for no other reason than retraining—all expenses incurred before benefits become apparent. After three years a snowballing effect of benefits kicks in as basic process reengineering gives back even more benefits to those further down the quality road.

Since the path you take during the first two to three years is "walked" at a steady speed because of the need to change culture, measurements, and organization, and to acquire basic skills, anybody ahead of you by just three years has, by definition, a competitive advantage over your firm. The challenge can be met by attempts to speed up the race through the awareness phase, but it still takes three years. If you allow that phase to take four or five years because the organization is too casual in its interest and approach, the competitive problem becomes greater.

What we do not know yet is at what point it is too late to even attempt to catch up. Recovery is possible on the brink of Chapter 11 bankruptcy; Harley-Davidson, the American motorcycle company, was within days of folding, and Xerox was losing market share rapidly because rivals were selling products profitably for what it cost Xerox to make them. So it is possible that you can put off implementing quality transformations for as long as five years, but after that it would cost too much to recover. At that point it might make more sense simply to sell the business or change its name. The message is that urgency to get on with the transformation today is crucial if you are to maintain pace with competitors.

If your rivals are not on the quality bandwagon, you can jump on it with the cold-blooded intention of using quality as a significant competitive strategy to sustain profitability and gain market share.

Conclusions

This chapter began with the statement that quality is becoming a major force in the world's business. Marketing and sales organizations are not immune to the ground shifting that is occurring. Richard J. Schonberger, in his highly acclaimed study of modern corporations, *Building a Chain of Customers*, argues that we need to build chains of customers to run world-class enterprises, stating the case positively:

> In marketing, the opportunities lie in an expanded view: Not just sales revenue, but locking into tight alliances with customers who prefer to deal with firms that are on a course of continual improvement.

Customer loyalty and repeat business—ideals desired by all marketing organizations—are only possible if the firm is improving its products and services, if costs (prices) are stable or dropping competitively, if response times to customers are improving, and if flexibility in meeting their demands increasingly is a way of life. Sales and marketing must work with all segments of the enterprise in new structures, relying on a new philosophy of operations, based on the use of the correct technologies and information and tightly focused on the wants of customers.

The rest of this book will point you in the right direction. How you travel to a more successful business is your choice.

References

American Society for Quality Control. *Looking for Quality in a World Marketplace*. Milwaukee, Wis.: ASQC, 1991.

Ernst & Young and American Quality Foundation. *International Quality Study*. Cleveland, Oh.: Ernst & Young, 1991.

Garvin, David A. "How the Baldrige Award Really Works," *Harvard Business Review* (November–December 1991): pp. 80–93.

Schonberger, Richard J. *Building a Chain of Customers: Linking Business Functions to Create the World Class Company*. New York: Free Press, 1990.

Thomas, P. R. *Competitiveness through Total Cycle Time: An Overview for CEOs*. New York: McGraw-Hill, 1990.

U.S. Department of Commerce, Technology Administration, National

Institute of Standards and Technology. *1993 Award Criteria: Malcolm Baldrige National Quality Award.* Gaithersburg, Md.: U.S. Department of Commerce, 1993.

U.S. General Accounting Office. *Management Practices—U.S. Companies Improve Performance through Quality Efforts* (GAO NSIAD 91–190). Washington, D.C.: Government Printing Office, 1991.

3

A Corporate Strategy for Quality Improvement

In times of crisis or high turbulence people
expect, indeed demand, great change.
JOEL BARKER

In this chapter I explore the features and benefits of a quality initiative at the corporate level, suggesting strategic initiatives, illustrating the process with the case of IBM's Market Driven Quality strategy, and concluding with a discussion of how quality efforts differ in manufacturing and service organizations.

Marketing and sales organizations do not function in isolation from other parts of an enterprise. Nor are they immune from the realities of the marketplace or the judgments of their customers. Marketing and sales can only operate successfully in the marketplace when working in concert with other organizations in the corporation, such as manufacturing, distribution, and headquarters. Therefore, if you are to implement the kind of significant transformation of marketing and sales required by quality, it must be part of a corporate assault on defects, improvement in business processes, and creation of a culture which is very market-driven and customer-focused.

The purpose of this chapter is to discuss some common environmental and market realities facing all corporations, tie those to some basic strategic elements of any transformation, and then illustrate the process through the case study of IBM's corporate quality strategy. IBM's experience is not offered as necessarily ideal or typical; rather, it is an instructive scenario since it involves a global enterprise that has decentralized accountability for all its parts, making it both a large and small company at the same time. The chapter ends with an exploration of marketing as it varies in manufacturing and service organizations, since in most instances the values of both must be merged for successful implementation.

The Marketing Environment

By now we have all heard about the global market. Our own staffs have drawn painful conclusions about the rapidity of change in competition and the fragmentation of markets into niches, and the phrase *new paradigm* has been burned into our senses. Taking all that information in and then turning around and asking what are we going to do about it, and how are we going to take advantage of the opportunity it represents, often leads to a strategy that absolutely requires increases in efficiency and effectiveness. In this context, the basic beliefs of the quality improvement world, such as cycle time reduction and getting closer to your customers, begin to make a lot of sense *strategically*.

In their practical book called *Strategic Choices*, Ken and Ed Primozic argue that in large part firms find it easier to thrive today if they can manage more by effectiveness than by efficiency. They call for identifying and improving key assets or functions, but then managing the links that those assets and functions have to extended enterprises such as suppliers and allies. To grow, they argue, you can essentially do one of two things: invest in more bricks and mortar for factories and sales offices or form alliances with other organizations for as long as they make sense.

Getting into someone else's envelope, the Primozics argue, makes a lot more sense than building more sales offices. You see the concept at work every month when you get a gas bill full of advertisements from other firms that have linked with your gas company to sell stereo equipment, entertainment, vacations, and luggage.

We need to know what our services cost today, how our services and offerings compare to those of the competition, where future investments should be made, what the priority projects are, and ultimately what impact our activities have on the corporate management process. Answers to these questions are almost the same as those in a Baldrige assessment, because both approaches come to the same point: to help us develop a comprehensive plan for future investments and activities.

Improving Efficiencies Is Not Enough

In the world of quality we must operate at two levels. The first is the efficiency level in which ongoing functions (such as payroll) must be improved dramatically in order to reduce costs and deliver services. The efficiency level of activity has captured the largest share of attention from quality experts, and it will be the subject of much of what follows in subsequent chapters. But these activities only affect cost reduction (e.g., accounts payable and receivable, and clerical and administrative expenses) and leverage (e.g., asset turns, return on investment [ROI], and cash management). While the focus on these activities has reduced operating expenses between 10 and 35 percent, and is thus important, efficiency will not guarantee a company sustainable competitive advantages or ensure prosperity deep into the future.

We also have to focus on the nature of product and service offerings, market share, and management activities such as acquisitions, strategic planning, and corporate transformation. Failure to work on these issues ensures that all quality improvements ultimately will be at risk. The Primozics have essentially broken activities into two categories: those that save us money (e.g., reduce costs and increase leverage) and those that make us money (e.g., market share and executive strategic decisions). Most organizations focus the bulk of their quality improvement activities on the "save money" arena, and yet quality efforts need to be achieved above that line in the "make money" arena as well. If you chart the waves of activities in a corporation, you quickly find that leveraging and cost-reducing activities flatten out as you become more efficient because of a declining marginal rate of return. In other words, you can make an organization only so efficient in its existing world before something has to change to get to a different level of effectiveness. To improve continuously you must change the fundamental marketing strategic plan. The speed with which an organization can move to a new paradigm in effect dictates its ability to obtain sustainable competitive advantage.

You can chart an experience curve for a particular activity, and the further down the curve you go the more efficient you become in that activity. A popular false assumption is that competitors are on the same experience curve; for example, that all microcomputer manufacturers are more or less as efficient as each other. Other false assumptions are that competitors have the same profit motive for the short term; that technology does not change; or that outside forces do not have an impact on cost curves. Moving rapidly from one marketing level of experience or products to another is the name of the game. In short, waves of change characterize a competitive environment.

For instance, in the retail industry, developing an on-line inventory system is fine until everyone has such a capability. Therefore the healthy firm will have found a way to move to a new curve earlier, that is to say, to bar codes and point-of-sale terminals before the competition does and before the last drop of profit is squeezed out of the on-line inventory control system. The surviving and thriving firm will have also gone from the point-of-sale terminal to a home-computer-based ordering process (e.g., Prodigy) before its competitors.

In manufacturing, the curves could have been efficient shop floor practices, then just-in-time manufacturing, then use of computer-aided design and manufacturing (CAD/CAM) and robotics, and now just-in-time distribution systems. One final example is from the insurance industry: moving from the automated home office to on-line regional offices to personal computers for agents, and then direct electronic links to other service organizations and people.

Applying Quality Principles to Reach New Levels of Competitive Effectiveness

The lesson from this wave perspective is that a major achievement in developing an effective quality-based marketing enterprise is the ability to identify when to get off an experience curve and onto a new one attractive to customers. Closely tied to the jump onto a new experience curve is the delivery of high-quality goods and services at levels at least as effective as on the earlier curve. That requires identifying opportunities, studying competition and market trends, and doing this work in a logical way. That is why the introduction of quality process management techniques in a corporation is so crucial and should not be left up to the manufacturing arm of the business. Marketing has to set the agenda in a market-driven customer-focused environment. How marketing communicates its findings and plans is a useful application of quality activities in the category we earlier referred to as managing efficiencies. In this approach, efficiencies are means to an end and are not allowed to be ends unto themselves.

Therefore, creating an environment in which the spirit of innovation and intrapreneurship exist becomes fundamental to a quality-based corporate marketing strategy. As John Masters said, "You have to recognize that every `out front' maneuver you make is going to be lonely, but if you feel entirely comfortable, then you're not far enough ahead to do any good. That warm sense of everything going well is usually the body temperature at the center of the herd." We all know that a "me too" strategy for a business does not work in the long run.

Using a Vision to Enhance Marketing and Planning

The heart of what gets done begins with what many call the *strategic vision*. Simply put, you picture where the organization needs to go, communicate and sell that throughout the enterprise, get buy-in from all levels, and then execute plans to implement it. This function of corporate management, as a critical element of quality, has changed over time. In the 1950s and 1960s, for instance, vision activity was executed with "management by control," by the 1960s we began to see "management of people," and in the 1970s we talked about "leadership styles." In the 1980s we went to school on "management by creativity," and now we find ourselves at the door of "management by innovation and entrepreneurship" but in a much broader market.

The Primozics have suggested a different strategic planning methodology as the first step in the implementation of any quality improvement in an organization. Well received is their concept of the Innovation Arrow illustrated in Figure 3-1. To use their description:

> Strategic thinking must be a continuous cycle. The cycle begins with formulating a strategic vision for the organization, proceeds through creating strategies that determine how the vision can be used to guide the organization's efforts, continues with developing appropriate tactics to implement the strategic plans, and leads to the implementation and operational steps that all members of the organization must carry out in the day-to-day running of the enterprise.

No step can be skipped and all steps must be repeated continuously in a never-ending loop. The continuous nature of effective vision-setting, market-focused activities is consistent with the beliefs of all experts on planning and quality and of executives of successful firms. It is one of the few issues on which there is little debate. The dialogue occurs down the arrow on execution, about which everyone has an opinion, but not on the concept that a seamless process must exist that goes from vision to execution and is comprehensive across the enterprise.

While how a vision is applied within the context of the waves of change is a large subject, suffice it to say that the way you develop new visions and get on the right curves at the right time is by thinking of your business on various experience curves, and comparing these to

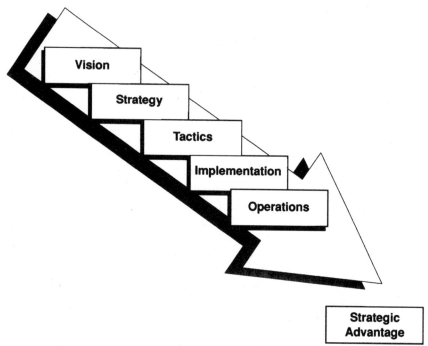

Vision

Strategy

Tactics

Implementation

Operations

Strategic
Advantage

Figure 3-1. Innovation Arrow. (Kenneth Primozic, Edward Primozic, and Joe Leben, *Strategic Choices: Supremacy, Survival, or Sayonara.* New York: McGraw-Hill, 1991, p. 15.)

your competitors' and to what your customers expect. Then plot your vision and plans to keep moving quickly into products or services that are on new experience curves long before your financial community wants you to. Cycle time reduction in getting onto a new curve is a critical success factor for any corporate marketing planning process.

Finally, organizations have to be structured to take into account the realities of new industry and market configurations and to be more capable of changing quickly as circumstances require. All segments of the empire must be networked together in practical interrelationships (e.g., business partners with specific lines of business and direct sales forces). Innovative projects that increase organizational effectiveness should be selected for support. Resources and talents within the organization must be made available quickly where needed in the planning and execution of marketing programs.

All these requirements call for less bureaucracy, flatter organizations with common visions and values, incentives and motivations that encourage change and alliances, and close ties to customers through extensive study of their needs and expectations, by benchmarking against the competition and the best functional practices in the economy. Doing all of these with speed and a profound sense of urgency requires organizations that can be changed quickly and that have very short lines of communication to "permission givers," who authorize activities. Empowerment of motivated and educated employees makes an organization light on its feet and with good prospects for success.

However, you have to be careful. Empowering employees without first making sure they have the skills with which to make a particular decision can be catastrophic. For example, if you empower a sales representative to negotiate price, that individual had better know what the profit margins are, what constitutes a profitable deal, and the effect of such a sale on the objectives of the organization. Those pieces of information and how best to apply them require training and constant communication. If those processes are not in place, empowerment becomes a liability. Each empowered act or process should have, as part of its definition, clear plans for education and communication.

Leadership also can be a problem. Who is in charge must always be clearly understood. Without that appreciation the aggressive employees will take charge (probably without proper training) and confusion will occur, with mistakes and delays inevitable. Delegation must be clear and precise. For example, if you are going to delegate pricing authority to a sales manager or sales representative, the executive who owns that authority today must be the one to publicly (and in writing most often) delegate that responsibility. He or she must then retain the authority and be required to inspect the process at work and to ensure people are correctly trained to exercise the newly granted responsibility. This sounds like basic management; however, we each know of many instances where these two fundamental practices are ignored in the euphoria of empowering employees today.

Strategic Elements of a Corporate Approach

The objectives of marketing are frequently defined as to:

- praise the firm.
- promote its products and services.
- help design and manufacturing come up with the right products and services.
- convince customers about the mutual benefits of working together.

Marketing managers argue about the priorities of these missions, but the reality is that each must be worked on because failure to perform well in any of the four makes success with the others virtually impossible.

Marketing must also be adamant proponents of quality in all that is done because that is what the customer is willing to pay for. Quality corporate marketing activities therefore focus on links to design communities, analysis of competition and customer wants, and ensuring quality of products and services. Marketing fixes problems as they come up with customers on the one hand, while proposing problem elimination at their source on the other. Marketing ensures that the best trained and most effective employees deal with customers, and that the firm is easy to do business with from the customer's point of view.

How Marketing Leads with Quality

Richard J. Schonberger, in explaining his notion of a chain of customers, has found that effective marketing organizations identify multiple ways of linking to customers as partners rather than just as procurers of goods and services: "Good customers are like money in the bank." Marketing is the customer's point of contact (through sales and service organizations) and thus a primary role must be to advocate the needs and interests of the consumer.

In the world of quality, marketing recognizes its role as advocate and implements "time-based competition." Better than most marketing experts, Schonberger has boiled the concept down to two ideas useful to us: that faster is better, and that predictable or invariable response time is good. Faster delivery, such as provided by some pizza chains (e.g., Domino's) or mail-order catalog enterprises, is very effective. But so too is consistency, such as is provided when we walk into a McDonald's restaurant anywhere in the world and receive the same consistent quality of products. Schonberger finds it advantageous to measure response time. At a sales organization level we will see examples in future chapters. But at a corporate level, measurement systems should reflect and give credit to faster responses to changing market conditions. Taking a leaf out of development and manufacturing, corporate management can measure how long it takes to create a new service, or to perform a new task, or to conduct a planning process. Make that measurement, and its attendant reward and incentive systems, as important as the actual output of the planning and visioning process.

Doing things quicker is not enough, however. We also live in a world in which part of competitive advantage is wrapping services and customer support around products that in time become commodities. The effort to become more service-oriented requires a different model of how both manufacturing and service organizations view their relationships with customers, and marketing is responsible at the corporate level for defining that model.

The Value of Relationships over Transactions

In the work of Christian Grönroos we have a useful model of what the end results should be. Grönroos, who has extensively studied service management and marketing, is best known from the phrase *moments of truth*, which was applied by senior management at SAS, the Scandinavian airline. In Figure 3-2 Grönroos shows a marketing strategy continuum that is long-term, suggesting that relationships with customers over the long term are more important. His studies have shown

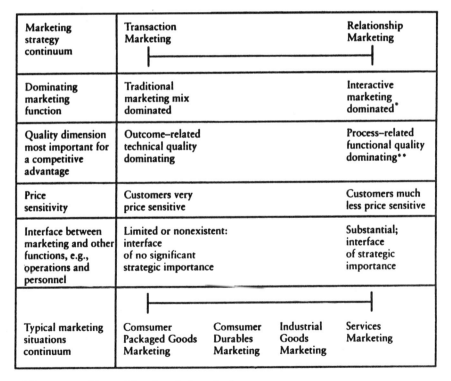

Marketing strategy continuum	Transaction Marketing			Relationship Marketing
Dominating marketing function	Traditional marketing mix dominated			Interactive marketing dominated*
Quality dimension most important for a competitive advantage	Outcome–related technical quality dominating			Process–related functional quality dominating**
Price sensitivity	Customers very price sensitive			Customers much less price sensitive
Interface between marketing and other functions, e.g., operations and personnel	Limited or nonexistent: interface of no significant strategic importance			Substantial; interface of strategic importance
Typical marketing situations continuum	Comsumer Packaged Goods Marketing	Comsumer Durables Marketing	Industrial Goods Marketing	Services Marketing

* But supported by traditional marketing mix elements
** Provided that the technical quality is at an acceptable level

Figure 3-2. The marketing strategy continuum. (Christian Grönroos, *Service Management and Marketing: Managing the Moments of Truth in Service Competition.* Lexington, Mass.: Lexington Books, 1990, p. 146)

that as an enterprise desires or is forced to become more service-oriented in approach, relationship marketing increasingly displaces transaction-based marketing. The driving forces are the obvious ones:

- better or more diverse technologies
- growing customer sophistication
- customer access to more options
- competition

To one extent or another, all organizations are on a continuum with transaction marketing at one end and relationship marketing at the other extreme. If a firm sells only commodities, then it is probably closer to the transaction end of the line and has to compete almost solely on price and availability—tough to do today. As you wrap services around products you move toward relationship marketing, which differentiates your products and firm from others. It gives your company the opportunity to acquire competitive advantages over rivals.

A customer's view of quality shifts too. For transaction-based firms it is the superiority of the product sold; at the other end, it includes the superiority of the services offered (such as how customers are treated and supported). I have found that customers become more sophisticated, requiring more of what you do well. In short, you meet their needs by shaping their wants in your terms.

The lesson is clear: determine what waves you are on and want to get on and what kind of business you are in (transaction versus relationship-based). Then develop a planning methodology that is continuous in its process of polling customers, measuring results, and supporting a vision in a disciplined manner.

How to Plan in a Quality World

All effective strategic planning models have some common elements, but the message from the world of quality is to make planning a process that has seasons of activities. These involve assessments (similar to Baldrige) done at a certain time annually, spring or fall scans of the competitive and economic environments as input for the planning process, periodic checks on the relevance of the vision (which should stay consistent over long periods of time), and so forth. Figure 3-3 illustrates a proven planning schematic that I and my colleagues use. It looks very much like many you have seen except it is a closed loop process. It works if an organization applies it first at the top, then cascades it down

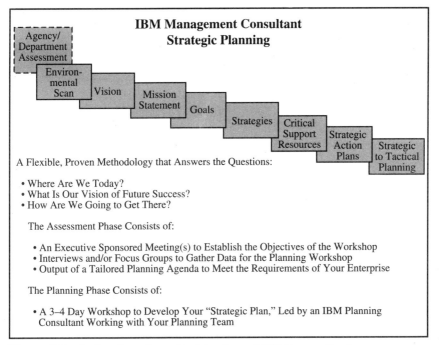

Figure 3-3. A planning schematic. (Courtesy of IBM Corporation.)

consistently through the enterprise. The schematic accommodates strategic and tactical planning for any activity: marketing, manufacturing, services, or quality, for example.

Two features are different from others, however. First, it calls for an assessment of the fitness of the organization to perform its duties. This can be done using, for example, the Baldrige assessment methodology or one that the enterprise creates on its own, but the assessment must be measurable and believable. It can also be used to assess the planning process of the organization itself. The point is that in a quality-driven organization, the planning cycle should begin with some assessment of fitness of vision, values, and capabilities.

The concept of the environmental scan covers a broad spectrum of activities but boils down to answering the question, "Where are we in what we do?" An environmental scan is simply the act of identifying forces that influence your activities. These, for example, can include government deregulation, the state of the economy, war, the changing nature of technology, and competition. This scan can catalog functions and relationships and links to customers and suppliers, while allowing you to conduct exercises to identify and analyze strengths, weaknesses, opportunities, risks, competition, trends in the economy, current strategies, and so forth. This part of the process is best managed and driven by senior management, because these executives can use this point in the cycle to educate themselves on current circumstances and trends in their business.

Visioning Is Crucial to Good Planning

Great leaders know the value of good visions. Martin Luther King, Jr., sparked the civil rights movement with his "I have a dream" speech, while President John F. Kennedy focused Americans on putting a man on the moon. The challenge, of course, is developing a vision that employees will endorse and support through their decision making. In marketing it can be as simple as to be a $100 million business by 1998 or to be seen by customers as the number one provider of a service, and so forth. Using quality language, however, helps raise the vision to a higher, more noble purpose, from building walls to building cathedrals. What is the best that we can be? The vision then speaks of quality, customer satisfaction, effectiveness, and productivity, and not just performance.

Assessments and environmental scans, along with the creative genius of employees, are good input for the vision. Visioning can be a group function, which increases the probability of buy-in. With a vision, the enterprise can then have guiding principles for its future. At Ford, the vision is "Quality is job one." Johnson and Johnson, when it faced the Tylenol tampering crisis, relied on its corporate vision of service to its customers quickly to reach the decision to recall every container of that product immediately, even though it appeared that the problem was limited to only a few areas. The firm also used its vision to rapidly design a tamperproof container, which immediately received public endorsement. Great visions do not have to be the preserve of generals and politicians; they move corporations toward greater quality too.

Assessments and scans are applicable at each level of the organization. Their content changes at each level because the scope of these exercises is limited to the area of the business controlled by an organization. Much below a sales manager's territory they lose their effectiveness. In sales organizations they become extraordinarily useful at the district level and up because national, industrial, demographic, and technological forces can be identified. I have found such exercises of value at each succeeding level because the environment and all assessments are defined in terms relevant to the participants.

Mission statements can be used to begin building the specifics of quality practices in a sales enterprise. Since a mission statement must help communicate vision to stakeholders, formulating one is a crucial activity. Mission statements are most effective if they are developed with the broader participation of a department or firm than the vision, because no sooner do you begin to describe the actions of an organization than you must set goals, which are often statements of how much you will achieve by when.

Quality-minded marketing enterprises craft mission statements and then goals that speak about increases in customer satisfaction, cycle time reduction in services provided, defect-free products or error elimination in tasks performed, and measurements of progress toward each goal. Goals should always be stated in measurable terms so you know how close you are to achieving them. Strategies that support each goal then can be constructed, linking vision down to mission and goals, approach and deployment. Later assessments of that organization's performance are increasingly based on quality indicators that track trend analysis of improvements and not simply on measurable goals. In short, you measure progress toward goals *and* quality indicators. For problems in attainment you study the causes, try improvements, measure their effectiveness, and then implement additional improvements as you learn and as your organization learns.

These improvements can be as simple as increasing the frequency with which the switchboard operator answers a customer's call in three rings or fewer. If last year that happened 50 percent of the time, this year's goal might be 90 percent of the time, and the third year's objective, 100 percent. Compare that performance goal to the more traditional type in which a marketing organization might have said its mission was to gain market share by selling more widgets and that its indicator of success was solely how much market share grew each year against some target, perhaps even quarterly in nature. A quality-driven enterprise measures the number of products sold as an indicator of customer acceptance of its services, and thus market share is a by-product of the firm's focus.

Strategies, when they have a quality bent to them, speak to issues such as how to improve the quality process improvement skills of sales or customer-contact employees so that they can increase customer satisfaction by a certain percent (goal). Quality elements in the strategy also include using more customer feedback (surveys, participation, and so forth) to ensure the activities of the organization are closely tied to customer expectations, hence increasing the odds of higher customer satisfaction. Satisfied customers in turn vote with their money, buying more of your goods and services.

Supporting Strategies with Tools and Training

We add the step of determining critical support resources simply because salespeople alone cannot do the job. Tools can be of great help. For example, to stay in closer touch with the customer, a salesperson might be given a car phone. To respond to customers with an order confirmation, a fax machine could be justified. Federal Express tracks the location of packages with miniature computers in their trucks, while packages have bar codes for scanning at every point in the delivery process. Information technology is a proven way to improve quality in services while providing a vehicle for collecting, organizing, and presenting information to help assess quality.

Training is a critical factor in the transformation of sales organizations. It is not uncommon for an enterprise to invest two to ten days per employee per year in education on quality awareness, process reengineering, and assessments. That is a major expense and a complicated but essential activity that more than any other set of tasks fundamentally:

- sells the vision of a new role.
- sets a new philosophy of operation in place.
- teaches employees how to implement it.

Sales personnel need this kind of education as much as manufacturing floor employees. Companies that have done it well began by educating the CEO, who in turn personally educated senior executives, who in turn taught their managers, and so on down the line, using consultants and in-house instructors. In each case quality training is led by the senior manager of the organization. The message of commitment becomes too obvious to ignore.

How Measurements Support Your Vision

The next chapter will discuss strategic action plans. However, the more common measurements of progress can be extended across the enterprise, the better. In this step achievable end results or outcomes and specific measurements are developed. This step also involves developing specific action plans and teams to carry them out, and establishing accountability for results within specified time frames. This task is fairly straightforward, but it must include quality results; otherwise, when you get to the last step, which is individual tactical plans, the process falls apart. At the tactical level, cross-functional teams looking at processes rather than at individual tasks cannot work effectively together if upstream activities have not been coordinated consistently.

This simple view of sales planning from assessment to tactical plans is a process. Viewed that way, inputs—the work done at an earlier stage—yield outputs, the inputs for the next phase. Thus, for example, input for the vision step would be assessments and environmental scans. The output is the visualization that offers guiding principles for the organization's future. Those working on the mission statement use the vision, and their output is the consensus they build on the future direction of the organization. In a good process, documented, disciplined outputs from one step are available to those downstream in the planning exercise. Thus people working on goals have as inputs not just mission statements but also the vision, environmental scans, and assessments. They may use them or not. Those setting goals may or may not have been involved in formulating mission statements. The point is, documented outputs upstream in the process become available to those working downstream.

In theory progress in each category gets reported up and down the line quickly so responses to problems can also be speeded up. In practice, that is not the case, of course. But when such reporting becomes a priority, over time relevant "top sheet" indicators of quality progress emerge and are taken seriously. This is so much the case that often the word *quality* in *quality indicators* gets dropped because quality is assumed and is in the fabric of the measurements of the business's success.

IBM's Market-Driven Strategy

IBM's application of TQM grew out of its three basic beliefs: respect for the individual, customer service, and excellence in all that is done. The TQM process that emerged, called Market Driven Quality (MDQ), led to a catalog of conditions for excellence across the entire enterprise:

- Executive vision
- Supporting strategies
- Management commitment
- Education
- Communication
- Customer involvement
- Supplier quality assurance

- Process management
- Visible measurements
- Periodic reviews
- Employee participation
- Rewards and recognition

Some of this was not news. In the very recent past (1984–1985), IBM sales employees had attended seminars by Deming and Juran to increase their awareness, process analysis had been done in the mid-1980s, and between 1987 and 1988 emphasis was placed on how to simplify business processes across the company. In 1990, IBM senior executives (most with extensive sales and marketing backgrounds) collectively set a "six-sigma" (six errors per million actions) goal for error defect activities across the company, including sales. The company has been measuring achievement and working toward this goal through the early 1990s. It also developed an internal quality assessment used by all large organizations within the company, including marketing and sales groups. Prizes for reaching certain point levels were established.

Lessons IBM Learned

The experience of applying MDQ across the enterprise taught the company important lessons. In the interest of saving time, I list only the lessons, leaving future historians to document the "guts" of the story.

- Continuous improvement only comes if top management is positively committed and involved.
- Vertical organizations must recognize that they are part of horizontal processes and that people tend to fix problems first before preventing defects.
- Education on quality cannot be an end to itself, but must be tied to changed behavior and to results.
- Education has to be tactical, and most important, just-in-time, applied the next day or lost.
- All employees can each day make improvements to IBM; they use many approaches to accomplish these.

Thus there was a growing acceptance that one thread did not make a tapestry. That realization encouraged empowerment and a flattening of the organization. The implementation of quality had to tie back to the values of the company. John Ackers, CEO, captured the essence of the focus with his admonishment that "IBM is about the value we create and the values we live by." Finally, paybacks in the cost of quality improvements were long-term, less frequently short-term. Over time, IBM had to travel through phases well understood by others already on the journey: first, awareness of change leading to understanding; second, changes in attitude, then behavior; and last, results. These conclusions were also reached by other recognized leaders in quality (Hewlett-Packard, Motorola, Xerox, and so forth). In particular, Xerox's former CEO David T. Kearns recently told the story of his firm's transformation in a book called *Prophets in the Dark*.

Tactical Plans for the 1990s

On May 15, 1989, the firm tied MDQ back to the basic beliefs and announced four market-driven principles to ensure clarity of common purpose in terms all would understand:

- Make the customer the final arbiter.
- Understand the markets.
- Commit to leadership in the markets we choose to serve.
- Execute with excellence across our enterprise.

These four principles govern many of the actions taken across IBM. On the customer as final arbiter: "IBM is in the business of helping customers achieve their objectives through the application of information solutions." And, "Customers alone decide the success of our efforts." Understanding the markets "means understanding current and prospective customers." On leadership in markets we choose to serve: "We must commit the resources necessary to achieve a leadership position." Offerings must be validated by customers. Executing with excellence is "the responsibility of every individual in IBM." Fundamental measurements of success are customer satisfaction, IBM revenue growth and market share, and finally profit and financial returns. These quotations suggest the kind of thinking that can be applied effectively in all sales organizations, not just IBM.

Goals for each organization were established so that all could be held accountable for progress. In the case of IBM U.S., they were measurable targets by year for defect eliminations, Baldrige-like self-assessment scores, customer and business partner satisfaction, and employee participation in the MDQ movement. Initial targets were set in 1990 and extend through 1994, with customer satisfaction (the most important) being the best in the world by mid-decade. These goals are simple and apply to everyone.

To implement these worldwide "strategic initiatives" with executive owners accountable for progress, local efforts started with the intent that all functions, including sales, would have activity in each. These continue to be:

- Definition of market needs
- Defect eliminations
- Cycle time reductions
- Increased employee participation
- Measurements of progress

U.S. marketing set as its mission to "create a long-term relationship with each customer by providing expert assistance and world-class offerings using the full breadth of IBM skills, products, services and business partners which all contribute to the customer's success." Its goals were to increase the number of customers, expand IBM's activities with these customers, and enhance IBM's value in their activities.

The mission and goals in turn led to a wide variety of activities designed to enhance IBM's skills in sales and support organizations, work in those sectors of the information processing markets that customers were most interested in, and increase customers' perception of IBM as the right choice, while improving both efficiencies and effectiveness. Targets were set for improving customer satisfaction as measured through a variety of national surveys, while looking at zero defects as the goal to achieve in process reengineering. Cycle time reduction became the way to increase responsiveness. The corporation also accepted the notion that all these activities had to function as a closed-loop system and thus had to interlock up and down the organization and as well as horizontally.

IBM's Critical Quality Processes

Over the years IBM identified key business processes requiring world-class performance, hence continuous improvement. The list has grown but the initial collection was comprehensive:

- Market information capture
- Market selection
- Requirements
- Hardware development
- Software development

- Plan integration
- Production
- Solution integration
- Marketing
- Customer fulfillment
- Customer relationships (marketing and service)
- Customer feedback

The framework for selecting these processes is illustrated briefly in Figure 3-4, but it also grew directly out of the Baldrige model.

Marketing and Sales Responsibilities

Marketing functions are responsible for collecting market data, doing competitive analyses, selecting markets, identifying and assessing capabilities, and developing strategies for offering goods and services. These include development of announcement plans, advertising, and support.

Sales organizations are responsible for improving the quality of delivering goods and services (customer fulfillment) and developing long-term relationships with customers by providing the right skills and excellent offerings. Both marketing and sales coordinate customer feedback to provide a closed-loop process back up through manufacturing and right to the market information capture process. Figure 3-4 illustrates the entire marketing-oriented process at IBM. It represents a useful model that can be applied by any sales organization, big or small.

Executive owners for each process were identified, and they have responsibility for working with all levels of the organization to ensure positive activity in each strategic phase.

Dedicated quality staffs are in place. A senior vice president, reporting to the chairman of the board, has overall worldwide oversight responsibilities. Within each national structure and line of business, including one for each division and large business unit, MDQ directors or managers are responsible for implementing quality improvement processes, providing education, and measuring results within their own organizations.

The critical message is that *how* processes were improved and *what* was measured became more consistent across the enterprise over several years as experience dictated what worked better. Clearly, teaching employees a single method of process improvement was very helpful.

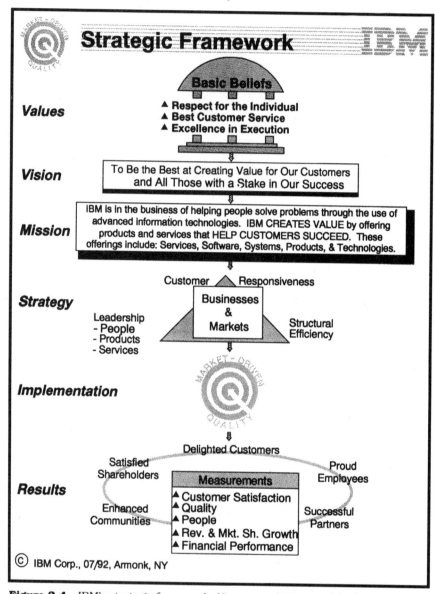

Figure 3-4. IBM's strategic framework. (Courtesy of IBM Corporation)

Because as individuals moved from one process improvement team to another, they all spoke the same language and used the same methodologies, saving time and avoiding confusion.

Since marketing and sales organizations have a long history of working with measurements, it should be noted that at IBM, guidelines for design of measurements were developed. The guidelines are applicable to sales, marketing, manufacturing, and service groups. Measurements have to be easy to capture, display, and understand; they have to focus on effectiveness (customer satisfaction) and efficiency (productivity); they must be presented graphically, indicating trends; and they must be visible to all those involved in or affected by what is being measured.

The Role of Education in Implementing Quality

The delivery vehicle for transformation and then tactical implementation of this strategy was education. It began with one- to two-day classes on quality improvement, with a little on why IBM needed to do this. Then came two classes, each two to three days long, that took employees through the rationale for transforming IBM, teaching that it was a journey, and then increasing their skills in setting visions for improvements, goals, and strategies. As individuals joined process improvement teams, they received additional training (one to four days) on process reengineering and basic statistical tools. The next phase involved education on empowerment and teaming. Employees also took classes in various colleges and universities, community-based quality organizations, and through such national services as the American Society for Quality Control (ASQC).

Results at IBM

Positive results occurred during the period 1988 through 1993. Employee commitment to MDQ and transformation of the company, as measured by employee opinion surveys, rose each year. Various measurements showed a decline in the number of defects in products introduced and serviced by the field. One manufacturing plant won the Baldrige Award in part because it could demonstrate effective links to customers for feedback, which had to be accomplished by working with sales and marketing organizations in IBM. Many processes, from payroll to accounts payable, improved, driving down costs and making possible a reduction in the number of employees without compromising support to customers. Customer feedback routinely influences types of products announced, and it encouraged a shift from products (machines and software) to services and consulting. Despite a battering of the industry by customers and the economy, customer satisfaction increased. Most important, the culture changed from an inward-looking one to a new, more customer-focused one.

But the tone internally is one of not being satisfied with success since there is more to be improved. Internally, assessments in the 1990s called for more work, while executives told customers that at best the company was grading itself a C+ despite having won numerous quality awards around the world. The call was for speedier change. Impatience for results created some frustration, which can test the commitment to quality for some. However, sufficient faith in the ultimate success of quality improvements prevented backsliding by the company and by any major part of the organization. In large part what helped was that quantitative results proved the value of the transformation. On a 100-point scale, MDQ-focused sales organizations enjoyed a satisfaction level 6 index points higher than their internal counterparts who were less focused. The same quality-focused group had a 7 percent higher market share, while revenue was 17 percent higher. In short, no organization could afford to ignore MDQ.

In the early 1990s more reviews involved looking "at the numbers" for quality indicators rather than just at how many products were sold or how much money was collected. Customer satisfaction data is taken with the same seriousness as revenues, and employees from executives to salespeople are paid for improvements in this area more than before the MDQ movement started. In short, a product manufacturing company has evolved into a market-driven firm that increasingly measures everyone's success more by what is important to the customer than by internal measures.

Manufacturing versus Service Marketing Perspectives

The IBM case study could just as easily have come from Westinghouse, Motorola, Xerox, Millikin, Harley-Davidson, or many others. They all traveled a similar journey. With over half of the economies of the western world manufacturing-based until the late 1980s, successful patterns for business were manufacturing-oriented. Since the early 1980s, however, that has been shifting to a services-based approach that, while it does not desert traditionally successful processes which result in new product introductions, better manufacturing, and good repair service, does require a different emphasis. Customer perceptions of quality involving both product and services formed. This acknowledged that the manufacturing of a service takes place at the time a service is performed.

The Nature of Service-Oriented Processes

How a customer receives is as important as *what* he or she acquires, placing an enormous burden on having processes for services at least as effective as those long in place for manufacturing. In some instances the "how" is more important today than the "what" since customers increasingly are concerned with the way they are treated. If they perceive that the "value added" in your business is service, then a different emphasis comes into play. For example, customers' view of the risks of doing business with a firm rises with services more than with products because the former cannot be tried out, touched, or looked at. They must be experienced when they are delivered. In short, it is harder to "kick the tires" on a service than on a product.

Conversely there is a move afoot among some service enterprises to become more manufacturing-oriented in their approach in order to acquire a repeatable level of performance. That is why, for example, consistency of service at a food chain, such as MacDonald's, or at some of the major hotel chains is stressed. At MacDonald's the primary product lines are produced at each outlet exactly the same way based on a documented approach taught to all employees worldwide. While experimentation might go on at individual locations (recently with Mexican food and before that with salads and low-fat hamburgers), the main items that draw customers in are always the same. Many of the disciplines required to ensure, for instance, the same hamburger wordwide or the same service at a Niko Hotel come largely from manufacturing disciplines. By the same token, manufacturing is becoming more service-based.

How Quality Influences Service Strategies

Several fundamental ideas must be understood when building a corporate quality strategy. First, presale marketing, postsale marketing (managing the experience for a customer), and word-of-mouth profoundly influence the basic functions of a services organization:

- creating awareness, causing a trial of the service
- demonstrating benefits of the service
- building loyalty to it

Preselling affects awareness and causes a trial of the service, while post-sale marketing most affects the demonstration of benefits and building of repeat business. In a manufacturing enterprise, the basic activities are least influenced by word-of-mouth and most by preproduction and postproduction marketing. Increasingly, applying the manufacturing lessons of quality to services marketing makes it possible for companies to compete successfully in a world where people buy products, support, and services. How these steps are carried out is the subject of the rest of this book.

For manufacturing companies, marketing involves enhanced efforts to provide service properly the first time. Sales and service personnel must deliver promised service more reliably than ever before and in a more timely fashion. Finally, empathy is essential. Empathy, to quote two experts, Leonard L. Berry and A. Parasuraman, is "the provision of caring, individualized attention to customers."

For a sales organization, defect-free activities are crucial. This means assuming the same rigorous disciplines of training and process management as exist in manufacturing. Customers must feel after the experience that their expectations were met. That requires creating a culture of "do it right the first time." Vision, measurements, and rewards are the best tools for accomplishing that objective.

Do not provide a service without first testing it, just as you would test a product. Pilot the activity in a small sector of the business to work out the process bugs. Focus on eliminating all errors rather than on simply reducing the number of problems, since a customer who experiences even one of the few remaining problems will not care that he or she was the exception. In their minds, the defect in service is an indication of how the entire enterprise functions. Rehearsing the service is like practicing for a play. Do it and you quickly find out what does not work well. We know today that this approach often has the added benefit of saving large sums spent on rework and correction of problems (from 15 to 70 percent of the cost of a service) while offering the potential of reducing the time it takes to do the work.

Marketing has long known that the quality of its sales personnel is crucial to success. So too is the quality of the backroom employees who service customers by processing orders correctly, generating accurate invoices, conducting timely customer satisfaction surveys, and ensuring sales-people are paid commissions correctly. This is people-intensive work and it must be managed as processes for hiring, training, supporting, measuring, and rewarding personnel who accept the gospel of quality and customer service, and who live in an environment that expects nothing less. The personnel element in the TQM equation is so crucial that we dedicate a whole chapter to the topic.

From senior management on down, communication on why consumer-contact employees must perform quality service is probably the single largest failure in firms attempting a transformation to TQM. People are simply not told frequently or effectively enough why they must be personally responsible for quality, nor are they taught how to achieve it. Management often is equally guilty of not creating circumstances that encourage effective teamwork. Management must train people to work on teams, assign individuals to teams, and create flattened organizations that are light on management and heavy on team responsibilities.

Experience dictates that senior management leadership on these points must be decisive and strong-willed. Nothing should be left to chance; so test services and measure their reliability and acceptance in pilot forums. The other two most effective levers for senior management are use of the perspectives that all activities are processes (not tasks) that must be improved and that highly trained and motivated teams of empowered employees can make the necessary changes to a business to fulfill the vision.

What might all of these activities lead to in terms of a strategy? It is helpful to boil many activities down to a few clear images so that everyone knows where they fit. Figure 3-5 offers a map of key marketing processes. Along the top are the basic activities and under each are components of those actions. Each item along the vertical and horizontal lines is a process. Each should have measures of success, be defined, and be tied back to what is important to the customer. That is how quality management is linked to what is important to the firm.

Note how similar it looks to a classic marketing value chain. Each set of processes is expected to add value as you move from left to right. You then make sure the whole collection represents a closed-loop system by making assessments of results available backward through the chain, so that at each point everyone understands how effective the activities are in satisfying the customer while supporting the marketing organization.

What Managers at All Levels Should Do

1. Marketing management must ensure their company is focused on its markets, and that means they must constantly advocate evolution and improvements in response to changes in customer or market conditions and demands.

2. If that activity is done before it is too late, then a second function is to take advantage of existing customer-contact employees to execute the company's plans by giving them incentives to offer goods and

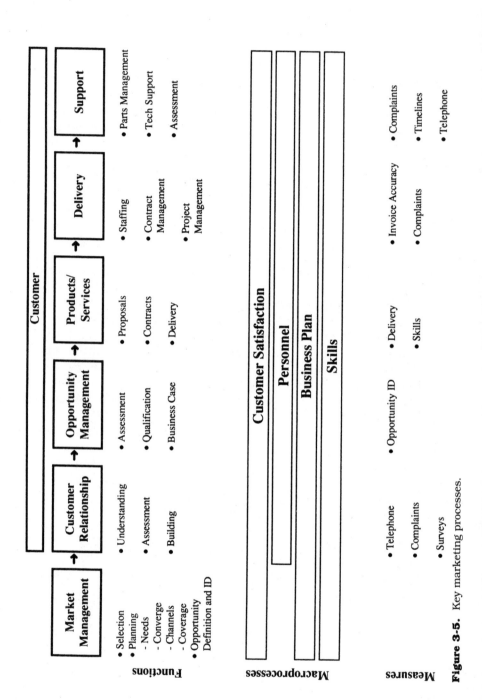

Figure 3-5. Key marketing processes.

services in a high-quality manner. This is in contrast to the traditional way of having sales, discounts, and monetary incentives to shove products at customers. Management can ease the process of employees' marketing to customers by training but also by making available information that facilitates their jobs (e.g., on-line product and customer files, product availability lists, and so forth). Senior marketing management should be the loudest champions of quality in the enterprise since they speak on behalf of the customer. That also means they must take leadership roles in showing the organization how to implement quality.

3. All marketeers are image makers; they are the company. If they preach quality values and spend time implementing and inspecting TQM initiatives, customers will come to depend upon that enterprise for goods and services. The data presented by the ASQC in its annual quality surveys strongly confirms the validity of this behavior. End results are repeat business, loyal customers, and a shift to relationship marketing instead of more traditional transaction-based selling.

References

Berry, Leonard L., and Parasuraman, A. *Marketing Services: Competing through Quality.* New York: Free Press, 1991.

Grönroos, Christian. *Service Management and Marketing: Managing the Moments of Truth in Service Competition.* Lexington, Mass.: Lexington Books, 1990.

Handy, Charles. *The Age of Unreason.* Boston: Harvard Business School Press, 1989.

Kanter, Rosabeth Moss, Stein, Barry A., and Tick, Todd D. *The Challenge of Organizational Change.* New York: Free Press, 1992.

Kearns, David T., and Nadler, David A. *Prophets in the Dark: How Xerox Reinvented Itself and Beat Back the Japanese.* New York: Harper Business, 1992.

Kouzes, James M., and Posner, Barry Z. *The Leadership Challenge: How to Get Extraordinary Things Done in Organizations.* San Francisco: Jossey-Bass, 1987.

Porter, Michael E. *Competitive Advantage: Creating and Sustaining Superior Performance.* New York: Free Press, 1985.

Primozic, Kenneth, Primozic, Edward, and Leben, Joe. *Strategic Choices: Supremacy, Survival, or Sayonara.* New York: McGraw-Hill, 1991.

Schonberger, Richard J. *Building a Chain of Customers: Linking Business Functions to Create the World Class Company.* New York: Free Press, 1990.

4

A Sales Force
Strategy for
Quality

*We realize that we are in a race without a
finish line. As we improve, so does our
competition. Five years ago we would have
found that disheartening. Today we find it
invigorating.*   DAVID KEARNS, XEROX

> This chapter focuses on specific strategies for implementing quality
> programs in sales organizations by describing the theory of quality
> in sales, the role of processes, and the first four critical areas to work
> on. It ends with tips on judging how you are doing in transforming
> your business.

The challenges facing sales management are to define how customer-
contact employees should behave, what services customers should be
provided besides simply a product, and to what extent offerings are
"pushed" on customers as opposed to executing a "pull" strategy.
Many factors influence choices: competition, the nature of goods and
services, industry practices, economic realities, quality of the sales
force, and so forth. Yet even at the sales force level, the basic elements
of TQM can and are being applied to implement marketing strategies.

The Theory of Quality in Sales

However you choose to implement quality principles, the elements are the same, regardless of whether they are imposed on manufacturing or any other part of the business. All good quality plans should have the following elements:

1. customer delight (customer satisfaction and feedback)
2. leadership involvement (directs and inspects)
3. continuous improvement (process focus)
4. employee involvement (commitments and empowerment)
5. quality assurance (assessment and process)
6. measurements (including self-assessments)
7. supplier partnership (sharing same disciplines of management)
8. strategic quality planning (by all involved)

At all levels of a sales organization, activities are looked at as collections of processes. All should contain each of the eight elements of TQM assembled into a cohesive plan that is implemented. Managing the effectiveness of these elements within processes is an important way to improve sales. Increasingly, leading with quality, rather than with price, is proving to be the more effective strategy.

Three Effective Attitudes toward Quality in Sales

Three perspectives apply at the sales level when implementing quality. First, activities performed always should be looked at as part of a collection of processes. Processes are the heart of any quality movement. Thus you can look at the order entry process, commission and compensation process, customer feedback process, and so forth. Customer-contact personnel can improve their efficiency by looking at their activities as a series of processes and, as they are asked to study these (because they are closest to the issues), they in fact can improve effectiveness with little or no management involvement.

Second, all processes, tasks, and measurements of effectiveness have an outward, or customer focus. Measuring how fast an activity is performed is of little significance if the customer does not care. For example, of what importance is it to a customer how fast your organization collects outstanding accounts receivables? It is very important to you, but if they are collected too effectively you might lose a customer. Much too frequently the tendency is to measure with inwardly focused indicators. The evolution of measurements should be to more outward, customer-focused indicators.

The third perspective calls for reductions in the time in which a cycle of events takes place. Cycle time reduction is of particular value in customer-contact situations for a number of reasons. For one thing, when you reduce the amount of time it takes to provide a service, customers like that and come back for more. That is why banks and fast food restaurants constantly worry about customer lines at counters and continuously try to figure out how to shorten them. For another, cycle time reduction means customer-contact personnel can service more customers, hence increasing both's productivity.

Reducing the amount of time it takes to execute a process often leads to reduced numbers of errors because, in many instances, cycle time reduction can only be achieved by simplifying the process you have today. That requires taking out more steps. Each time a step in a process is eliminated, you reduce the risk of an error. That is theory and often reality. However, since you can also create unanticipated new problems, it becomes critical to document the changes (so you can go back and see what is different). It also becomes crucial to measure the consequences of as many steps as possible, in order to learn how you are improving, what causes fewer or more errors, and to suggest possible opportunities for continued improvement. The errors will still occur, the changes will not always please you, but in aggregate, the process improves.

Common examples of simplification include reducing the number of approvals and "signoffs" required, the number of forms to be filled out (thereby eliminating redundant data that might be entered incorrectly anyway), and the number of people who have to touch a process. That is why more authority and responsibility is increasingly being placed in the hands of those actually performing tasks. Another approach is to delegate responsibility for an entire process to a small team (typically fewer than 10 individuals), who can decide at a tactical level how best to perform tasks. Both approaches decompartmentalize activities, *integrating* them more closely. The result is that they get done faster and more accurately.

Why You Should Focus on Customer Satisfaction and Cycle Time Reduction

Customer satisfaction and cycle time reduction represent the two most useful points of attack when searching for better ways to run a business. By asking how we might increase customer satisfaction, we immediately place ourselves in the position of our customers. We become more inclined to find out what they want next, crafting new offerings as a result. All the literature on quality and marketing harps on being fanatical about customer satisfaction; experience indicates that this is a good perspective. However, too often, even in well-run organizations, internal views are too dominant. Thus the culture constantly must be redirected outward toward customer satisfaction. This can be done by implementing measurements of customer satisfaction as opposed to tracking internal productivity achievements and by building processes that address customer needs before those of the firm.

Cycle time reduction can be used to lead employees to new ways of thinking about process reengineering. This is a technique well-understood in manufacturing. Ford executives like to cite the example of accounts payable, where they went from having hundreds of employees in each plant to fewer than a handful. They asked the question, How can we do accounts payable more quickly with fewer employees? By setting expectations on what "more quickly" meant, they forced thinking away from incremental improvements in their accounts payable process to fundamentally new approaches. Now suppliers get paid as soon as parts are shipped, not 30 days or more later.

Using the Eight Elements of Quality

The same can be done in sales. By setting a dramatically high level of expectations for a particular process, by default you force the process owners to develop bold new approaches. Along the way they can add customer satisfaction indicators, make more decisions based on facts that can be trapped more effectively than before, and give both customers and employees confidence about the possibility of even better service.

Process owners play a special role. They "own" responsibility for improving a process and should enjoy the fruits of their success. Since "their" process usually crosses conventional organization lines, they must be given responsibility to act and recruit cross-functional teams (people from various departments), as well as to be held accountable for results. These responsibilities often mean, in practical terms, that the process owner has to be high enough in the organization to understand how the process will be affected by the reduction of corporate coordination of activities across various departments and divisions. In other words, process owners must understand the context in which their responsibilities lie. My notion of ownership is crucial to the successful implementation of a process because it is best handled in the same way as, for instance, the delegation of re-

Culture Changes in Sales Organizations

Transactions	➤	Relationships
Product	➤	Service
Centralized Management	➤	Decentralized Management
Individual Performance	➤	Team Performance
Bureaucratic	➤	Entrepreneurial
Inward (Upward) Focused	➤	Outward (Customer) Focused
Slow to Change	➤	Quick to Change
Measures Efficiency	➤	Measures Effectiveness

Figure 4-1. The transformation of a sales organization.

sponsibility for generating sales, using all the same motivational tools such as compensation, rewards, and accountability.

Figure 4-1 summarizes on the right the kind of behavior wanted in a quality-driven organization and on the left the kind of behavior that generally exists today. To move from left to right, you use the eight key elements of TQM and rely on customer satisfaction and cycle time reductions as compasses to guide you. The necessary task improvements can be done using the process management reengineering techniques we are increasingly studying and applying today.

Figure 4-2 illustrates conceptually how all of these elements work. As you develop a plan for quality improvements, it is helpful to document these actions in a visual manner so that everyone understands how specific activities fit into the big picture. Figure 4-2 is a simplified form of an actual blueprint for excellence employed by a sales organization.

Existing models of how quality-driven organizations view themselves apply in a sales enterprise. For example, Figure 4-3 looks at sales as one large process and uses the Baldrige framework to express its various components. As with the pieces depicted in Figure 4-2, we see common elements:

- the leader driving a vision that is heavily value-based (e.g., market-driven, customer-focused, quality-dependent)

- the collection of information used in fact-based decision making, planning and deployment, and improving the processes of the enterprise

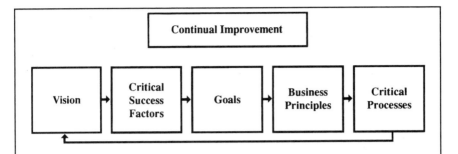

<u>Vision:</u>

A view of our environment that will enable our tremendous future success.

<u>Critical Success Factors:</u>

Areas requiring continual improvement through quality to successfully implement our vision.

<u>Goals:</u>

Measurable targets that support our vision and ensure focus on the critical success factors.

<u>Business Principles:</u>

The manner in which employees approach their responsibilities to achieve our goals.

<u>Critical Processes:</u>

The most important processes requiring a discipline to support the actualization of our vision.

Figure 4-2. A simplified blueprint for excellence.

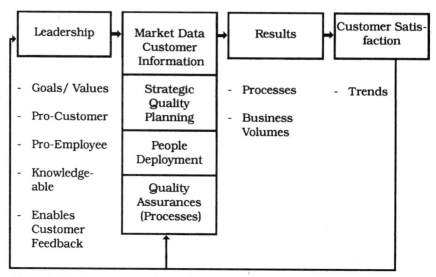

Figure 4-3. Process view of a market-driven sales organization.

- the measurement of both results and customer satisfaction

Results then influence the leader's vision and the process starts all over again.

The Role of Processes

The core of a quality-driven sales organization's activities is its collection of processes with which the business is run. In addition to providing leadership and measuring results, the lion's share of the work in transforming an organization rests on the collection of tasks performed on a daily basis. The sooner you can identify these, measure their current effectiveness, assign process owners, and begin improving critical processes, the faster you get going on the quality journey.

How to Apply Planning Elements

The beginning is the creation of a vision of where the organization is going. Visioning as a process is more appropriately discussed by experts on leadership and need not detain us here. However, having a leadership vision, as well as a mission statement about what the role of the sales organization should be, are preliminary steps to working with processes.

The mission statement should be profoundly customer-driven. For example, "thriving by helping our customers gain competitive advantage in their markets through the use of our services," suggests a focus. Some organizations also add a statement concerning their employees; for example, "We are also committed to continually improving the skills, performance, and job satisfaction of all employees." Most will also make a statement of success: "A key measurement of our success will be our growth in revenue," or "in customer satisfaction."

Traditional critical success factor analysis typically leads a quality-driven organization to the conclusion that improving customer satisfaction is the most important issue to focus on, followed very closely by employee success (morale, skills, and so forth). Other critical success factors involve an organized approach to identification of sales opportunities, application of teamwork, use of process reengineering, and so forth. Results usually are measured in one of three ways:

- customer success or satisfaction
- employee success or morale
- company revenue or profit success

Typically, indicators of success and continuous improvement are developed for all three categories, as it is impossible to do well without performing effectively in all arenas. Examples of quality indicators are percentages of telephone calls answered, measures of how fast proposals are answered over time, or surveys of how customers feel about a particular service or offering.

Goals help point to the specific processes that must improve and become more effective. Goals also serve as a good link back to vision and categories of successes. In sales organizations effective common goals are statements of values and expectations. Examples include:

- delighting customers
- improving employee skills
- implementing "world class" quality
- enjoying market share growth
- experiencing increased profitability

Setting Priorities for What Gets Done

Firms that have experienced successes in the implementation of quality in sales organizations, such as IBM, Motorola, and Xerox, will argue that (1) you cannot fix all processes at the same time because boiling the

---

Important Sales Process

Opportunity Identification	Competitive Analysis
Customer Feedback	Compensation
Communication	Employee Feedback
Skills Development	Order Processing
Accounts Receivable	Distribution/Delivery
Service and Repair	Recognition
Revenue and Profit Accounting	Pricing
Telephones	Business Partners
Supplier Relations	Facilities Management
Advertising	Sales Planning
Quotas and Measurements	Suggestions
Resource Deployment	Inventory Management
Organization	Strategic Planning
Quality Assessments	Personnel Practices
Complaints	Market Segmentation
Product Liability	Brand Management

Figure 4-4. Important processes in a sales organization.

ocean will take too much focus off day-to-day business and (2) thus you must set priorities on processes targeted for improvement. Experience shows that working on a few at a time (say a half dozen or fewer) in a disciplined manner is extremely effective. Once a set of processes is improved, stabilized, and put on a course of continuous improvement (and with some early results achieved to encourage others), then the next tier of processes can be addressed.

It is not uncommon to catalog a list of 15 to 20 critical processes that need improvement. Figure 4-4 lists some of the more obvious ones evident in all sales organizations. Yours probably has some additional ones. No list is absolute except the one your organization creates. But any list is very long.

Depending on which planning methodology is used, it is best to lump all obvious processes into groups based on importance to the organization and to its customers. Linkage analysis methods, for example, point out dependencies among processes, which leads to one list of what gets worked on first, then second, and so forth. Self-interest and management philosophies about how things get done will lead to another. Sporadic or even thorough surveying of customers generates a third. Any of the major planning methodologies in use today will generate useful lists. In the final analysis, your list will be a blend of what is important to customers, your employees, and the firm as a whole.

However, experience shows that there are several very obvious processes and issues to begin with, regardless of what list is used. They are (1) measurements, (2) organization, (3) compensation, and (4) education on quality. All four are admittedly inward-focused, pay too little attention to customers, and allow maximum politicking in the existing culture. However, they are the crucial early processes to work on because they represent the bedrock of incentives that historically have encouraged employees to perform the way you want. By the same logic, these tools, when managed as processes, can be applied to improve all other processes, to learn about quality improvement techniques, and ultimately to change behavior to conform to the vision. Organizations that have transformed their sales organizations understand the logic of why these four are first and in the order listed; the literature on quality is only just beginning to catch up with this reality.

Measurements

People work on those tasks for which they are being measured. That is one reason Deming, Juran, and all the other quality gurus spend time on the pros and cons of various types of measurement systems. In order to improve continuously, processes have to be measured statistically; yet even before going to work on a process, individuals must have incentives to perform well. Part of how that is done is through measurements. Nowhere is this more so than in a sales organization, where we have developed a type of worker whose performance is rewarded according to measurable results, usually sales volumes or profitable sales volumes. Their managers are also products of a system that rewards them with money and promotions based on their performance against a measurement system. Often this measurement system created incentives for individual results, not for team results. The incentives also encouraged many sales regardless of what the market (customer) wanted—the "push" approach.

Sales personnel traditionally compete against each other, as well as against other competitors outside of their firm. By not cooperating across a larger base of customers, they suboptimize the capabilities of the entire enterprise to get many sales in order for the individual to gain a few orders in a particular sales territory.

In a shared circumstance, someone with deep skills in a particular aspect of your services or product line could focus just on that, bringing in more sales because of his or her continually improving skills. But when more skill is focused on a narrower area, a larger territory or customer set is required. This is the reason for finding ways to share resources across a broader customer set.

The theory behind traditional measurement systems is that sales personnel work best when rewarded for individual achievements (sales) and that they will not attempt high performance if not measured and rewarded on a transaction-by-transaction basis, in other words, by commissions and quotas. A backward look in time indicates the wisdom of this approach, as most successful sales organizations have compensated and rewarded their staffs that way.

How Measurements Influence
Your Sales Team

However, it is becoming increasingly evident that the nature of measurements profoundly supports or inhibits the cultural transformation of an organization, particularly manufacturing sales teams that need to become more service-oriented. It is difficult to get the attention of a salesperson to improve a customer-related process if he or she is only being measured on sales achieved this month. In other words, the measurement system in an enterprise must support the vision, goals, and objectives in terms that are quality-driven.

Jump-Starting Transformation
with Shared Measurements

Several very simple methods are frequently used to jump-start the transformation. First, in order to get disparate sales offices or sales units working together to optimize the use of resources, have them share a common quota. If an individual's reward/compensation/career is dependent on the success of specific others, he or she will quickly want to learn to function in a team environment. The process is most successful if managers of a sales office within a district are first put on the district manager's quota, because then they have an incentive to alter their own and employee's behavior.

This shared measurement approach should not be limited just to quotas, but should include expenses, resource allocation, market share, and overall customer satisfaction. By being forced to help others be successful in order to succeed individually, executive management can then turn to this team to determine better how to allocate resources across various sales offices, share resources, or combine processes to improve overall effectiveness. In time, the sales organization can also improve the measurement and reward processes of the firm to reflect the new realities values.

How far down the organization should shared measurements go? The cautious approach is to begin with just sales management at the district and sales office levels sharing common measurements. However, it quickly becomes evident that unless a common measurement system exists up and down the line from sales representative up to sales executive, contention and conflict occur. Therefore, common measurements have to be pushed as rapidly as possible down the organization. Team successes then become more valued.

Initial reaction to such an approach is anything but wildly enthusiastic, particularly among outstanding sales personnel who fear commissions being "socialized" as they "carry" weaker performers. They also experience difficulty relating to successes that are much larger than they are accustomed to tracking. For example, if salespeople used to chasing $100,000 worth of revenue annually and are now being asked to contribute to the success of an organization selling $5 million in goods and services, they may not relate their contribution to the $5 million as easily as to the lower number.

However, if expectations of how much individuals should generate for the common good are defined and the results of those salespeople and the enterprise are communicated constantly, they soon come to relate to the welfare of the whole. For example, asking salespeople to grow their sales volumes by what is anticipated across their industry, knowing that expectations may rise or fall during the course of the year depending on how the whole team does, helps move the process along. Then broadcasting how the entire enterprise is doing monthly, quarterly, and annually lets management communicate whether as a team everyone is on track to success or if additional efforts are required.

Thus measurements in a quality-driven organization tend to be broader in scope than in traditional sales structures. Instead of just measuring an individual's sales revenues or number of products sold, other measurements, such as customer satisfaction indices (for which you need a customer feedback process), skill levels, profitability, and team participation, are added. This requires reward and recognition systems to change so that a salesperson can actually thrive because of outstanding contributions in areas other than just revenue volumes. For many, that notion is radical, a profound departure from how we have measured sales personnel in the past.

A Case of the New Measurements

Perhaps no greater stereotype of the traditional commission-hungry predatory salesperson exists than that of a car salesperson. Yet it is this community that provides a dramatic example of what happens when measurement systems are changed. Carl Sewell's Cadillac dealership—the most successful luxury-car business in the United States—illustrates the lesson. Sewell begins with the concept that if something is important then it should be measured so you know how you are doing. Second, he believes in setting measurable targets for performance, e.g., number of cars sold, bills collected, customers satisfied, and so forth. He argues that "the secret is to set goals that are in the best interest of the business," which ties back to the vision of what the business should be all about. Sewell believes in competition and thus makes available to all employees results of individuals. But he also expects the team as a whole to be successful.

Sewell argues that measurements can be compared to baseball performance. You want measurements that indicate whether or not the baseball team won and individual statistics on the performance of each player. Using the same analogy, individual performance indicators can be accumulated for the team while the team has a common goal: to win today's game, to get to the World Series, to be world champions. As individuals—and thus the team as a whole—perform better, expectations can be raised and measurements can document results. Thus a combination of what the individual and the enterprise do together provides the design point for measurement systems that encourage continuous improvement.

Sewell preaches the gospel of measurements. Simply put, his experience shows that you should measure things that employees can relate to, affect, track easily, and understand. One added-value tip from Sewell is to state your measurements in positive terms, not as targets missed but as progress toward a goal. His success is built on the vision of customer satisfaction; no measurement is implemented that does not support that notion. The result: his is one of the most successful automobile businesses in America as measured by repeat business, growth in sales, and earnings of sales personnel.

Focus on Measurements

Lesson Number One.   Focus early in your transformation on what gets measured; later we will look at what gets rewarded as linked to performance against measurements. Changing measurements may in fact be the easiest element of a transformation process because the senior manager of an organization can almost single-handedly implement these. He or she would then require the help of staff to trap data on these measurements and ideally would engage employees in designing measurements in the first place to gain buy-in and understanding.

Organization

Chances are your organization is a marvelous example of what your firm needed to perform well in the past. It probably is not well structured for today's market realities because it is very difficult to change structures. Changes are attacks on little kingdoms, sanctuaries of inefficiency, and comfortable zones of operation. Most companies reflect a time when efficient organizational structure involved a command-and-control approach to business. That required many layers of management and staff, often leading to ratios of staff to customer-contact employees of 5 to 1 up to 8 to 1. Changes to policies, practices, and offerings had to work their way through a hierarchy to ensure that coordination occurred across the empire and that innovations were the "right" ones.

Times have changed. Symptoms are everywhere. Product introductions need to come every year or two, not every three to seven years. New competitors appear from out of left field, especially from overseas. Market opportunities are identified more quickly, and you have less time to take advantage of them before they change, disappear, or are occupied by a rival. Microcomputers and telecommunications have democratized access to information in all organizations, allowing a decision maker to act faster. This access reduces or bypasses traditional staff functions. Costs are too high, given what goods and services have to be sold for, so overhead must be slashed, and quickly.

Then, of course, change is not what it used to be. In a marvelous book, *The Age of Unreason,* Charles Handy shows that change is not part of a pattern but appears more "discontinuous" than ever before; thus it's disturbing to decision-makers. He argues that "it is the little changes which can in fact make the biggest differences to our lives" and that "changes in the way our work is organized...will make the biggest differences to the way we all will live." We do not need to go through his defense of these ideas because we all are already noticing the effects on our businesses.

What Today's Organizations Must Look Like

Let's get to the heart of the matter. We need to structure organizations that satisfy several basic requirements reflecting current realities:

- the majority of workers placed in direct customer-support functions; fewer in staff positions

- fewer levels of management, driving down overhead costs while shortening the decision-making process

- flexibility to change quickly to support new sales opportunities

- continuous improvements in the effectiveness of the enterprise

As sales increasingly move toward a market reality that involves adding services to products, deliverables become more of what an individual does in front of the customer. Instead of just delivering a product, you frequently have to perform a service associated with that product. That circumstance can call for more labor-intensive tasks and, at a minimum, requires people in front of customers. In a market-driven organization, backroom personnel are of less value to customers. So, from a design point of view, we need more sales and service personnel and less staff. It is no accident that major corporations throughout the world are slashing staff functions in order to supply sales offices with people.

As market conditions change, the ability to make decisions more quickly and to deploy resources equally as fast requires us to reduce decision-making cycle time. The only way to do that is first, by reducing the number and levels of decision makers, and second, by giving greater authority to make decisions to lower levels of an organization. The ideal situation is a customer with a salesperson who has been properly trained, who can negotiate a profitable deal on the spot, and who can close some business without having to run to a manager for permission. That is cycle time reduction at work!

The smaller the transaction value, the easier it is to empower employees to make quick decisions:

- the waiter who rips up a dinner bill because the meal was poorly prepared

- the automobile salesperson who adds a half dozen oil changes to clinch a deal or to thank a repeat customer

- the clerk who takes back a piece of merchandise with no questions asked because customer satisfaction is paramount

We have all heard about the extreme cases of people renting helicopters or jumping out of airplanes to deliver goods, and Japanese store clerks delivering flowers and products to people who bought faulty electronics. But realistically, the required decision making is more than just having customer-contact employees enjoy greater leeway in making decisions. It also involves giving managers greater responsibility and authority to decide what products to sell, what services to offer, and how best to organize without having to seek permission. That is the goal you should strive for in restructuring organizations.

Why We Need to Change Organizations

The logic for changing organizations to meet new market conditions is fairly straightforward. Organizations function best when they support groups of work activity and if these groups of work activity respond in time to existing marketing opportunities. So the ability to change an organization's structure quickly is very important. It's also significant to have measurements that encourage an organization to change in a timely fashion in response to market conditions.

An example illustrates the case. IBM in the 1980s did a fine job in selling computer hardware. It became very obvious as the 1980s passed, however, that the slowest growing portion of the market was hardware and that the two fastest expanding segments were software sales and services (e.g., programming, project management, and consulting). Being outstanding in the fastest shrinking segment of the market was not going to be a long-term winning strategy. IBM therefore poured dollars and people into software and services. That led to major reorganizations as resources shifted to these growing market segments. As a result, contract services business grew at double-digit rates in the late 1980s and early 1990s, rapidly contributing larger portions of the overall revenue of the corporation. A whole new consulting business emerged that, by mid-1993, had become a very large enterprise in itself, generating hundreds of millions of dollars in revenue around the world. Meanwhile hardware revenues, still enormous, remained relatively flat as product costs declined and expenditures by customers shifted to software and services.

Hardware firms that did not make the shift quickly enough either suffered terribly or went out of business. IBM, although it was not entirely immune to the negative effects of the transition, nonetheless moved rapidly from being just a vendor of machines to being a service company with positive results. Internally, the same kind of impatience exhibited in process reengineering and cultural change appeared with the movement to new markets. Executives wanted the process of migration to software and consulting to go faster than it did; but change came and at about the same speed as in other firms that transformed their businesses.

Other examples abound. Airline companies now think of themselves as service companies, with their "moments of truth" coming when customers deal with employees. Sewell uses the notion of service more frequently than the concept of sales to attract business. Today all the literature on marketing and manufacturing identifies with the concept of service.

How to Change an Organization

The fastest, easiest way for organizations to change is to reduce their size. That means taking out layers of management, changing spans of managerial control from 5 or 6 employees to 10 or 30 employees. Alteration of spans of control in turn forces managers to become facilitators of change, cheerleaders, and visionaries, because otherwise they become huge bottlenecks for employees. Changing spans of control also forces organizations to delegate more responsibility and authority to the lowest levels. If you have intelligent, positively motivated employees who are well trained to make decisions and support and understand the vision, the process works. Those closest to a situation or a problem often are the best individuals to find a solution. Organizations, therefore, become smaller, hence easier to change, and migrate to structures that support the work that has to be done.

There is no ideal organization. At one enterprise sales and administration may form a team to concentrate on a specific set of clients while at another, a group of product experts may band together to increase market share in a specific geographic area. In the consulting world, teams of experts from all over the nation come together for a specific engagement and then disband at the end of that effort. Often they operate with little management interference because all are being measured by a common system focused on making the engagement successful.

Increasingly evident is the rapidity of "unofficial" changes in organizations. Traditionally, management announces a restructuring and produces an organization chart with people's names in boxes. We have all seen examples of how in practice people cluster together differently than on the "org chart" to get tasks done. What is happening more today is that the informal organizational structure is the norm, and that it changes much faster. Access to telecommunications, data bases, microcomputers, fax machines, and air travel has democratized business structures, taking away from senior management the authority to design the organization. The challenge for management is to make those changes public to improve their efficiency and effectiveness.

Individuals increasingly are working out of their homes and cars, may or may not be card-carrying members of your firm, and already are specializing with deeper skills in narrower functions. Charles Handy has statistics that bear out this reality; the point is you have to make organizations work in this new world.

Focus on Organizational Change Early

Lesson Number Two. Make organizational change as early as possible in the transformation of a sales enterprise to a quality, market-driven one. Encourage change organizationally and use measurements, flatten enterprises, share resources across traditional departments (e.g., sales office to sales office, store to store, district to district), delegate more responsibility (empower) to employees. To make that happen, all have to be accountable for common results, share a universal set of measurements applicable to various types of organizations (e.g., customer satisfaction indices, profit targets, etc.), and be knowledgeable about a common business plan.

Compensation

No issue creates more controversy faster in a quality-driven organization than how sales personnel are paid. The debate is an unresolved one and yet it strikes at the core of what an organization values. In the eyes of sales personnel "walking the talk" is most reflected in their compensation plan. The jury is still out on what constitutes the best strategy for balancing revenue generation with continuous improvements within a customer-focused enterprise. However, the battle lines are drawn and you have to choose which side to fight on.

The traditional school of thought holds that salespeople perform best when they are paid for transactions (things sold, billable services performed) in the belief that only in this way will their productivity be maximized. In this paradigm sales representatives are usually paid some salary (or none) and then commissions for either goods and services sold or how they do against preassigned quotas. There may or may not be any limits to their earnings, and all are encouraged to make more money by selling more products. For over a century this approach has characterized the sales compensation plans for most manufacturing companies with direct sales forces and for retail sales operations.

The benefit of such an approach is that sales personnel have to hustle to get paid and also fear being fired for not making objectives. It fosters self-initiative and independent action, and it keeps sales personnel focused on results, usually in individual territories.

The downside of this approach is that salespeople do not have incentives to develop relationships with clients that go beyond the sale of specific types of products. Concern, for example, for the overall welfare of a customer has to take a back seat. Resources are collected by salespeople into concentrated masses focused only on their territory with little or no regard for the welfare of the enterprise at large. In their world it is more important that *they* make quota than the corporation. Sharing of resources and help is less evident in this kind of environment. Development of additional skills also is minimized since it takes away from selling time. Frequently products that get sold most are those on which there is a bonus.

Problems with Traditional Compensation Methods

Besides these drawbacks, given what has been occurring in the world economy, the debate on how to compensate sales personnel has once again surfaced. For one thing, in a quota-driven environment, it becomes difficult for an organization to gain the full cooperation of sales personnel in identifying sales opportunities. Sales personnel fear that once additional leads are identified, their quotas will go up and hence put their earnings at risk if performance is measured against percent of quota attained. Yet sales personnel frequently have the most detailed view of opportunities, even if theirs is a constrained view (based only on what they see on the horizon in specific accounts). Not to use salespeople as full players in opportunity identification makes it difficult for a firm to respond quickly to changing market conditions.

A second problem is that a transaction-based compensation plan does not sufficiently encourage relationship-building as the organization becomes more service-based in performance of its marketing and sales functions. As it becomes increasingly important to employ teams working continuously or in narrow engagements with customers, the old compensation system is perceived simply as not motivating cooperation. Sales personnel tend, therefore, to "work the sales plan" to their advantage, which would be fine if corporations developed sales plans that elicited the exact kind of behavior wanted from the sales force. Few ever do, however; they always seem not quite perfect.

New Ways to Compensate

Against this background is another school of thought very different from what sales management has ever known. Deming, for instance, attacks quotas since they do not account for either quality or methods. He argues that to make quota, a salesperson will burn up as much of the company's resources as he or she has to.

Put in a more positive way, there is a school of thought that says, pay your salespeople a good salary and then allow them the opportunity to earn bonuses based on their performance in a number of areas, of which revenue generation is only one. This approach says that you pay less attention to "pushing" specific products on customers and more on encouraging (pulling) customers toward you, by emphasizing relationship-building instead of just transactions performed.

In order to alter behavior to mimic service-sector performance more closely, bonuses are paid based on management's assessment of performance in specific categories that are often defined in some detail in performance plans developed jointly with employees. These might include bonuses for achievements in the following categories:

- revenue generation
- team participation
- quality process improvements
- suggestions implemented
- skills developed
- customer satisfaction improvements
- sales opportunities and leads identified

Various models of bonus structures exist to implement these. Most are consistent from salesclerk and representative up through ranks of sales management.

Approaches vary. One way would be to assign point values for each category and then allocate available bonus money divided by the number of points, then multiply the number of points earned by an individual during a specific appraisal period by the bonus amount per point. Another would place an employee in one of four levels from high to low and assign bonuses as a percent of assigned salary with the people in the highest level earning the greatest percentage of salary (e.g., 40 to 90 percent) and those in the lowest level receiving nothing. This approach protects the ideal of attempting to feed the eagles and starve the turkeys. It has the added advantage in that the bonus pot is never overspent, as happens frequently in traditional percent-of-quota-attainment-based systems.

What Customers and Employees Want You to Do

Compensation systems are viewed very differently depending on where you perch in the customer–sales personnel chain. So far we have talked about a sales perspective. What about customers and the firm? Customers generally want sales personnel to treat them fairly and honestly keeping their short- and long-term interests at heart. At the other extreme is the firm which desires to influence the activity and results of both sales personnel and customers.

Salespersons in the middle want a link to the firm that pays their salary and compensation at least commensurate with the results they achieved, and ideally with the efforts they expended. Studies on motivation notwithstanding, there is a higher percentage of individuals working in sales who are motivated by money than in most other professions, and salespeople have less regard for job security than many other professionals. Those are the realities facing sales and marketing managers designing compensation plans.

The Conference Board, in a 1979 study about sales force motivation, learned that the top five motivators for sales personnel, ranked in descending order, were:

1. Recognition for outstanding performance

2. Promotional advancement opportunity

3. Management encouragement

4. Personal bonus incentives

5. Incentives in the form of commissions

Overall compensation was sixth, skills development seventh, and prizes eleventh. As an incentive, quotas were twelfth!

So should you assign quotas or not? In either extreme you can or cannot; what you do is a function of what your culture can tolerate. More important, which approach alters behavior to achieve what you want the entire organization to display?

A third variant, usually applied in addition to a base compensation and bonus plan, is some form of profit sharing. This approach is becoming increasingly popular in organizations that want (1) employees to work as teams, (2) employees to watch bottom-line expenses, and (3) to reward the effectiveness of the organization as a whole. The corporation assigns a percent of its profits to a bonus shared by all employees. The bonus is either a flat amount paid equally to each employee or a percentage of an individual's salary. Thus a salesperson who made more money this year than another would receive a larger profit-sharing bonus in recognition of his or her greater overall contribution to the corporation's profitability.

A middle ground between the old commission structure and the "let's get rid of all quota" approaches has been employed successfully by Sewell in his Cadillac business. Individual targets are set, results publicly posted, and payments made against revenue and other targets achieved. The business as a whole has targets that are communicated continuously to employees. At IBM, a combination of salary, product sales and/or behavior (e.g., acquisition of skills, implementation of process improvements, etc.) is generally in use, and in 1992, a profit-sharing bonus was implemented.

Develop a Compensation Plan that Supports Your Vision

Lesson Number Three. Getting to the right compensation method is crucial for an organization. Two suggestions work well.

First, form a team of sales personnel and sales management to develop a compensation methodology consistent with what the enterprise expects in the form of rewardable behavior, namely an overwhelmingly procustomer emphasis with an eye cast on the bottom line, too. They will do the job better than any personnel or compensation consultant because they are closest to the situation.

Second, treat compensation as a process that needs to be studied and continuously modified as circumstances warrant. If employees come to see that it is *their* process, they can be expected to take ownership of tying its rewards to their business objectives.

Now let me complicate the process further by reminding you that as sales personnel get older, their interests change. Between roughly ages 21 and 30, people are developing, learning, and exploring possibilities, and therefore they are very interested in things such as improving selling skills, job satisfaction, and positive feedback. In the next period—roughly from about age 30 to 45—research shows that career enhancement is of utmost importance while their managers are viewed less as guides and more as role models. Rewards have to be more than money; promotions are crucial. In the period from the late thirties to early fifties, competition for success and promotion generally declines, employees see themselves as guides, and immediate rewards have to be monetary. They worry about making money, relationships with coworkers, and how their job identifies with specific organizations. As they approach retirement, sales personnel begin to change their images, identifying with other interests outside of their traditional career. They are more interested in what psychologists and sociologists would call "lower-order rewards," like money.

So why go through all of this? As you change your organization into one valuing continuous improvement and renewed customer focus in a service-based world, each age group has to be treated differently. This is particularly difficult with older employees, a problem since 22-year-old salespeople are becoming as rare as hen's teeth thanks to demographics throughout North America and Western Europe.

The problem is fixed the same way smart sales managers have always properly fixed sales contests. Involve the right age mix of sales personnel to design your reward and compensation system to conform to your requirements and values and to their needs and desires. Treat it as a process and the incentives to motivate correctly will emerge.

Quality-focused firms find that compensation strategies can be developed that support business objectives. Hewlett-Packard pays better than the average company and for merit—with bonuses, commissions, and base salary an outgrowth of sustained performance. Many of its competitors follow a similar approach. Honeywell pays competitively by business type, fairly in comparison to other employees in equal positions; the process is communicated and each business division is responsible for establishing and administering its plans. In Chapter 5's discussion on recognition, we address some additional ideas about compensation.

Quality Education

The fourth process that must be attacked early and with enthusiasm and care is education to make employees aware of the principles of process reengineering, the realities of changing markets, and the definition of their role. Some skills transfer can also occur in this early stage of movement to a more quality-driven company culture.

Just as measurements, organizational changes, and compensation systems remain forever with the enterprise, so too does education on quality. Each of the Baldrige winners in the United States and Deming Prize winners in Japan will tell you that it is not uncommon to spend up to 4 percent of their budgets educating people on quality continuously for a number of years. Why? Because the results can lead to a 10 to 40 percent reduction in waste and associated costs while gaining several points of market share within three to four years of initial investment in quality education. Money in the bank or invested in stocks hardly matches those yield rates.

Every case of quality transformation I have studied has placed education at the forefront of implementation. Larry McMahan, vice president of human resources at Baldrige-winning Federal Express, stated what the first task hads to be: "All managers must be required to take company unifying courses in teamwork, customer/supplier alignment and systematic quality." Brenda Sumberg, director of quality at Motorola University (Motorola was also a Baldrige winner) argues that "initially, training's role is to change the attitude of the people, then skill-based training encompasses quality tools, related to their jobs." I could fill pages with such quotations, but the message is obvious enough.

While education will receive more attention in subsequent chapters, it is important to note that just as the first three most crucial processes should be attacked in the first six months of a move to quality-based management, so too should quality education.

Two Strategies for Quality Education

There are two typical approaches to quality education. The first approach, and the one most appreciated by sales personnel, involves a one- to two-day awareness class on why the enterprise needs to apply quality techniques, identification of TQM's basic elements, and some exposure to statistical methods of measuring activities. This is then usually followed up later with seminars on process reengineering (usually one or two to five) in which specific problems are worked on. At this point employees are exposed to statistical process control (SPC) tools such as Pareto charts, fishbone diagrams, and so forth.

A second path, the fire-hose approach, sends everyone off to five to fifteen days of education on the above topics and then drops them back into their work environment. If the measurement system has been altered to give incentives for process reengineering, then results can reasonably be expected; if not, then you can count on having wasted their time while frustrating employees now hopeful that things will change.

I personally have found incremental education programs substantially more effective. Providing adults with training when needed with a "just-in-time" approach works better and creates expense only when needed, when it makes sense. Each successful education program recognizes that employees need hard skills to transform their business and that those skills involve process reengineering, problem identification, analysis, and resolution. Education must allow employees to link their quality activities back to their real jobs. Finally, good education programs must by necessity evolve over time as the skills and needs of employees, individual by individual, change.

The better programs, like those at IBM, Xerox, Milliken, Federal Express, and Florida Power & Light, are also aimed at altering cultural values. For example, at IBM, a two-day class, known as "The Journey Continues," is given a year after initial TQM exposure to show employees the power of vision, the benefits of working more closely in a team environment, and how to encourage and support each other in quality improvements. It is based on the work of James M. Kouzes and Barry Z. Posner. Theirs is a simple message: to get extraordinary things done in an organization, five practices must be alive and well:

- challenging the process
- inspiring a shared vision
- enabling others to act
- modeling the way
- encouraging the heart

The job of leaders is to make these five practices come alive. By challenging the process, you search for opportunities to change the status quo, with risk-taking allowed and encouraged. Inspiring a shared vision calls for envisioning a better, specific future and attracting others to the common purpose of implementing the vision. Enabling others to act is simply fostering collaboration and teamwork and sharing power and information. Modeling the way is setting the example, leading by doing. Encouraging the heart is recognizing contributions, linking rewards to performance, and "valuing the victories."

The class is unique in that it works on the values of an employee as applied to quality and not on the mechanics of applying process reengineering. Many of the same sentiments are reflected in Stephen R. Covey's *The 7 Habits of Highly Effective People.* Approximately 25 percent of the course content is directed to altering attitudes, another 25 percent to teaching skills, and the remainder to transmitting knowledge about transformation, vision, and so forth.

Nobody is exempt from quality education. In many firms the standard approach is for the initial awareness education to be taught by the highest ranking official of the firm to his or her direct reports; they in turn teach their direct reports, and so on down to the lowest level. This process ingrains in management the principles and values involved and is proof of commitment to employees up and down the line. Later, when skills, such as statistical analysis and problem solving, are of greater importance, instructors on staff (full- or part-time) usually do a better job in providing the training.

Increasingly, particularly with industrial products, customers are asking for proof of a vendor's commitment to quality. This is done not just to ensure quality goods and services but also because manufacturers are finding it more cost effective to have fewer suppliers, upon which they become more dependent. To have a supplier that is not dedicated to providing high quality goods can be disastrous. Thus just to be competitive, many suppliers have to prove what they are doing to implement TQM. For instance, at one point Motorola insisted that its suppliers compete for the Baldrige Award!

We already saw that customers at the retail level are increasingly relying on quality of products to make buying decisions rather than just on price.

Invest in Employee Education

Lesson Number Four. Educating employees about quality is thus a crucial and early requirement.

Tips on Knowing if It All Is Working

A large number of processes has to be improved to make an organization more effective. The real test of whether or not the initial attack on quality, with its attendant recharging of the customer-contact community to place customer satisfaction at the top of its priorities, begins by assuming nothing. A number of tests to gauge progress should be performed, starting at about the six-month point and continuing periodically afterward.

To begin with, the first four processes targeted—measurements, organization, compensation, and education—are inward-looking and do not involve customers or take into account where your competition is on quality. (The processes involving customers come next and are the subject of Chapter 5.) However, nobody goes to market without first doing some preparation internally, e.g., building a product or service to offer. So it is with transformation to a quality-driven organization. The initial measurements are simply a step to alter behavior and will be replaced with others more specifically tied to tactical processes of concern to customers. Organizational and compensation actions are taken to align resources with the vision of your firm's future. Education simply greases the wheels of progress.

However, while a new vision and focus may look good on paper, in reality they will be resisted. First, there are those who feel that the way things are today is just fine, so why change? A second group will conclude that the kinds of changes being asked for are different from what made them successful so far. A third perspective will be that these changes just will not work. This group—usually cynics—will argue that they have seen this all before: quality circles in the early 1980s, excellence as the program *du jour*, and so forth. The skeptics are the best allies because once converted they can be the nucleus of a new way of doing business and they ensure that reality does not give way to euphoria and wild abandon to TQM.

But because change is difficult for many people, the nature of the difficulty must be understood. That is why formal assessments are very helpful. Several techniques work well in taking the pulse of the transformation.

How to Assess the Status of Quality among Employees

Employee opinion surveys are very useful tools; many companies apply them effectively. If you do not have such a tool, get to work on one right away and make sure its anonymity is preserved no matter what the cost, because the knowledge gained can set the quality agenda for years. As you begin to preach the gospel of quality and customer focus, two or three questions in employee opinion surveys allow you to determine progress or at least buy-in. If the questions are asked exactly the same way over the next several years, the first round serves as a base line against which to measure progress over time. The kinds of questions to ask include:

- To what extent do you believe senior management is committed to quality improvement at XYZ Company?
- To what extent are you personally willing to apply principles of quality improvement to your job?
- To what extent is your manager (or department) committed to quality improvement?

You also want to know how your managers feel about these issues both as employees and as leaders of the firm because in the final analysis, if management is not on board with quality, it will not come on its own. Senior management needs to monitor commitment on the part of those individuals who ultimately have the authority and capability of energizing the entire enterprise toward quality.

Statistically measure responses to the questions on the roles of management, department, and individual. Then also measure answers to the following:

- To what extent do you understand the company's quality improvement strategy?
- Which of the following best expresses your views on being customer-driven? (Pick 3 to 5 variables relevant to your industry and business.)

Initial responses will probably range from a low of 20 percent positive to perhaps a high of 50 percent. Incremental improvements in buy-in of 5 to 10 points per year would not be uncommon, meaning that the *total* transformation of the culture will require up to nearly ten years, although three to five years is more normal. As successes mount along with peer pressure (due to growing buy-in), some will leave your firm, others will be eliminated for taking too long to convert, and the rest will embrace the new approach at their own pace. The point is that it takes time to gain buy-in and to effect a real service-oriented transformation. But it then sticks as a permanent part of the corporate culture.

Using Quality Indicators

To use measurements as a tool to influence activities as early as possible, begin by developing a short list of quality indicators that measure progress against goals and add to it as necessary. Practical criteria for these should include:

- one page of measurements only
- quarterly publication
- numeric (percent, index, ratio, etc.)
- easy-to-understand trend indicator
- this year's achievement goal (a number)
- measurable from salesperson to sales executive

There is no black magic involved. For example, I worked in one sales organization that set five goals involving customer satisfaction, employee morale, quality, financial contribution, and community involvement. Ultimately we had 2 to 5 measurements for each category, and all of them fit on one piece of paper, serving as a barometer of the health of the business.

For customer satisfaction we began with what was available: a national blind survey that generated a satisfaction index. We then added local surveys, a complaint process measurement, and so forth. For employee morale, we began by using results of a national survey, added a local one to generate data on our issues and then a skills index (which measured the percent of skills we had to go after quantifiable opportunities). Then we added percent of employees submitting suggestions (as an indicator of ownership for change) and other measurements as new processes came on-line.

For quality we did a Baldrige assessment, graded ourselves terribly with an awfully low score, and then built upon that platform.

Financial contribution was obvious: customers voted with their money, which we could measure with existing data: percent of revenue growth, index of market share, and profitability.

Community involvement was measured by the number of employees active in community affairs (e.g., political office, charities, United Way, and so forth).

Another tactic is to put together a team representing various segments of the organization to advise, preach, and report on progress.

Respected floor leaders can craft a program for quality while preaching, explaining, and defending its purpose.

One final recommendation: ask peers in other firms about how much progress they made and over what period of time. Their advice is priceless; they too want to ask you the same questions. Many firms find it expedient to form councils made up of customers or peers to trade war stories and get advice. While more will be said about quality councils in subsequent chapters, suffice it to say that asking others about their initial processes and programs is just good benchmarking and common sense. The support they give is vital in this early stage when most em-

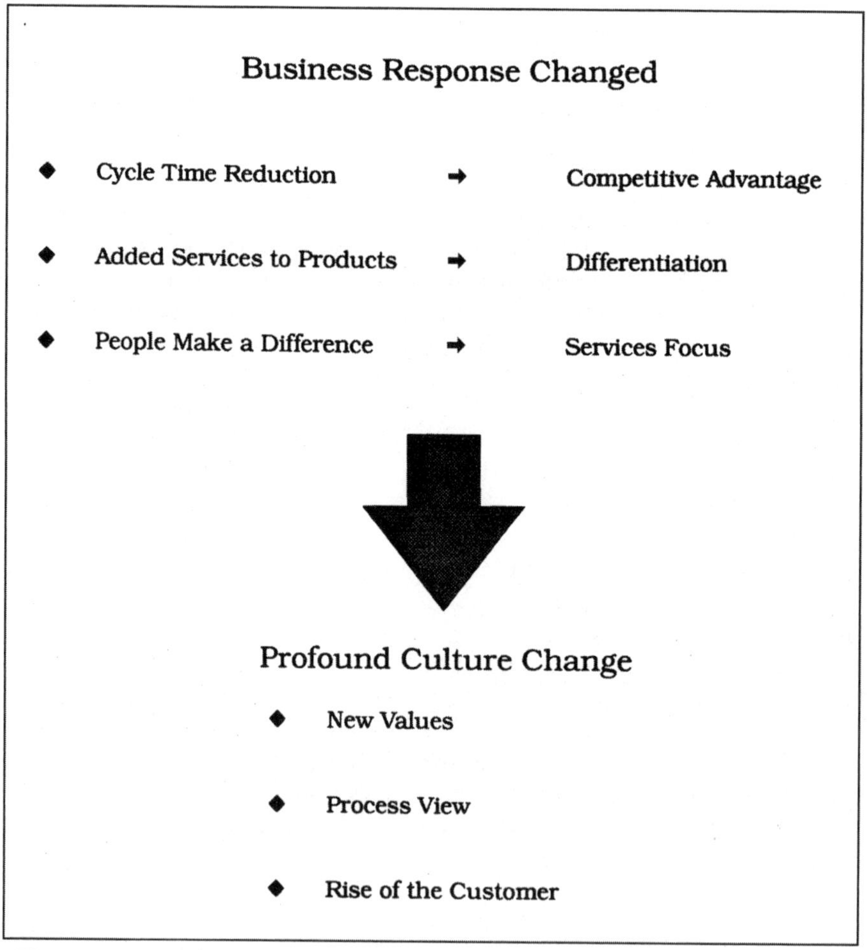

Business Response Changed

◆ Cycle Time Reduction   ➡   Competitive Advantage

◆ Added Services to Products   ➡   Differentiation

◆ People Make a Difference   ➡   Services Focus

Profound Culture Change

◆ New Values

◆ Process View

◆ Rise of the Customer

Figure 4-5. The quality transformation.

ployees have doubts and are insecure about the outcome of what obviously does not appear on the surface to be good old-fashioned tactical selling activities!

Conclusions

Earl C. Conway, director of corporate quality improvement at Procter & Gamble, stated the message clearly: "Quality is the unyielding and continuing effort by everyone in an organization to understand, meet, and exceed the needs of its customers." Others have lined up behind this same message to all managers. An editor in chief of the *Harvard Business Review*, Rosabeth Moss Kanter, spoke for many executives when she warned that "cowboy management is a disaster for the company that seeks quality." If you have any doubts about the need for quality, remind your employees that customer focus in a global economy is the central issue. "The Japanese are consistently disciplined. They seem to have the ability to stick with a task until they reach a goal. And that's not true for Americans," says Marilyn Zuckerman, quality manager at AT&T. I could fill many pages with similar statements, but they would all simply reinforce the same message and provide sales management with a wonderful reaffirmation of what we have always known: that the customer is king and the king wants quality (see Figure 4-5). And isn't the customer always right?

References

Bowles, Jerry, and Hammong, Joshua. *Beyond Quality: How 50 Winning Companies Use Continuous Improvement.* New York: Putnam, 1991.

Covey, Stephen R. *The 7 Habits of Highly Effective People.* New York: Simon & Schuster, 1989.

Handy, Charles. *The Age of Unreason.* Boston: Harvard Business School Press, 1989.

Kouzes, James M., and Posner, Barry Z. *The Leadership Challenge: How to Get Extraordinary Things Done in Organizations.* San Francisco: Jossey-Bass, 1990.

Rackham, Neil. *SPIN Selling.* New York: McGraw-Hill, 1988.

Ries, Al, and Trout, Jack. *Bottom-Up Marketing.* New York: McGraw-Hill, 1989.

Ries, Al, and Trout, Jack. *Marketing Warfare.* New York: McGraw-Hill, 1986.

Sewell, Carl, and Brown, Paul B. *Customers for Life: How to Turn That One-Time Buyer into a Lifetime Customer.* New York: Doubleday, 1990.

5

Quality-Focused
Core Processes

*I am the world's worst salesman, therefore, I
must make it easy for people to buy.*

F. W. WOOLWORTH, 1888

This chapter is devoted to a discussion of some of the earliest customer-focused core processes that should be implemented in a sales
organization. It illustrates actual examples and then a case study.

The activities of a business can be viewed as collections of processes that
need to get done daily in order for the firm to be successful. What you
see quickly enough is that there are certain functions that are crucial for
success with customers (e.g., processes for taking an order or for delivering goods and services) and others that may or may not be so critical
(e.g., administrative processes for running your building). Finally you
can also look at processes as either very efficient and effective or in need
of much work. A sales organization that has caught the quality "bug"
sees its activities as collections of processes that it prioritizes first by importance and next by need for redesign, or reengineering.

No two organizations ever come up with the same list and never do
their processes have the same features. But then who ever admits that
his or her business is the same as someone else's? Therefore, in this

chapter a number of processes are presented to illustrate the idea that collections of tasks should be viewed as processes. The processes below are not comprehensive nor are they prioritized. All, however, are outwardly focused on the customer. Processes that are really customer-focused increase the chances of providing goods and services right the first time, hence ensuring repeat business and high customer satisfaction. Many organizations find that even in the best of circumstances, "doing it right the first time" can only occur up to 80 percent of the time. Twenty percent of the time you have to manage complaints, about which I will have more to say below.

If you have started to work on measurements and organization, then the kinds of processes described below are most likely to be the next collections of activities to improve.

Processes Linked to Business Plans

In defining collections of processes, there is much to be said in favor of the technique of approaching them much the way zero-based budgeting is done. Essentially once a process or activity is identified, you ask how relevant it is to what the business is commissioned to do. If it is not very relevant then it is a candidate for elimination; if it is critical it is studied, continuously improved upon, and measured for effectiveness. For example, say you run a real estate broker's office with 15 agents. After mapping all significant processes you find there is a small process used to file information about real estate agencies in other cities in a file cabinet. Years ago this was done in case your agency had to refer your clients moving to another city to other real estate agents. Today you are tied into a national real estate network via computer. Thus you no longer need to maintain this paper file, which is hardly used and out of date anyway. So you stop collecting data manually but make sure that the computer referral process meets the current needs of your clients.

Where zero-based approaches work is with reports that have been generated for years, often long after they are no longer needed or wanted or read. A common example in sales is the computer-generated report of sales activities published one to three months after they occur, especially if the information is already available on-line. Expense reports are usually another good example since they are produced at least 45 days after expenses are incurred. A better process would be to develop a reporting system that gives you data about the previous month's expenditures on the first working day of the new month.

Use Your Business Plan to Set Priorities on the Value of Processes

But zero-based approaches alone do not help define what is important. More critical is to have a frame of reference against which to measure what are critical and effective processes. The best way to get that frame of reference is to have a business plan against which you can measure all activities. Those activities that support the business plan are kept and improved; those that do not are thrown out. The business plan needs several critical elements, however, to be useful in zero-based approaches to priorities.

1. *The business plan should have a value-laden vision to guide those making decisions about processes* because no business plan is detailed enough to cover all activities. If employees have a vision of where the firm is going and what it values (e.g., total customer satisfaction), then they have a frame of reference to operate within an empowered environment. They can make decisions with greater confidence.

2. *The business plan has to include specific statements about mission and goals* because employees will want (rightfully so) to ensure that processes exist to support achievement of all goals. Since measurement of progress toward goals is such a critical aspect of TQM approaches, linking processes to goals is essential.

3. *Processes should be viewed both as collections of tactical actions that efficiently implement the business plan and also as routine activities performed daily as core elements of your business.* For example, if you have a goal to increase sales by 7 percent and your plan to implement involves increasing the sales force by 2 percent, you may need a training process to bring new sales personnel up to speed quickly. Since turnover is always an issue, training would have to be ongoing throughout this and many subsequent years. You would thus develop a training process that exists as a routine part of the business.

4. *Things change so you need a way of revalidating the relevance of your processes and measuring their effectiveness.* This is where the notion of using a process such as the Baldrige Award assessment comes in very handy. Designing statistical measurements into processes will indicate if what you are doing is actually improving. Self-assessments and built-in measurements together give an organization the ability to ensure linkage of activities and processes back to a business plan. Indeed, the Baldrige approach requires first that there be a business plan tied to a vision of where the enterprise is going precisely so that all activities can be assessed against the intent of the enterprise.

Xerox's approach to its sales representatives illustrates all four points. Xerox intends its field personnel to understand and satisfy customer requirements in such a way that the firm also is profitable and grows market share. These objectives must be achieved through quality in sales. Xerox defined six collections of processes to achieve quality in sales: training, support systems, tools and measurements, communications, management behavior and actions, and recognition and rewards. Within each of these families of processes are more narrowly defined ones. For instance, under the heading of management behavior and actions, the firm has processes to broadcast success stories, manage for results, conduct roundtables, publish newsletters, and develop quality communication strategies at the sales unit and representative level. All of these activities are expected to be at the unit and branch office level in addition to the corporate level.

How Processes Affect Customer Satisfaction

But more important than our four points is measuring performance against what would satisfy and exceed customer expectations. To a large extent what is involved is delivering what the customer expects you to. In other words, customers want your processes to satisfy needs and wants. While the literature on customer satisfaction is vast and need not detain us here, several obvious issues need to be kept in mind when determining which processes to improve. You should ask how each process satisfies the needs and wants of customers.

Needs are things expected minimally by customers and are not negotiable; you either have them or not. Wants are the ill-defined things customers desire over and above the minimum. Since delivering on needs and wants always requires a combination of products and services, well-executed processes, and effective personnel, a quality-focused organization will test processes against all three elements. That is why we are deluged with lectures and books on setting customer expectations (product needs management) and on why giving more than needs creates significant added value or, in Michael Porter's thinking, strategic competitive advantages.

The issue of expectations can also be complicated. Minimal requirements can and should be documented by constantly asking customers. These expectations can include a basic menu that never changes (but which can be added to), a consistent service (the time it takes to get your teeth cleaned by a dentist), a product (size of memory on a microcomputer), or the appearance or actions of a vendor (IBM and its blue suits). Once you understand these, then you earn the right to exceed expectations.

Such additional actions can involve doing the work in less time or for less cost, or adding to products. The quality gurus are almost universal in their thinking, and students of customer satisfaction concur, that it is more important to meet minimal standards of expectations first than to exceed what you think a customer wants. Yet the dialogue that got you to an understanding of minimal expectations also can be used to define what would exceed expectations and hence delight customers. With very complex products (such as computers, airplanes, and weapons systems) there is the added requirement and opportunity to delight that comes from suggesting new products and services to customers that they had not thought about before. But they will only pay attention to you if you constantly meet normal expectations.

Research has suggested that the greatest points of leverage on customer satisfaction rest with the effects of processes and personal actions, not with products because things can be made equivalently by many vendors. That is why well-run organizations look at customer feedback processes, cost-free telephone calls (like 800 telephone numbers in the United States), order entry, automated teller machines, and so forth. All processes that touch a customer ultimately become more important than the product being sold.

Customer Feedback Process

All effective sales organizations have created customer surveys of various types. The effective ones have defined customer feedback as a process that takes into account all types of customer input, such as surveys, telephone calls, complaints (both written and oral), suggestions for improvements, and what they do or do not acquire. The smart organizations have woven customer feedback into all their business processes. Thus, for example, at Xerox, one-third of a sales representative's appraisal is dependent on customer satisfaction. At many companies, all field executives have the amount of their bonuses tied to a similar measurement: happier, more satisfied customers trigger larger bonuses. Targets for year-to-year increases in customer satisfaction are tied back to bonuses. Well-run organizations also have figured out how to get the data from customer feedback into the enterprise so that products, services, and processes can be designed to improve customer satisfaction. In short, doing an annual survey is in itself not a process but one task within the customer feedback process.

Figure 5-1 is a highly simplified flowchart of how one firm assessed the needs and desires of its customers. It begins with an assessment of the current relationship with a customer, then flows down through a

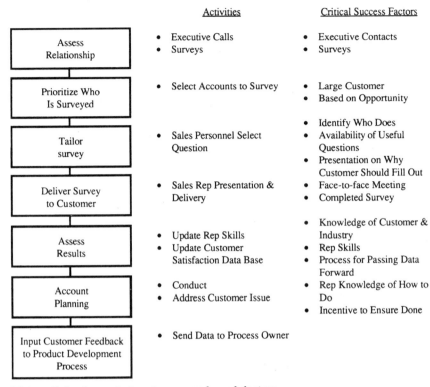

Figure 5-1. Assessing customer needs and desires.

process for continuously gathering account data, which then is used to plan how best to service that customer. Note that the survey is only one part of the whole process.

In this particular example, survey questions are designed to elicit responses that can be statistically collected. Thus trend analysis can be done over time and reported in normal bar charts. In addition, a select number of questions concerning products, customer-contact personnel, and ease of doing business is clustered together to create a customer satisfaction index—a percentage of satisfaction—that serves as a macroindicator of whether relationships are improving or deteriorating. Figure 5-2 offers another customer satisfaction survey process to illustrate again the basic elements of such an approach to disciplined understanding of customers.

Most sales organizations do some sort of survey work. Typically these are done in one of two ways: either a central office mails out surveys to all customers or to a statistical sample and over time feeds results back

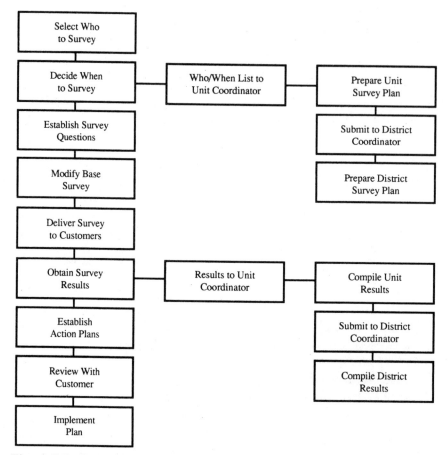

Figure 5-2. Surveying customers.

to local offices, or local offices mail surveys to their own customers. Sometimes a firm employs a combination of the two approaches or uses an outside company to do the work. In most cases, surveys are done several times on one customer to measure levels of satisfaction with the relationship between the two enterprises or between the individual customer and the firm, and several times during the life of the product that a customer uses.

Surveys are designed either to indicate long-term macro trends in customer attitudes or to provide sales with actionable feedback. The first type is done, for example, by conducting blind telephone surveys across samples of customers on a regular basis. The result is a set of percentages of satisfied/dissatisfied per question. These frequently are presented as rolling averages over four or more quarters and suggest broad national trends. A second type of survey is mailed or called in to specific customers, data is gathered, and then it is returned to a sales office for each account. A sales representative then can follow up on concerns expressed by each customer.

Large firms like Xerox, IBM, Ford, and others conduct tens of thousands of surveys by mail or telephone monthly, measure return rates (of written surveys), trap statistical data on responses to questions, then distribute results to those who can actually do something to improve them (e.g., product designers or local sales offices). Typically such a critical process has national and local process owners whose job it is to ensure the process is executed, results delivered, and the efforts improved.

What actually gets asked varies so much from firm to firm that I could fill pages with examples, and in the final analysis you would have guessed most of the questions anyway.

Feedback processes ideally cover all aspects of the relationship between customers and the firm. That is a tall order. Figure 5-3 is a catalog of most activities of a typical sales organization that affect customer satisfaction from the customer's perspective. Your firm probably has some others unique to its own customer set. Each needs a definition in your firm, which then can be translated either into action or feedback questions.

Figure 5-4 takes several of these attributes of customer satisfaction and defines what they mean to customers, to illustrate the kind of clarity a sales organization must have on these important points.

It is very important to ensure that a couple of features exist in the feedback process regardless of its form.

Features of Good Customer Feedback Processes

First, while write-in comments are useful, *make sure all questions are designed so that answers can be swept up statistically.* Thus a survey with multiple-choice answers (e.g., very satisfied, satisfied, all the way to very dissatisfied) is quick to fill out and gives you needed data.

Second, *ensure a routine exists for reviewing results on a regular basis (e.g., monthly or quarterly) and for determining what people are going to do to improve them.*

Third, *if in doubt about what questions to ask, how often, and of whom, form a task force made up of customers and your people to design questionnaires.*

Fourth, *ensure there are other means of obtaining feedback from customers.* This is crucial because each medium for collecting data—written forms,

Categories of Actions Affecting Customer Satisfaction

Sales	Products	Service	Administration
Affordable Solution	Meets Needs	Quick Problem	Ordering Efficiency
Defined	Quality	Identification	Delivery Speed
Expectations	Good Functions	Responsive	Billing Accuracy
Knows Needs	Timely	Knowledgeable	Telephone Support
Provides Products	Availability	Parts Available	Terms and
Understands	Low Price	Single Contact	Conditions
Customer	High Performance	Quick Fix	Empathy
Easy to Do Business	Good Value	Low Cost	Politeness
With	Ease of	Frequency	
Handles Complaints	Maintenance		
Well	Reliability		
Professional			
Customer Education			
Loyalty and Trust			
Distribution			

Figure 5-3. An organization's actions from the customer point of view.

Sample Attribute Definitions

Attribute	Definition
Billing	Accurate, easy to understand, timely, with flexible payment terms.
Understands Customer	Understands customer's business, competition, needs, and how to apply products to customer.
Customer Education	Providing training that meets customer needs, where and when needed is affordable.
Professionalism	Customer contact employee has integrity, is responsive, enjoys trust and confidence.
Low Price	Product/service is efficient and effective for what it costs and what customer is willing to buy.
Responsiveness	Meeting and exceeding customer expectations on speed and quality of service/inquiry.
Parts Available	Refers to ability have working parts in timely manner that are cost effective from customer's viewpoint.

Figure 5-4. Precise definitions of several attributes of customer satisfaction.

telephone surveys, face-to-face meetings—has strengths and weaknesses and generates different forms of information. Each can be used as a check on other methods to ensure statistical validity and to flush out details. For example, if written survey data suggests growing dissatisfaction with your sales operations in a particular city, conducting round tables with, or calling on, customers in that city will probably lead to details on why service is declining and what they would recommend to improve it. Such round tables and calls, when done on a routine basis, keep management close to customers. In turn, customers appreciate their ideas being taken seriously.

The literature on customer surveys and customer feedback is massive and growing all the time. But the basic elements remain the same. What we know is that in a quality-oriented organization customer feedback is treated as a comprehensive process crucial to the success of the firm. Haphazardly executed customer feedback processes are next to useless because nobody believes the data gathered, which may actually not be of the type that can lead to corrective action.

But surveys themselves are a complicated issue. Many factors outside your control influence customers. For instance, a product of yours that does not work may generate a complaint or a desire to complain that is directed to you when in fact the problem was caused by a distributor. You get blamed for the problem because your logo is on the product. Therefore, looking at all kinds of influences on customer expectations in any feedback process is crucial, especially today when many businesses have alliances and partnerships with organizations that can enhance or hurt how customers view them. Anticipating customer needs and wants in terms of required processes can then be measured with customer feedback that takes into account both direct and indirect influences on your business.

Customer Complaint Process

A variant of the customer feedback process is the all-important customer complaint process. In some organizations it is treated as a subprocess of customer feedback and surveys, and in other organizations it is an independent process. Either way it is an important vehicle for giving the enterprise an early warning signal that something is not right. Surveys of customers in the United States have shown that 60 to 70 percent of complaining customers will do business again with the organization with which they had a problem providing their concerns are resolved. Ninety-five percent of complainers said they would be willing to do business again if their complaints were resolved quickly! However, there is a dark side to customer complaints; 50 percent of all customers with a problem never bring the problem to the attention of the vendor, 45 percent typically do but only to clerical or customer-contact individuals. That means that as a manager, you only stand a 5 percent chance of receiving customer complaints. Encouraging complaints is thus the only way you have of finding out what is wrong with your goods and services while showing your concern and demonstrating your corporate commitment to the best quality service.

You Need a Definition of a Complaint

How you define a complaint is critical to implementing a good response system. Narrow definitions, such as customer letters written to executives about problems, while widespread, do not even begin to approach the issue. Well-run organizations look for very broad definitions of complaints and identify a growing number of sources for these.

A starting point for a definition is that a *complaint* is any response or thought of a customer about any product or service that does not meet their expectations, no matter what the reason.

Customers who have been surveyed believe all vendors have a lot of room for improvement. TARP (a Harvard University research company) has determined that customers experience problems with banks 26 percent of the time; auto repair shops, 50 percent; auto rental firms, 36 percent; all salespersons, 40 percent; and utilities, 33 percent. So no industry is really immune from problems. TARP's research shows that in 91 percent of the cases involving over $100 in customer losses, non-complainers simply will not do business with you again. Complainers will not do business with you again in 81 percent of the cases if their complaints are not resolved. Yet if problems are resolved quickly, 82 percent of complainers will come back, 95 percent for small ticket sales ($1 to $5).

Understand How Your Customers Use Complaints

To remind you of the obvious, survey work in the United States shows that an average customer with a problem tells ten other people about it, and 13 percent tell more than 20 people! And the group that just keeps quiet and takes their business elsewhere is too large to ignore. TARP found repeatedly that customers just do not like to complain to vendors: 39 percent of the time in banking, 26 percent in auto repairs, 55 percent in car rentals, 62 percent with direct salespeople, and 45 percent with utilities. Yet resolving complaints keeps customers loyal. Since we know serving loyal customers costs far less than recruiting new ones, it makes sense to welcome complaints to fix problems. As Bill Harley, president of Harley Davidson Motorcycles, likes to put it, "When people have brand names tattooed on their chests, it's hard to change brands."

TARP's research has documented some very good news. Complaint handlers yield a very high, "real money" return on investment (ROI). In packaged goods companies, for example, ROIs ranged from 15 to 75 percent and in banking, from 50 to 170 percent. Retailing ROIs start at 35 percent and have been documented as high as 400 percent. Consumer durable goods come in at about 100 percent. In short, most firms can make money by having an effective complaint-handling process and organization and most important, all should seek out complaints to fix as a strategy for growing sales!

In quality-focused organizations, customer complaints are not viewed negatively but rather as an opportunity to improve. Measurements and incentives are designed into the culture to reinforce this positive approach. That it is still seen as a negative aspect of doing business cannot be denied; but customers who are always delighted cannot necessarily help a firm continuously improve—for that you need the complainers.

What a Complaint Process Should Look Like

A complaint process can be used to empower employees with a mechanism for feeding the concerns of customers back into the enterprise, particularly to those designing and building products or creating the terms and conditions under which goods and services are provided. Done nationally, such a process can be an analytical tool for identifying problems systematically, based on statistical data, not on impressionistic evidence. It can serve as a checklist of what needs to be improved. Such a process then becomes an effective monitor of actions taken to fix problems.

Figure 5-5 illustrates a simple complaint process. When a team actually designs one, it becomes very apparent in the first team meeting that complaints come into the organization in a variety of ways: letters, survey results, telephone calls, comments to sales and service personnel, and even irate customers putting up billboards on highways!

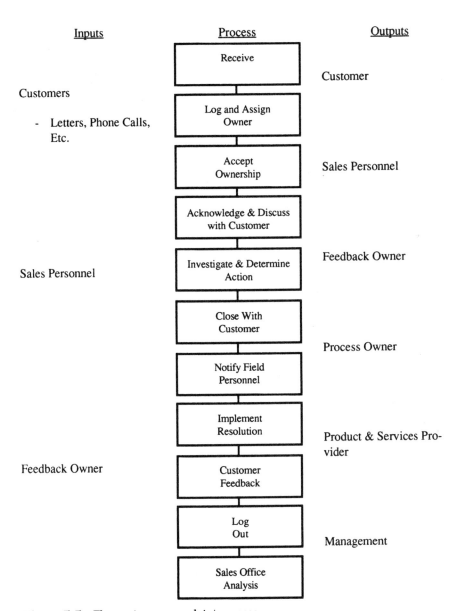

Figure 5-5. The customer complaint process.

Effective complaint processes are owned by the organization closest to a customer, for example, the local sales office. There is a defined process with a process owner responsible for the integrity of the system. The best processes have a computer-based data gathering and dissemination feature rather than the old manual logs kept by receptionists or secretaries. The best processes also have the following features:

- time frames for performing various steps
- time targets for closing out complaints
- customer determination of when a complaint has been resolved
- feedback to ensure management knows status of resolutions
- tracking of number of lost customers versus number gained
- statistical records
- all employees responsible for resolving problems in their areas

Information capturing is increasingly computer-based because the process must easily collect large volumes of data and aggregate the specifics of complaints into totals for trend analysis, either locally or nationally or by product or service. Good systems attempt to minimize data entry requirements (e.g., using imaging technology to scan letters) yet have query capabilities so that analysis can be done regularly. Such systems also produce either routine reports (e.g., monthly or quarterly reports on trends and even more frequent reports on unresolved complaints) or ad hoc reports as required. Regardless of whether or not computing is used, data collection and analysis is a closed-loop process just as the complaint process itself should be. Only in this way can you ensure systematic problem identification and resolution in terms acceptable to customers.

What to ask in survey and complaint processes is fairly straightforward. However, there are several tricks you can use to improve. My favorite is to pay attention to how my complaints are handled. I also collect questionnaires from other companies trying to survey me. Going to benchmarking organizations (about which more will be said later) for ideas is a priceless and very quick tactic as well. The bottom line is to treat these as processes, using common sense management infused with deadly seriousness of purpose.

Communication Process

A set of activities that does not get enough attention as a process in all sales organizations is communication with employees. Yet most managers would suggest that good communication is essential for transmitting vision and goals and for ensuring quality performance. Survey data confirms this. For example, a 1988 Harris poll established that workers most value managers who are honest, ethical, and who encourage a free exchange of information among employees. Organizations bent on continuous improvement have found communication to be a critical success factor because it is a primary element involved in the delivery of quality to employees and customers. Data and trend analysis is an obvious example of that at work, but so too are the one-on-one communications between employees and their managers or between employees within teams.

The old notion that perception, not reality, counts is addressed through clear and effective communication. Sharing of information is best when done with employees (fellow little *c* customers) and also with big *C* customers—the people who buy our goods and services. Good communication strategies recognize that sharing information is part of the quality education process for employees. Nowhere is communication more urgent than in organizations that have flattened their reporting structures, because traditional channels of information disappear and need to be replaced with more peer-to-peer sharing of information. For senior managers, communication becomes one of the top two or three most important functions that they must spend time on with their employees.

Since communication can involve a vast array of activities, it is a process unique to each organization at each level, and it grows in complexity and volume over time. Communication can involve advertising, direct response mail, sales promotion literature, business shows, media relations, and publications—and all of these just to big *C* customers! For employees there are all those just mentioned and management communications, bulletin board announcements, newsletters, recognition events, internal television, internal mail, electronic mail, round tables, speeches, unit meetings, annual reports, quarterly progress reports, process reports, team meetings—all providing the information needed to perform their jobs as well as a great deal considered irrelevant. Effective executives and managers should have a process to ensure adequate, timely, and relevant communication with employees, customers, and stakeholders within their own firms. Each customer-contact employee should also figure out what level and kind of communications are required with customers and treat those communications as a process.

How Communication Helps in the Sell Cycle

From a marketing point of view, communication can facilitate selling at four points in the sell cycle. The first point is when a potential customer becomes aware of a need and you want that individual to think that your firm can satisfy it. A second phase is customer interest in what you have to offer and the wish to see your offering. A third point is desire: "I want something" and "I believe your firm can best provide it." The fourth is the action of purchasing goods and services from you.

At each stage, different types of communication with customers and employees are required. Thus from a marketing perspective, communication must involve use of different types of tools to accomplish the tasks. These typically are:

- *awareness*—media, advertising, business shows, literature

- *interest*—advertising, media, sales promotion, direct mail literature, publications

- *desire*—media, direct response marketing, sales promotion, advertising

- *action*—sales promotion, advertising, media relations, personal contact

Within an enterprise, a variety of communication vehicles is also used. However, remember that the ones used with customers have the same effect on employees and often serve as a simultaneous method of communicating certain types of information (e.g., product specifications and benefits). Internal communications can address other issues more specifically related either to the quality movement or to sales results. The latter, for instance, would involve routine reporting of sales volumes and events. Encouraging the practice of quality requires more imaginative approaches. Figure 5-6 illustrates some examples from various American corporations. Corporate-level communications also work to disseminate company or brand image more than field sales organizations do, and increasingly national programs are becoming processes. This is true, for instance, at Xerox, where the quality image portrayed to the public is "Leadership through quality"; at Ford, where "Quality if job one"; at Milliken where they speak of "Pursuit of excellence"; and at Motorola where the objective is "six sigma" (4 defects per million tasks) performance.

What You Personally Can Do

Common personal communication activities for a sales manager or executive involve a combination of the following:

- written summaries on status at predictable intervals (e.g., monthly)

- round tables with teams of 6 to 12 employees on a regular basis (e.g., a different group every week)

Sample Quality Communication Programs

Company	Program
Transamerica	Lunch and Learn Program
Westinghouse	Quality Fair Day
Dow Chemical	Quality Performance Newsletter
IBM	Electronic Quality Bulletin Board
Corning	Quality Rally with Improvement Teams
Milliken	Sharing Rallies
Florida Power and Light	Exchange Expo

Figure 5-6. How quality is communicated at several companies.

- one- to two-hour interviews with employees to discuss anything employees wish (preferably with employees reporting to managers working for you and done with absolute confidentiality of the subject matter) but as a published process (e.g., executive interview)
- quarterly "town hall" meetings in sales offices to answer questions and discuss issues on the minds of employees
- speeches at employee gatherings
- staff meetings (but organized as a structured process so that they are effective and short)
- messages using the company electronic mail or internal television network
- joint sales calls with employees on customers

These various techniques have been used for decades, but in a market-driven world they are organized, predictable events. For example, scheduling and tracking one-on-one meetings with employees three times a week ensures that a certain percentage of employees is covered and the results of those sessions are documented. This is a way of using a tried-and-tested communication method as a process. Having a secretary ensure that you visit every sales office in your district at a predetermined level of frequency which is tracked and managed is also a quality-driven tactic. Comparing the effectiveness of these various communication techniques with each other, such as through employee opinion survey questions, also permits continuous improvement of the communication process.

Repair Services Process

Vendors of complicated products, such as computers, some home electronics, and industrial goods, pioneered the way in which service-oriented organizations improve performance and track successes. They can teach marketing and sales organizations a great deal because many of their activities seem unstructured and seem not to lend themselves to the rigors of process management. However, nothing could be further from the truth.

Take the repair of computers as an example. Customers have one fundamental requirement when a machine breaks down: get it fixed quickly. Even better is not to have it break at all. All IBM service personnel log every call made into IBM for repairs, and every repair person logs onto a portable terminal the nature of the repair, how long it took, and other particulars. These data are tracked by individual, unit, machine, and machine type, and are statistically measured to determine trends. The five critical quality indicators used are:

- customer contacts
- customer callback
- first-time fix
- fix time
- cycle time

All are measured as percentages achieved; each has an annual target defined as a percentage; all are measured by month to see trends of improvement or deterioration. Several are good quality indicators of speed of service: percent of customers contacted within two hours (customer callback) and fix time. The quality of the activity is measured by what percentage of repairs worked the first time they were performed (first-time fix). Automobile repair shops increasingly have adopted similar repair quality indicators. Sewell has such measurements in his Cadillac dealership. He can use the information to determine, for example, if an auto mechanic needs additional training, if one particular type of repair work is more of a problem than others, and how customers respond to the work being done. That last piece of intelligence is the kind that helps all service organizations set target performance objectives that meet customer requirements and desires.

Using Service Quality Process Indicators as Competitive Tools

Increasingly, time-recording processes are being improved because they help provide quality indicators in sales organizations. In the past time recording was done to determine how much an employee worked, to calculate pay, and to satisfy tax regulations. While those reasons remain, increasingly time recording is being used to determine how resources are being deployed. Firms that have made available to their sales personnel electronic mail and laptop computers are beginning to track information such as number of hours spent on selling, servicing, internal meetings, administration (e.g., internal paperwork), education, sick leave, vacation, and so forth. Others are breaking down selling activities into more finite detail by using a menu of options that the recording salesperson can select when logging data. When accumulated by unit, sales office, district, and higher levels and by activity type, the information gathered helps the organization understand the cost of selling and how better to deploy resources.

A second movement under way which, because of its obvious competitive implications, is hardly broadcast, is taking time-recording data and comparing it to information in computer-based opportunity identification processes to determine to what extent current resources are matched to areas of business potential, and to model changes. These two processes—time recording and opportunity identification—can also be matched up against a third process, tracking skills of individuals or business partners, to understand which skills are needed to go after opportunities, which skills no longer need to be cultivated, and which ones are required. The skills issue is an important one since customers are increasingly demanding that people who provide services know what they are doing, whether it is knowing your product or repairing home electronics all the way to understanding and supporting computers, rockets, and telecommunications.

Because firms that have such processes are very reluctant to share details, we should assume that these are useful quality improvement exercises. My experience confirms that it is impossible to run a large sales organization today without this kind of intelligence.

Building Three Critical Data Bases

What is the best way to build such a process? It makes sense to think of these as a collection of processes, some of which can be constructed independently of each other and then married later and by different parts of the organization (see Figure 5-7). However, since they are most useful if computer-based, some common standard user and computer interfaces should be established so that data from one process can be shared or compared to data from another.

Opportunity identification is typically the first application that sales wants and for which there probably are already rudiments of a computer-based process. If not, it is relatively easy to set up since sales organizations understand very well what kind of information they need and probably know how to get it.

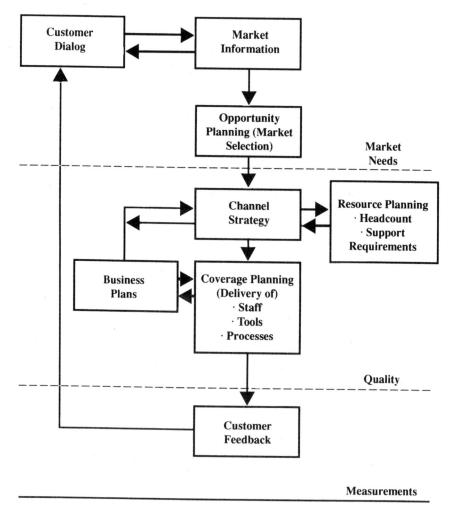

Figure 5-7. Service quality processes.

Skills data bases are also fairly easy to construct since these are just files on individuals using standard lists of skills which then can be sorted to say how many people are available with one skill or another, and to what degree of proficiency (e.g., a level of proficiency expressed as a number).

The *time recording* application is complicated and requires thought, particularly since it affects personnel directly and can be viewed as a "big brother is watching you" tool. It should *never* be used to appraise performance because people will be reluctant to report their true use of time.

All three applications are initially resisted by the sales force, so their benefits must be "sold." However, as employees begin to see resources shifted toward emerging opportunities, with positive effects on their own performance, buy-in increases. Skills data bases need constant supervision because employees rarely assess their own skill levels correctly; the confident employee overstates his or her skills while the humbler one understates. Since cold-blooded accuracy is needed in this data base, a process for validating the accuracy of skills is essential.

Time recording is resisted because there are probably other administrative forms employees have to fill out at the same time anyway (such as punching in to work, expense reports, etc.) that initially do not lend themselves to replacement with an integrated time-recording system. You may simply have to mandate it (and pressure the resisters until they too have recognized the wisdom of such additional work) because everyone has to participate; partial implementation is useless. The objective, after all, is to deploy the most skilled person on the right opportunity at the correct time. This would lead to closing more business, servicing customers better, and doing it faster—all benefits that employees appreciate but only when they become evident through their daily activities.

Telephones and Your Customers

You have an urgent need to call your most important customer about something of great importance that needs resolution by the end of today. You dial the number, it rings five times, and then you hear your customer's recorded voice say: "I am sorry that I am not here to receive your call, but if you leave your name and telephone number, I will call you by end of work today. Should you need to speak to someone right away, press zero and the pound sign on your phone and you will be transferred to an operator."

Over the past decade it seems everyone got an answering machine. On the phone we all speak more to voice mail than to our own employees! This has changed the way we view telephones, yet telephones remain as critical as ever to the success of a sales and marketing organization. Like other critical activities of the firm, how telephones are handled is crucial to improving customer relationships. The best way is to view the telephone system as a critical process.

Ideally, if the party you want is not in, you would prefer to talk to a knowledgeable person about your business or at least determine when you can talk to the individual you called. For many reasons, all of which we are familiar with, recorded messages often are all we get. However, properly managed, telephone technology is a very effective support mechanism for sales. For one thing, most telephone calls are made simply to transmit information, not to carry on extended conversations, so recording machines are fine in these situations. Most telephone calls are also brief. Relationship-building, therefore, is rarely the most critical reason for using a telephone; at best it simply preserves relationships by allowing you to stay in touch.

Surveys show that telephone effectiveness can improve or frustrate relations with customers. Telephone surveys with customers, for example, show that satisfaction with the company's telephone quality declines sharply as clients move from one person to another before getting the answer they want.

When you attempt to document the many ways telephones are used, you quickly realize how complicated telephone processes are and also how heavily telephones are used. The monthly phone bill will remind you of that obvious fact. But increasingly today, firms install telephone systems controlled by a minicomputer capable of providing considerable information while allowing you to program functions that will improve customer relations.

Use Measurements to Improve Telephone Effectiveness

Take measurements as an early step. With today's technology a firm can measure how frequently phones ring before they are answered. That means, for example, that you can program a phone to ring only once before moving to a recorded message, saving time for your customer calling in. Phones that ring a certain number of predetermined times (no more than four times is ideal) can be transferred automatically to an operator. If that individual is knowledgeable about your business, that "live" person can do wonders with your customer. Both sets of activities can be measured down to the individual phone level, by department or by function. This allows you to track trends, set objectives, and improve. Such a fail-safe approach, however, works only if:

- customer requirements are met.
- sales participates in the development of that process.
- all employees participate.
- defects are eliminated vigorously.
- results are measured continuously.

Also, you cannot forget to address the issue of after-office-hours coverage. Today phone audits are another form of measurement frequently used to identify quality or service. Someone is designated to call all or some telephone numbers within the enterprise to determine what percentage of the time the phone owner personally answers the phone, how frequently the recorded message indicates when a return call can be expected, what percentage of times a caller is given directions to a live person, the frequency with which the call was either picked up or transferred to a recorded message, and so forth. Any deviation from a prescribed set of guidelines on phone usage (such as forgetting to turn on your answering service when you leave your office) can be viewed as errors, measured statistically, and presented as a number or percentage of defects per month or quarter, and by organization. Figure 5-8 illustrates a sample monthly report stating errors in sigma (errors per million).

	June 1992 Audit Results Area Branches Six-Sigma Goal: 99.9999966% Pass					
Operating Unit	Coverage		Phonemail Greetings		Number Audited
	Pass/Fail	Sigma	Pass/Fail	Sigma	
Central Illinois	93%/ 7%	3.00	98%/2%	3.59	90
Central Plains	92%/ 8%	2.91	92%/8%	2.89	125
St. Louis	89%/11%	2.72	95%/5%	3.11	108
Greater Chicago	88%/12%	2.69	93%/7%	3.00	170
Minnesota/North Dakota	83%/17%	2.47	91%/9%	2.87	120
Wisconsin	81%/19%	2.36	95%/5%	3.15	113
Indiana	76%/24%	2.20	94%/6%	3.06	128
Area Branches Total	86%/14%	2.57	94%/6%	3.04	854
U.S. Branches Total	86%/14%	2.58	92%/8%	2.91	5535
June 1992 Goal		3.05		3.05	
December 1992 Goal		3.15		3.15	

Figure 5-8. Sample report of errors in sigma.

Targets can then be set. For example, defects per million can be presented along with a target for this year and next, striving for zero defects (six sigma or better). Thus an organization could be at 1.2 sigma (awful), improve to 2.5, then 3.5, then 4, and so forth. Each jump in whole number is a quantum leap, and therefore it becomes harder to reduce defects per million. But you can set the target for all telephones answered with 3.5-sigma quality this year, and then 4.5 next year, and so forth. Having a current greeting (e.g., one that says you will be back in town at some future date, not on a day already two weeks past) is another common measurement.

To close the loop with approach, deployment, and results called for in the Baldrige model, you must have questions in your customer surveys about the importance of good telephone communications, and customers' satisfaction with the issues being measured above. The data will then allow you to make ongoing changes in measurements, targets, and processes to continuously satisfy customers with regard to your phones.

Use Surveys to Identify Areas of Improvement

Customer satisfaction survey questions on phone systems are frequently employed because companies have found increasingly over the past ten years that an organization's accessibility by telephone is a major factor in determining customer satisfaction.

When surveying customers, relevant questions concern their level of satisfaction with the number of rings, the qualifications and effectiveness of those who answer the phone, the percentage of times the customer's questions or issues were resolved, and what kind of after-hours message greeting was present. It is not uncommon for customers to complain that even with a warm body on the phone, that person could not satisfy their needs as much as 40 percent of the time. Once problems are measured and recognized, a sales office can fix them and track improvement.

Consequently, in addition to taking advantage of the technology and measuring telephone effectiveness, businesses are also investing in better-quality receptionists and phone operators. They are concentrating on friendly phone voices and in training operators on:

- how to handle various types of calls (e.g., complaints).
- who different employees are and what are their responsibilities.
- how the organization functions so as to direct calls correctly.
- how to use computer-based files to answer questions.

Thus a combination of operators, better technology, measurement systems, and trained employees increasingly is making more effective use of telephones in quality-focused sales organizations.

Surveying your own people also makes sense. Many companies do that today and find responses similar to those of customers. For example, an internal survey of the phone system at one large firm several years ago showed 37 percent dissatisfaction—roughly the same as customers. When broken down by job type, satisfaction varied with executives least satisfied and staff most. You can also survey which functions of a phone system are most important and rank them, thereby determining which ones must work well. Listed in order of most importance to employees, the top five features are: transfer, volume, hold, speaker, and connect. At IBM, marketing and sales use the following five features the most in descending order of importance: delete, save, forward, replay messages, and external greeting. Your organization is probably the same.

Reporting results of such surveys to employees, along with targets for improvement, is a useful way of sensitizing them to customer needs. When they see how customers and they themselves feel about telephone quality, the importance of good telephone management becomes very obvious to all. Since we use telephones every day, if we are reminded of their effect on customers, telephone disciplines help keep all employees conscious of customer service. It works better than posters or puffed-up executives pontificating on the need to serve the customer.

Case Study of Customer Satisfaction in Action

Can these various processes be brought together in a coordinated strategy? Since all processes are at different levels of effectiveness, the question always has to be asked. However, a quick look at what goes on at the American Society for Quality Control (ASQC), a world-class center for quality and clearly a market-driven organization preaching the religion of continuous improvement as part of its support role in the Malcolm Baldrige Award, illustrates what can happen.

The ASQC has a staff of about 150 employees, and their tens of thousands of customers are all experts on quality! The ASQC has recognized that dissatisfied customers tell others about poor service. At the ASQC the staff has learned that satisfied customers may not tell others of their pleasure but also that "delighted customers brag about you and tell others." They have learned through experience that converted dissatisfied customers, although tough to win over, are loyal forever and tell all their friends. These are the same lessons learned by other organizations and confirmed by academics studying the issue.

The ASQC enlists its customers, therefore, to help sell the society by (1) delighting them by design rather than by accident and (2) being very responsive to their complaints. ASQC also recognizes that it is not the only quality association in the United States and thus sees other quality-expert societies as competitors to beat through outstanding service.

How ASQC Knows Its Customers Well

Satisfaction is defined by measuring customer needs and expectations and through analysis of how well ASQC's products and services perform. Listening to customers is done through a variety of means: telephone calls, market research, surveys, focus groups, complaint letters, service staff, and personal dialogue.

ASQC has learned that expectations vary by customer while needs are very situational, since not all requirements are created equal. Even tougher is the realization that expectations on the part of customers rise over time, which means continuous improvements have to keep up. Measurements of how ASQC does are tied to what customers directly offer ASQC through its various processes and also based on actual performance (e.g., how fast orders are met, phones answered, etc.).

In May 1987 the ASQC adopted as its mission "to provide performance leadership in association management by delivering products and services that meet customer needs (and expectations)." ASQC then established four guiding principles:

- customers as focal points of all activities
- total quality performance as the basis of all actions
- staff and teamwork as keys to success
- ASQC as partner to members, fulfilling their goals

Its employees were also taught that customers expected to reach them, have easy and pleasant interactions with staff, get what they wanted quickly, and have problems resolved quickly.

With values in place, moving to create standards of performance came next (what we would call goals and targets). Thus, on the goal of being able to reach the ASQC, it established how many hours per day the office should be open (7 a.m.–6 p.m. CST), measured how many telephone callers as a percent hung up because they could not get through, and set an objective of answering every telephone call within three rings. On customers getting what they asked for, targets were set for availability (95 percent) and accuracy of order processing and fulfillment (100 percent). On getting helped quickly, ASQC established a 48-hour window of time to get orders for publications out the door. On fixing problems, it decided to set a 100 percent target for same-day resolution. Each of these targets was then measured regularly to understand progress toward achievement.

As measurements were created, the ASQC realized it had a number of universal issues to deal with. Each goal needed a numeric measurement, and it had to be the easiest way to measure. ASQC had to determine how frequently to measure and how best to report performance. Each goal had different requirements. But across the board, this service organization's measurements focused on trends, shifts, volumes, cycles, and spotting dissatisfaction.

ASQC found a number of ways to get its customers to respond to the quality of services provided. For example, when books are shipped to a customer the package contains a feedback card that can be returned with comments on service. These cards are timely and accurate (since they come directly from customers), permit comparison to other ASQC services, are statements of satisfaction with products, and serve as a source of suggestions for improvements.

Periodic surveys of the membership look at the validity of ASQC's mission and how it is performing against it, product satisfaction (e.g., courses, conferences, publications, etc.), and services (courtesy, knowledge, and promptness). Finally, actually listening to customers in meetings and telephone calls is another source of feedback.

How ASQC's Management System Is Quality-Based

To ensure the staff is committed to customer satisfaction, ASQC's incentives and rewards are tied to its vision. Continuous-improvement values are espoused and groups are rewarded for achievements. A variety of indicators of customer satisfaction is used to measure the effectiveness of the organization and hence of the staff. These include service levels, course satisfaction indicators, satisfaction with quality-expertise certification of members, membership retention, and adherence to such critical deadlines as mailing ASQC's journal or financial statements to members.

ASQC can tell you precisely how well it is doing. When it first measured how effectively it filled orders, ASQC determined it was accurate 91 percent of the time. It reached 96 percent accuracy in 1991 with an objective of 100 percent. On-time delivery went from 75 percent to 96 percent; days of invoice delay went from 79 down to 7! The percent of problem calls went from 27 percent to 8.2 percent, while calls abandoned, first documented in March 1990, was 68 percent and then moved to 5 percent. That latter measure is an example of how an unknown problem, once identified and measured, can be fixed quickly to the delight of customers.

The ASQC represents an interesting combination of marketing and sales. It does not have a direct sales force, nor is it a retail operation with a storefront. But it practices marketing and selling, experiences competition, is well known, and has a unique set of customers. It is a wonderful example of quality principles applied effectively in a marketing world. The ASQC is also an ideal example because its customers are already quality-focused. In reality, sales organizations would argue that only some customers are as quality-disciplined. However, the trend data presented in Chapter 1, and the obvious lessons which many businesspeople are learning concerning their own enterprises, are leading to customers more in tune with the kinds of expectations demanded by ASQC's customers. That is why the ASQC case is so instructive.

The values ASQC espouses and the focus it maintains—squarely on the customer—can be found in other organizations and in similar terms. For example, McDonald's Corporation, with its thousands of outlets selling fast foods in a ferociously competitive environment, succeeds the same way. It has its phrases, of course, such as "Customer Care Culture," but it too strives to know the needs of its customers and empowers employees to satisfy those. Yet all store-level work is done in the context of consistent product delivery since customers want McDonald's food to be the same everywhere. The common goal for all employees is "McDonald's success is dependent upon providing services and products that meet or exceed each customer's expectation. Therefore, the goal of each of McDonald's employees is total customer satisfaction." And further, "each employee's success will be based on his or her contribution to the goal." Processes were developed as at the ASQC, that made it easier and consistently possible for employees to TLC—Think Like a Customer!

References

Albrecht, Karl, and Zemke, Ron. *Service America! Doing Business in the New Economy.* Homewood, Ill.: Dow Jones-Irwin, 1985.

Bauer, Roy A., Collar, Emilio, and Tang, Victor. *The Silverlake Project: Transformation at IBM.* New York: Oxford University Press, 1992.

Czepiel, John A., et al. (eds). *The Service Challenge: Integrating for Competitive Advantage.* Chicago: American Marketing Association, 1987.

Davidow, William H., and Bro, Uttal. *Total Customer Service—The Ultimate Weapon*. New York: Harper and Row, 1989.

Liswood, Laura A. *Serving Them Right: Innovative and Powerful Customer Retention Strategies*. New York: Harper and Row, 1990.

Peters, Tom. *Thriving on Chaos*. New York: Alfred A. Knopf, 1987.

Shaw, J. C. *The Quality-Productivity Connection in Service-Sector Management*. New York: Van Nostrand, 1978.

6

Personnel Practices in a Quality World

There is dignity in work only when it is work freely accepted. ALBERT CAMUS, 1953

In this chapter I describe how sales and marketing personnel practices change in a quality-focused world. Topics include teams, performance evaluations, skills development, recognition, suggestion processes, and employee feedback.

Any effective transformation of an organization occurs at the level of the individual. Organization charts, commission plans, products, and advertisements are all important, but people buy from people. Customers judge service-focused marketing and sales organizations at the human level. Therefore nowhere is it more important that the gospel of quality be embraced and applied than with employees. Those of us in sales know that no product just "sells itself." We know that customer-contact employees do that. As we move increasingly into a world with self-directed work teams and less management command and control, in which services performed by employees are the added value wrapped around products, the way we deal with employees is crucial. Yet tradition, past experience, legal requirements, and poor management will work against changing personnel practices, particularly in well-established firms that have succeeded in the past.

If you foul up the quality transformation of your employees through ill-conceived personnel practices, your future chances of success go into a free fall. A quick story illustrates the risk. Disney Corporation, which most people would agree is an extremely well-run company that invests great sums in training its personnel to deal with the public at its theme parks, also has a long-standing tradition of quality in all that it does. Quality appears in the unique superiority of its full-length animated movies, its dolls, T-shirts, and of course, its theme park rides. In the 1980s the firm decided to open retail outlets in the United States to sell Disney products, such as Mickey Mouse dolls and clothing, and it almost failed.

What Disney found out very quickly was that employees in the pilot stores were hired just as other retail stores hire, and of course, these members of the Disney world acted like those in other retail establishments. Yet the public had come to expect a certain style of behavior on the part of Disney employees—and that was missing. Disney officials quickly realized the problem and responded correctly by training retail employees the same way other Disney employees are trained at the parks, and used the same personnel practices they used around the company. Thus the politeness, the "look," the style of dress, and the celebration of quality came to the stores along with rapid increases in sales and profits, making the move into retail successful.

How to Make Employees Customer-Driven

All excellent sales personnel understand very well that the personal influence they have on customers is profound. Thus all internal processes should be geared toward rewarding behavior that delights customers, exceeding their expectations. The processes largely involve training and rewards. Training can involve increasing employee's skills concerning products, industry, marketplace, negotiation, and so forth. On a more personal basis it involves developing listening and communication skills, and encouraging responsiveness, courtesy, leadership, creativity, trust, and credibility. Since surveys suggest that, at least in the United States, customers expect relatively poor service (unlike in Japan), exceeding customer expectations should not represent a major hurdle.

In fact, customers argue that they become satisfied when employees are responsive, demonstrate knowledge of products and how to get things done in their own organizations, exhibit the capability of setting realistic expectations, and always perform in an honest and ethical manner. If you have poor personnel performance then you have no choice but to offer a better quality or cheaper product. Good people actually take the pressure off price and quality to a great extent. The one characteristic that makes all of this very difficult, however, is that delight with an employee is a subjective matter, hence difficult to measure.

Yet even in the area of personnel management quality principles are being applied effectively. We are finding that what the Baldrige criteria call for, what Deming has preached for years, and what successful marketing and sales organizations have learned, are all compatible with human nature. As with other aspects of business, personnel activities should be looked at as measurable processes. Those that most influence employee behavior become the earliest to be subjected to the rigors of quality improvement. As in earlier chapters, I will describe some processes—not all—that illustrate how to apply quality in the world of sales and marketing personnel.

A World of Teams

In a firm committed to continuously improving its performance, teams are to people as processes are to tasks. Businesses have become more interested in deploying personnel in teams and judging the work of groups rather than individuals. But why team building? Many reasons are given today for clustering employees in teams. First, as products and services become increasingly more complex, no one individual has all the skills to accomplish a task; hence a group of people with multiple skills is focused on a clear objective. Selling a complicated computer, for example, may require the services of a salesperson, a systems engineer, a financial expert, and someone conversant with a particular software application.

A second reason is that it becomes easier to improve processes if a group works together, combining various components of a collection of activities to reach a result. For instance, a sales organization cannot be effective unless sales personnel work efficiently with administration to ensure timely and effective processing of orders.

A third common reason is that as the ratio of managers to employees decreases, it becomes easier to allow employees to self-appraise, peer-appraise, and develop their own priorities. A related idea is that as circumstances change more quickly and the knowledge required to react to them grows, only those closest to the situation can determine what needs to happen next, not managers. This situation requires more peer cooperation and communication.

Increasingly, research is showing that teams of people are more effective than individuals in getting things done well and quickly. Finally, as organizations flatten, they must hold employees more directly accountable for results, and hence must delegate increasing responsibility to them. Such enterprises find teams a logical cluster of employees.

As with so many other innovations in organizations implementing continuous improvement processes, teaming first emerged in manufacturing plants but now is rapidly spreading through service organizations, including sales.

How Sales Teams Work

Before I summarize how best to use teams in sales, some definitions are in order. We frequently hear the phrase *self-directed work teams* in quality-focused companies. Such teams are highly trained employees given complete responsibility and authority to perform specific sets of tasks. They are given authority, training, and freedom of action, and they are held accountable for the results of their work. Teams range in size from as few as 5 or 6 people to as many as 18; however, experience suggests that fewer than 12 but more than 5 is optimal. In sales, a self-directed team might consist of a salesperson, an administrative individual who processes orders and generates bills, delivery or maintenance personnel, and others who are required in order to sell a product or service.

Self-directed teams tend to look at themselves as responsible for one or two broad categories of activities, while more conventional task forces have a very narrow focus. Traditional teams in American business have been managed by supervisors, while self-directed teams make decisions by consensus and control their own activities. In a more conventional environment individual performance is rewarded, while in self-directed teams rewards are tied to how the team as a whole performs. The former cherishes the lone cowboy and seniority, the latter, the skills and ability to work with others.

Peter F. Drucker, in a February 1992 *Wall Street Journal* article, points out that there are various types of teams evident in business today. Using sports as an analogy, he speaks of baseball, football, and tennis doubles teams, each characterized by a group focus but playing by different rules. His point is that teams behave in different ways and thus must be constructed to meet the needs of the task at hand. His is a useful perspective.

Baseball teams are good in factories where everyone plays a position on a team. Each player can be measured individually but the team operates with highly defined, repeatable processes. In football teams, more commonly seen in service organizations (e.g., hospital emergency rooms or symphony orchestras), players are in fixed positions because of the "instrument" they play, but they work as a team, and for a manager. You see this model used frequently in flexible manufacturing plants (e.g., Japanese car manufacturing). In tennis doubles, the team does the performing while the individuals contribute, much as in a jazz combo. Positions in doubles are only relatively fixed, since people adjust to cover the strengths and weaknesses of fellow team members. The team has to be small (e.g., 5 to 9), well-trained, and work well together. It is a useful model for sales teams.

Drucker makes a strong case for treating each type of team differently and not attempting to make a hybrid, arguing that once they are set up it is difficult, if not impossible, to change their nature. And he reaches the obvious conclusion: once your people are on a team, their performance, appraisals, and rewards must be dependent on their new roles; the old personnel process—one that focused on individuals—simply spoils the use of teams.

The need to ensure that teams work effectively is borne out by the benefits gained. Increasingly the evidence shows that teams are more productive than individuals. They streamline functions (improve processes) faster, are more flexible in changing offerings and responding to customer needs, drive up quality in all that gets done, find employee commitment to the team's objectives stronger than to anybody else's, and result in greater customer satisfaction as they respond faster and with better quality.

How to Make Sales Teams Successful

The literature on how to set up and run teams is vast and will not be discussed, just as the dynamics of how processes are reengineered is best suited to other books. However, because use of teams is a strategic imperative in the successful implementation of a quality-driven marketing or sales organization, the keys to success should be understood. Fortunately, useful studies have identified what is really important. One of the best is by Carl E. Larson and Frank M. J. LaFasto, *TeamWork*, from which we can learn what is critical for teams.

1. *Clear goals.* Teams that succeed understand exactly what the end goals of their efforts must be. They also appreciate that these goals are important and worthy of achieving. Some sales teams even use the phrase *sense of mission* to describe what they are focused on when detailing their goals. The old story about the bricklayers being asked what

they were doing illustrates the point. The first said he was laying bricks, the second answered he was building a wall, the third proclaimed he was building a cathedral. Clarity and elevation are important elements of successfully defined goals. They help teams ensure focus and concentration—two key requirements in sales.

2. *Results-driven.* Larson and LaFasto found that how teams are organized influences whether the team is successful or not. It should be organized to facilitate communication among team members and most important, to perform efficiently the tasks for which it was set up. Different structures are required for various tasks. For example, creative teams that must develop new processes need to be organized to optimize autonomy. Tactical team structures are used when you want to execute a plan. This type, more frequently seen in sales organizations, has self-defined roles for each individual that, when performed according to a plan, result in a task being completed effectively and in a timely fashion. In all such teams, important factors are clear roles and accountability, effective communications, checks on individual and group performance, and judgments made based on facts.

3. *Qualified team members.* The authors use the word *competent* to describe the kind of team members required. I prefer *qualified* because that implies a process to continuously improve skills can be put in place (the subject of discussion below). Regardless of what teams you have, competency involves both technical knowledge (e.g., features of the products being sold) and personal characteristics required to get along with fellow team members. These are the kinds of interpersonal skills that we have always looked for in good customer-contact employees: compatible personalities, good appearance, similar social or ethnic backgrounds, communication skills, intelligence, organized behavior, results-oriented, ethics and honesty, and so forth. They must also be able to sublimate their desire for individual achievement to team accomplishment.

Successful tactical teams, because they are highly focused with clearly defined roles, require members who display the characteristics of loyalty, commitment to the team, action-orientation, urgency, and responsiveness to big *C* and little *c* customers.

4. *Unified commitment.* Simply put, effective teams have members committed to the success of the team. We know this commitment as team spirit, while others would characterize it as esprit de corps—intense loyalty such as seen in certain military units or, for that matter, Notre Dame football fans! Tough to define, it brings out the sense of urgency and desire for success in ways not otherwise possible. In sales we can see it in the desire to be the number one sales team, best sales office in a district, first group to obtain $1 million in sales, and so forth.

5. *Spirit of collaboration.* Teams function well when managers and team members all work to create an environment that is collaborative—in other words, teamwork. In sports we understand the concept; in sales, it is everyone in the car dealership doing their work well and on time to ensure that the customer buys a car, gets proper financing, has a clean restroom to use, is offered a hot cup of coffee, gets good service on the car, and leaves pleased with the experience.

Trust is the operative word to describe this environment. Right behind it is respect. If you create a working environment in which employees trust and respect each other, there is less hesitancy to take risks, learn new things, and improve processes. Being cheered on to new success is more effective than being punished for losing a sale. The values most cherished by successful teams in an organization attempting to improve continuously are:

- honesty and truth
- openness and sharing
- consistency and predictability
- respect

Since collaboration fosters trust, and trust can be lost quickly and hardly ever regained, it is imperative that from the start, as managers, we create a spirit of openness and support. That is why the spirit of continuous improvement and investment in skills are so crucial while we are celebrating victories along the way.

6. *Excellence.* Every important sales organization cherishes excellence in its culture because only then can it do more than before. Since the pressure to perform in sales actually increases in organizations that are continuously improving—because they must gain more sales and improve processes at the same time—excellence has to be cherished almost as a religion. Indeed, all the quality gurus speak about employees naturally desiring to do well, and thus processes should be designed to make that happen. Pursuit of excellence also leads to bolder goals, particularly for results of process improvements. It gives purpose to work and inspires loyalty to the mission. Breakthrough improvements only come from boldness of purpose and that requires a culture of excellence. Goals, excellence, and clarity all in turn lead to standards of performance that are benchmarks against which to measure subsequent achievements.

7. *Support and recognition.* Support can range from your giving teams the resources required to do their work (e.g., office space, fax machines, product brochures) to protecting teams politically from those who would resist their innovations. And there is also recognition for performing effectively as a team in carrying out goals of the enterprise.

Protection is particularly important if your organization is in an early phase of implementing quality-based management principles and still formulating a new culture. Since employees judge management's true values by what it supports, giving teams resources, protection, and recognition becomes a critical bellwether signal to others about what management really values. Lack of tangible support is usually one of the greatest failings of management, regardless of whether in sales, manufacturing, services, or the public sector. Yet it is where "walking the talk," or as many in sales like to say, where "the rubber meets the road," occurs.

8. *Principled leadership.* Larson and LaFasto, like all experts on teaming, as well as Stephen R. Covey on managing our own affairs, indicate that team leaders need very specific attributes and attitudes. Briefly put, they are:

- consistent goals and message.
- clear perspectives on expectations.
- supportive decision making.
- suppression of personal ego.
- creativity.

This brief overview of teaming is no substitute for more detailed study. However, my central message is that marketing and sales organizations have been successful in achieving quality improvement by using teaming as a critical strategic imperative. No significant quality improvement effort has been achieved without equally successful implementation of teams as a fundamental way of organizing the work force to focus on tasks.

Performance Evaluations

Teaming and continuous improvement do not mean that employees are not appraised. We already saw that, for example, in the case of the Cadillac dealership, individuals were measured on their own performance and against that of the dealership as a whole, much as baseball players have statistics assigned to their performance and also others that benchmark the results of teams. In a quality-focused world appraisals are subject to much debate because they go to the heart of the management role, the values of the organization, and the culture of the society in which a firm operates. Like teaming, appraisals have a vast literature of their own. Each of the quality gurus focuses considerable attention on the topic, and every manager is also experienced in this area.

Deming, for example, believes workers normally want to do well. When they do not it is usually management's fault because it either created an environment that failed to bring out the best in people or it measured them incorrectly. Deming would, for instance, get rid of quotas for salespeople. However, looking at what the quality community thinks of the worker can help you decide how to appraise employees and hold them accountable. Quality experts argue that variation in performance is more a function of the process or work than of the personal characteristics of the individual. *But it all begins with accepting the notion that people want to work, like doing it well, and are prepared to accept responsibility.* Those three premises require that we allow people to do the work they are capable of performing. In this model managers focus on eliminating obstacles to good work, instead of watching employees to make sure they perform.

At the one extreme, as proposed by Deming, is that annual merit ratings or management by objectives destroy pride in workmanship. Appraisals require an environment in which you control instead of give direction, push for results instead of improve processes that lead to results, and evaluate employees instead of give feedback, which encourages improvements in performance.

Joiner Associates, long tied to Deming's point of view and a firm more experienced in manufacturing than sales organizations, makes a strong case for eliminating performance appraisals:

1. Appraisals ignore the reality that employees do work within groups or teams. Individual evaluations undermine teamwork.

2. Appraisals ignore the reality that employees work within systems or processes, not as individuals acting as masters of their own destiny.

3. Appraisals ignore the reality that employees work with variability and instability. Put in nonstatistical terms, workers perform differently on different days and appraisals may not take into account that variability. Take a salesperson who has a strong first half year then a weak second half year but is appraised on the second half only. Does that person get a favorable appraisal? Simplistic, yes, but the example challenges how we view people. This is especially significant in sales where significant appraisals are done on a monthly, quarterly, or half-year basis.

4. Appraisals ignore the reality that appraisal systems are biased and inconsistent. The current system may call for managers to skew statistically how many workers are appraised high and low. There are biases on the part of the manager doing the appraisals, and variations in his or her philosophy concerning such things as whether or not to socialize earnings, treat all employees equally, and so forth. Appraisals therefore are at one extreme too lax and at the other too harsh.

Shift Emphasis from People to Process Performance

Deming and Joiner Associates argue that one should focus on improving processes rather than on controlling people to generate output. In fact, this approach is beginning to surface in sales organizations ranging from small retail operations all the way up to such large enterprises as IBM and Xerox. Actual case studies show that it is more effective to measure and study processes, which are then improved by employees, and then measure the results of processes to gauge how additional progress can be made. This approach provides the benefits that managers traditionally have attributed to appraisal systems (e.g., the ability to direct employees, provide useful feedback, determine training needs, communicate, and so forth) but without the negatives identified by Deming.

What Quality-Based Performance Plans Value

When looking at the performance planning process, you can see that appraisals of processes (based on statistical or hard evidence) rather than just of individuals make sense, and lead to change. Performance plans focus on helping people to do better. Teams are cherished because they optimize use of an organization's resources by focusing on customer-oriented tasks rather than on inward-looking bureaucracies. Leaders set visions and goals so that individuals can frame team activities and make decisions that optimize implementation of visions. Managers understand the concept of variation in performance, accept it as normal, and use it to improve processes and hence the performance of individuals in an environment of continuous, positive improvement.

The values cherished in performance and development plans for individuals are:

- continuous improvement.
- continuous learning.
- learning in depth.
- measuring performance factually.
- interpersonal skills.
- joy in work.
- excellence.

Outstanding sales managers have always known that happy sales personnel make good salespeople. They also understand that salespeople are happy if they are confident and recognized for their contributions, as well as when business is good. While teaming and proper performance and appraisal processes must be in place to create the effective sales employee, other processes are needed as well. These include skills development, recognition, and suggestion processes.

Skills Process

If the only significant asset an organization has is its people, and good people really make a difference, transforming an organization into a quality-oriented one, then it stands to reason that investing in their skills is crucial to success. How to improve skills in an organized and cost-effective manner is always important, but so too is what gets taught.

All large corporations and many state governments have established training facilities to invest in their personnel. At McDonald's it is Hamburger University, at IBM it is a variety of facilities in Thornwood, New York, Atlanta, Georgia, and elsewhere, and others, such as Xerox and automotive manufacturers, have campuses too. Instructional facilities have been established by the leading corporations in Japan and Europe as well. They have all found it cost effective to do a certain amount of training on a wide variety of subjects ranging from product knowledge to general business topics to personal skills such as communication.

But all effective skills processes have three common features.

First, every employee has a written development plan that states what skills that individual will develop this year and how.

Second, the development plan is owned by both employee and his or her manager; they review it just as they might a business plan and execute it accordingly.

Third, the best skills development plans are tied to the needs of the business. These needs are (1) related to the outcomes of forecasts and opportunity identification processes, (2) weighted against anticipated turnover or availability of personnel, (3) measured by the cost of hiring necessary skills versus developing these in-house, and (4) defined by customer needs.

The quality-driven organization takes skills development further to include a variety of skills, independent of products and services, that all employees must have. These include, but are not limited to, the following:

- leadership
- how to work on teams
- communications

- conducting meetings
- negotiations
- empowerment
- process reengineering methods
- statistical measurement techniques
- Total Quality Management
- visioning and goal setting
- business issues

How to Use Training to Build Skills

All the companies that have undergone profound transformation say that the primary vehicle for change is education. Over a period of several years they have spent up to 4 percent of their budgets on education programs involving just quality. Once basic education on quality has been provided and then applied, employees generally switch (as they do in Japan) from formal class instruction to department meetings focused on specific quality improvement methodologies (e.g., how to apply fishbone analysis techniques to determine why sales are lost). It is a process that evolves from teaching employees to employees sharing knowledge with each other and finally to employees sharing with their customers.

In the beginning, education is offered by management; later employees foster it themselves (e.g., as brown bag universities with one-hour sessions at noon or at breakfast). Eventually, education may take the form of meetings with customers on specific quality-related issues.

When employees are trained on quality disciplines, the normal cycle of instruction first involves running seminars on why the firm, along with the industry and the economy at large, has to change. Then what typically follows is some detailed training on process reengineering involving looking at tasks as processes, doing root cause identification analysis, then planning process improvements, all laced with a dose of skills transfer on statistical measurements.

A third phase involves education on how to work in teams and how to create visions, missions, goals, and plans for improving. This is followed by specific subject education relevant to one group or another. This education varies from one- to two-day doses all the way to three-week total immersion. The best programs employ a combination of classroom lectures, case studies, experiential activities, and on-the-job applications working with real processes. Employers keep lists of who has gone through the various stages of education and provide additional opportunities for training to those who have not gone through a structured program. Feedback is obtained at each class so that the training itself is improved. The best programs tend to have dedicated training staffs who get better at it, combined with all managers doing some teaching as well.

On a broader basis, all skills development follows similar lines. But how are skills considered a process? Figure 6-1 illustrates a high-level flowchart for one skills process. In this particular example, data is gathered and stored in a computer to ease the process of comparing needs to availability of skills, and of tracking who has what skills or needs more training. In some cases these data bases are parts of other processes (such as sales opportunities and customer satisfaction), but they are linked together through programming to provide insights into the organization not otherwise available.

In the model cited in Figure 6-1, all aspects of a sales organization are involved. Managers offer training and computer facilities, and employees participate in the training and improvement of their skills and are responsible for keeping their personal skills data file up to date. Sales and marketing personnel own the opportunity identification process. Figure 6-2 illustrates a model of how all these elements come together in an integrated fashion to ensure that quality is built into the daily activities of each process.

Using the Concept of Skills Data Bases

Some standards for skills have to be set along with goals for improvement. For example, some organizations have defined from one to five levels of skills in a number of predefined subject areas. Each skill level is assigned a number. Someone can look at a skills data base and see how many skill level 1 or 3 or 5 people there are for a particular assignment or type of opportunity. The original concept of a computer-based skills file dates back to World War I and the U.S. Army, which collected skills of individual soldiers and kept them on punched cards. It could find out, for example, how many French-speaking chauffeurs it had in France in May 1918. The same concept applies in business today.

In my firm, I might want to know how many skill level 5 (the highest level) people we have in telecommunications so that I can determine if I have enough people to go after all the opportunities in telecommunications products identified by sales personnel. If not, I know I have a

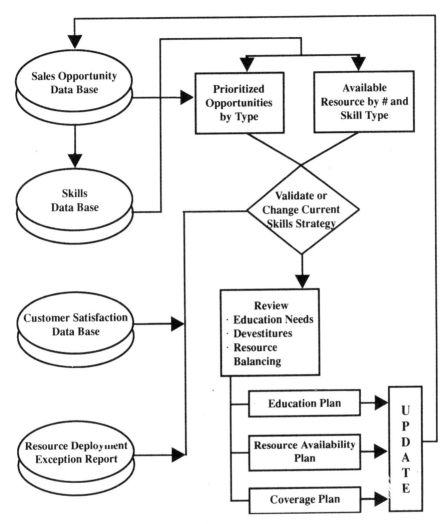

Figure 6-1. Skills process flowchart.

Communicate Vision & Results	Educate & Train	Empower & Delegate	Incent & Recognize	Measure & Evaluate
Customer and Employee Feedback				

Figure 6-2. People and quality.

problem to fix right away. Figure 6-3 suggests the kind of data such a skills data base can produce to help sales management. This data was drawn from an actual IBM skills data base in use today in one sales district. Such a report is produced on a regular basis or as needed. An optimal arrangement is to study all skill levels once each quarter to determine what percentage of opportunities is covered by the correct skills and what holes either have to be plugged or can be ignored. You can even see what percentage of employees has updated the skills data base within the last six months (as illustrated in Figure 6-4). In this particular example, the organization also set targets for improvement: everyone updates their file within six months, and all sales personnel acquire a minimum of one level 5 skill per year. Such a skills process also can be used to determine what kinds of people to hire, yielding another quality improvement in your human resource pool.

The skills process has not yet received the same level of attention as other human resource topics such as quality education or recognition. Yet increasingly skills is becoming a critical process as customers be-

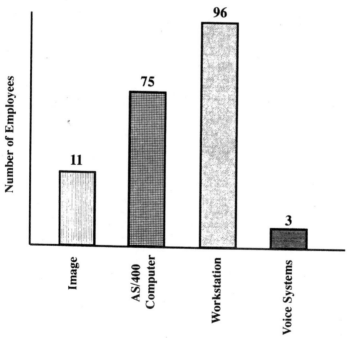

Figure 6-3. Typical information generated from a skills data base. (Courtesy of IBM Corporation.)

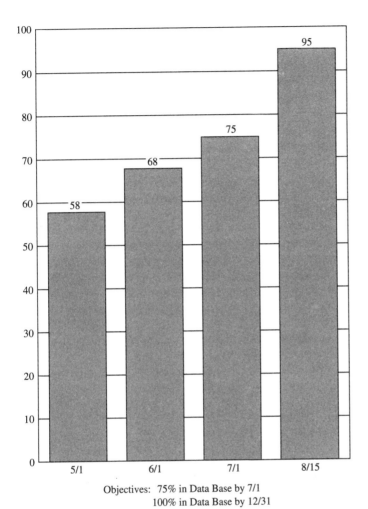

Objectives: 75% in Data Base by 7/1
100% in Data Base by 12/31

Figure 6-4. Chart showing progress toward 100 percent current skills information.

come more influenced in their buying by how employees perform. Therefore skills should be one of the earliest processes to address. It is also one that has universal features applicable across the entire enterprise regardless of job title or function. Employee surveys also confirm that investments in education make people more loyal, happier, and devoted to excellence—all wonderful traits to have in employees coming into contact with your customers.

Recognition Process

Recognition processes represent one of the most exciting new areas of quality improvement. Rewarding employees is a crucial "must do well" process. As a firm's culture changes, so too must the manner in which recognition is given for a job well done. Converting old recognition methods to new ones is crucial if new values and changed patterns of behavior are to be positively encouraged. For those focusing on recognition processes, it almost feels like a new field of study, with new lessons still being learned.

The first lesson is that recognition systems reward what organizations value most. For instance, if a salesperson is given a large cash award for selling a product but the person who fixes that product is given only a lapel pin, we quickly see how little the firm values customer service!

The second lesson is that recognition processes continue to be a form of feedback on employee performance, rewarding idealized behavior by thanking people and making them into heroes.

Because recognition is such an important form of communication as well as of corporate values, how it is done is more important than the actual gesture. For instance, public recognition broadcasts corporate values and is preferred by most employees. Cash awards, while very popular, may confuse employees as to what is the key priority since only one is the top priority—the one for which there is a cash reward. Frequent cash awards quickly become viewed as part of an employee's compensation. When that happens, recognition no longer is an effective communication vehicle of corporate values and priorities.

Increasingly, there has been a growing dialogue over whether there should be individual recognition or team recognition. If you are fostering team activity, individual rewards can get in the way; on the other hand, individual efforts might also warrant reward.

It is becoming very clear that recognition must be separated from compensation. The former recognizes an immediate success (and should be tied to quality of activity) and the latter rewards long-term performance, skill achievement, and responsibility. Recognition can be for various activities, more timely than a salary increase, and very personal.

Delegate Recognition to Employees

As organizations expand employee empowerment, they are finding it's also practical to delegate recognition activities to them as well. What a change this is, given the fact that historically all recognition was the preserve of management. By delegating you can move recognition into the realm of joint celebrations of special events treasured by the corporation. Thus instead of simply recognizing the accomplishments of one salesperson, the entire sales unit can be recognized for its overall accomplishments or for working together to close an important sale. Delegation also increases the odds that the right people are recognized since employees always know who really did the work!

Without going through Maslow's hierarchy of needs, suffice it to say that recognition meets an important need for all people, and the best recognition is that which reinforces an individual's confidence and self-esteem. The best processes are often those developed by teams of employees or outside consultants; but, in either case, with very careful planning.

Results evident in many companies suggest broad possibilities. While cash rewards remain very popular, so too now is peer-to-peer recognition. Awards that go only to teams that did process improvements are becoming more common, as are team awards to other teams. Milliken and Xerox recognize teams by having them present results of their work at Sharing Rallies in which they "pitch" their story to peers. One IBM organization gives out a large silver medallion to team members for a major quality accomplishment but only if they are nominated for the award by another team.

Opinion surveys tell you quickly how well current and new recognition systems work. For example, you can simply ask in a survey, "How satisfied are you with the recognition you receive for doing a good job?" That data can be statistically gathered by location and job group (e.g., sales personnel versus secretaries) and compared year to year. Outside survey data also helps grade your process. For instance, in a 1987 survey the American Productivity Center and the American Compensation Association found that only 46 percent of all firms contacted even had a recognition process. Of these, only one-third reported that these processes had a positive impact on performance! The survey led to the conclusion that recognition systems that foster too much internal competition, creating a situation of winners and losers, should be avoided. The point is that this is one process that applies to all people, can be measured easily, and can then be improved. Ideal systems balance individual and personal recognition and avoid creating barriers to cooperation within the organization.

Many successful sales executives have learned that employee-developed recognition systems that reflect the real values of the organization, such as quality improvement, are essential. Roger Milliken, CEO of Milliken and Company, argues that "recognition drives the process of change." Like Milliken, David T. Kearns, CEO of Xerox Corporation before it won the Baldrige Award, focused considerable attention on recognition, which he defined as "noticing a person or group doing a good job." Deming acknowledges the value of rewards and recognition as a way of bringing "joy in work, joy in learning. Everyone will win; no losers." In short, a variety of activities associated with rewards and recognition leads to a motivated work force.

Use Many Ways to Recognize Employees

Sales personnel have a strong heritage of needing recognition and encouragement, which should come in a variety of ways: recognition events, personal awards, sales contests, benefits, commissions, incentive payments, peer-to-peer recognition, and feedback from customers. So why limit a recognition process just to money?

What can be recognized in a quality world? Some examples suggest the new thinking:

- measuring processes, e.g., number of defects eliminated
- rewarding participation in teams that accomplish improvements in processes
- making quality recognition an award of its own
- celebrating customer satisfaction or service levels
- catching people doing little things that symbolize commitment to quality
- making certain quality achievements are prerequisites for traditional awards

The last point is so important that it needs to be expanded upon. Many firms recognize the "sales office of the year." Historically such recognition relied heavily, if not exclusively, on business volumes and profitability. What is beginning to appear, however, is a modified form of recognition in which minimum levels of customer satisfaction and process improvements are required before an office can even be considered for the award. Another example, used to foster teaming, is not to give one salesperson a $10,000 award but rather to give a salesperson $10,000 or $15,000 to distribute among the team that made his or her achievement possible, with the salesperson sharing in the financial recognition. Mementos also offer an opportunity. Instead of one individual getting a glass eagle or a piece of wood with a pen sticking out of it, give the same item to all members of a team or unit, and include a team photograph suitably framed and annotated. In short, firms are finding ways to integrate quality into the framework of recognition rather than simply recognizing quality achievements with separate awards.

Benchmark Recognition

How do you measure the recognition process itself? The answer is not so easy. However, what some organizations are doing is measuring the rate of participation in a recognition process and then surveying employees on its effectiveness over time. Thus, for instance, with peer-to-peer or team-to-team recognition you can look at the number of business units participating as indicative of usage and relevance. These indicators illustrate "in process" measurements as the recognition process is being used. For end result measurements opinion survey questions about specific types of recognition can be asked. Last, there is always benchmarking how your process works against someone else's. In fact this method is so important as a source of good ideas that Appendix B is a minitutorial on benchmarking.

Benchmarking will quickly make obvious what constitutes some "best practices." For cash awards, for example, you must:

- understand their pitfalls.

- publicize awards with write-ups.

- award teams and individuals, not just individuals.

- explain why an award is being given (tie to corporate values and priorities).

- customize awards (e.g., maybe a day off is more meaningful to a person than a memento).

- personalize it (e.g., running shoes for a jogger).

For several years in its midwestern U.S. marketing operations IBM has conducted a major recognition study that promises to offer new insight into reward and recognition processes in sales. At the end of its first year of work, the recognition team learned that:

- individuals preferred to hear about recognition rather than read about someone else's accomplishments.

- employees recognize peers for accomplishments management never sees.

- every location wants local awards—the "not invented here" mindset still exists, even though in a quality-driven world benchmarking would encourage you to steal good ideas shamelessly.

- new ideas have a limited shelf life and thus must be implemented quickly.

- new recognition takes time to start but is a process that gains momentum and a life of its own.

- management resists new recognition processes (largely it does not want to give up the power to give awards).

- each organization likes to give awards a local, unique name, so let the process be flexible enough to do so.

One final observation on recognition: salespeople pay very close attention to it. In a Conference Board study ("Motivating the Sales Force," 1979), when 127 sales executives were asked what motivates a sales force, over-all financial compensation ranked only 6 out of 17 possible motivators. The first was special recognition for outstanding performance. Second was opportunity for promotion and third, encouragement by management. Various compensation factors were fourth, fifth, and sixth.

When tied to a comprehensive compensation strategy, recognition processes are a powerful way to motivate employees to do what needs to be done. Given that the nature and location of work are changing so rapidly today, compensation experts are focusing more than ever on new ways to pay and recognize employees to foster changes in behavior. The bottom line is that the ability and incentives to accomplish such changes must come from reward processes that more closely link the interests of employees to the objectives of the firm.

Suggestion Process

Suggestion process is a weak phrase to use in a book espousing continuous improvement; but the expression is so well ingrained that it serves as a good introduction to an important concept of quality in a sales organization. Suggestion systems work on the assumption that employees have good ideas about how to improve the business. We also know most suggestion programs are terrible because employees make very few suggestions. Quality-focused enterprises prefer to think in terms of continuous improvement processes or of ideas generating improvements. Looking at how to extract good ideas from employees as a process is a different way of taking advantage of the most precious resource at your disposal: your employees, who happen to know a great deal about how things work well and poorly in the firm.

Why Suggestion Systems Are Useless

Typical suggestion programs do not work well for several reasons.

First, like little battered poor boxes at the back of churches, they are ignored. The boxes or little stacks of suggestion forms are there. If someone bothers to fill one out, he or she has to mail it somewhere. Nine months later the employee gets a form letter rejecting his or her idea. It is not uncommon in traditional suggestion programs to see only 10 to 20 percent of employees ever submitting a suggestion in their entire work careers! Of those suggestions submitted, only 10 to 20 percent are ever implemented.

Second, the suggestion program is typically not linked tightly into the culture of the firm or into the job of an employee. Nobody talks about it; once in a while somebody gets attention and a check for submitting an idea, but employees are *not* expected to submit any.

Third, suggestion programs are not treated as processes with the kind of discipline and focus that an important process would require.

Finally, senior executives generally do not recognize that suggestion processes are very powerful tools to improve the overall welfare of an organization interested in continuous improvement.

In addition to these four problems, other difficulties sometimes plague more traditional programs. Too often the focus is just on cost savings; programs that pay for ideas create a "lottery mentality" that encourages people to submit only those suggestions that might generate a fat reward check; and they have too many restrictions, such as suggestions cannot be related to your job! There is limited management involvement, and evaluators find them annoying to deal with.

On the other hand, if you are going to ask your employees to direct their own affairs, work in self-managed teams, take responsibility for their own actions, and improve processes and increase their effectiveness, then as a manager, you must given them the resources with which to carry out their responsibilities. Many of the tools they require are as simple as methods for getting things done. One of these tools is an effective suggestion process, a vehicle for collecting their ideas for improvement, getting them channeled to whoever can implement them, and then rewarding the generator of the idea. A suggestion program, as a vehicle for continuous improvement, must be one of the vital processes of the organization.

How to Make Suggestions Work for You

When treated as a process for continuous improvement, suggestion programs can have spectacular results. Companies all over the world are beginning to report that when suggestion programs are treated as a process, participation by employees rises to above 70 percent per year, and acceptance and implementation also rises to over 50 percent per year. Milliken is recognized as the leader in suggestion processes in the United States, but the list of firms that have replaced old programs with new processes reads like a who's who of corporations: American

Express, Caterpillar, CIGNA, Dow, IBM, Federal Express, Hewlett-Packard, Kodak, Matsushita, 3M, Mitsubishi, Nissan, Siemens, Toyota, Xerox, and many others.

They have all learned some basic lessons about how to get meaningful suggestions for improvements.

1. *Employee participation.* All employees are eligible to participate, not just nonmanagement employees. All teams can participate.

2. *Recognition.* Small and large suggestions are recognized and celebrated. Taking a lesson from baseball, base hits win games, not home runs. Thousands of little suggestions are sought, tracked, and celebrated, not just blockbusters.

3. *Management participation.* Outstanding processes require involvement of the manager of the suggester in advocating and supporting the idea for improvement until it is implemented. If the employee thought enough to make the suggestion, then the manager, in his or her role of creating and facilitating an environment in which employees can perform their best, takes the suggestion as one of the most important items he or she can work on. Rather than seeing suggestions as additional work, managers see them as agenda-setting items for their contributions to the organization.

4. *Types accepted.* Rather than just focus on accepting suggestions that lead to cost savings, encourage suggestions on any subject, from anybody within the enterprise. Suggestions might save money, increase efficiency, improve the quality of any product, service, or process, or generate revenue.

5. *Feedback.* One complaint that employees have about traditional suggestion processes is that they would submit an idea and never hear what happened to it. In a good process, there is continuous communication between suggester and manager or company until the idea is implemented or killed. Feedback does more to generate new suggestions than just about any other action because then employees realize their ideas are appreciated and, when implemented, that they can make a difference.

6. *Job focus.* Quality-driven organizations expect their employees to improve the enterprise as part of their job and therefore, a suggestion process is a tool for them to carry out one of their central responsibilities. It is not uncommon in such organizations to see a line item in an employee's performance plan saying that he or she should submit suggestions (but no quota for these, please). When appraisals are done or bonuses and rewards extended, they often are in response to the role in-

dividuals played with suggestions. This means you should give bonuses to sales personnel for making your organization better and not just for selling more products. Xerox, Milliken, and others even host national recognition events in which teams present to each other process improvements, often initiated through their suggestion processes.

In short, *quality-driven organizations treat the suggestion process as one of a half dozen absolutely critical strategies for continuous improvement.* Efficient suggestion processes typically are as disciplined as any other process, rely on computer technology to facilitate capturing and measuring suggestions, and are simple, repeatable, measurable, and feedback-driven. Good ones encourage ideas on any subject from any employee, secure the involvement of his or her immediate manager, offer quick feedback and adoption, often do not pay cash awards since suggestions are considered part of the job, and challenge employees to unleash their talents. The best also require all suggestions to be calls to action—not statements or complaints.

How to Design a Good Suggestion Process

A typical suggestion process or, as it is known in many organizations, a process for generating ideas that improve other processes, has a fairly standard format. An employee submits a suggestion on-line to his or her manager, who acknowledges receipt within 24 hours. Within two or three days the two talk about the idea and jointly determine how to have it analyzed or implemented. If the suggestion is within the manager's immediate area of responsibility, it can be implemented immediately. If it is beyond the manager's responsibility, he or she takes primary responsibility for advocating its study and, if appropriate, implementing it in a larger organization (e.g., sales office, sales district, or corporation).

Since suggestions are submitted on-line, the computer can track them by individual, unit, suggestion type, quantity, and source. It can also show whether or not the process is working. Every 30 days good systems trigger a reminder to manager and employee that the suggestion is still "open" (not implemented or rejected by either manager or employee or both) so that they can communicate on progress. Trend analysis shows the organization what kinds of suggestions it is getting and which populations provide more or fewer.

Trend analysis is important because it gives the enterprise insight on how much commitment employees have for personally suggesting improvements. Historically, salespeople provide the fewest number of suggestions, yet in a market-driven world, they should be providing the most if they truly are to represent the interests of their customers. The only way to know if they are actually proposing changes is to have a suggestion process.

Once suggestions are implemented, they are communicated back to the suggester and his or her manager and are publicized with appropriate recognition. The latter can come in a number of ways: a better appraisal, a bonus, a small token of appreciation, name and picture on a bulletin board, or a promotion. After a while the culture changes and you actually see lists go up of how many suggestions came from one organization versus another. Challenges between units or offices are made to see who can implement the largest number!

There are some dangers to avoid, however. The most obvious is not to measure an employee on the number of ideas submitted for appraisal purposes because that just causes more suggestions, not necessarily better-quality suggestions. You should strive for better-quality ideas instead. To improve quality, keep the suggester involved and responsible for helping to implement his or her own suggestions.

A second danger, now seen in some Japanese companies with very high suggestion submission levels, is encouraging the trivial suggestion just to get one in. Moving the proverbial doorknob from the righthand side to the lefthand side makes measurements look good but does not really improve things. Emphasis should be on ideas that make a difference, so reward and compliment quality.

Measure Progress and Expect Improvements

As with all good processes there are certain measurements made continuously that are sensible. The typical ones are:

- number submitted by organization, office, and person.
- number implemented by organization, office, and person.
- type (e.g., process, product, facility, customer satisfaction, health and safety).
- origin by geography or type of employee (e.g., factory worker, salesperson, etc.).
- rejection and acceptance rates and ratios.
- cycle times (time between suggestion and implementation by type).
- money saved, revenue generated, customer satisfaction improved.

Implementing suggestion (improvement) processes is complicated. The most difficult problem faced by any organization replacing an old suggestion program with the kind of process just described is getting employees, especially salespeople, to use it. The old paradigm, in which suggestions were not taken seriously, is a real problem.

Successful implementation requires management attention, lots of recognition, teams developing local processes or emphasis programs, and patience. It is not uncommon in the first year to see only one suggestion for every four employees. But it will rise to 4 or 5 per employee within a couple of years and then as high as 15 or 20 per employee per year. Most executives do not understand that constancy of purpose in implementing this process is required; this is another reason the process fails to take off as quickly as it should in many sales organizations. But imagine the power you gain if every sales employee you have submits 15 suggestions each year and 10 each are implemented! Imagine if these suggestions overwhelmingly came out of your employee's direct knowledge, out of their jobs! Imagine the effect on the bottom line if all employees make suggestions and implement most of them, all directed at improving customer satisfaction!

Employee Feedback Processes

Employees are the most important resource in the firm. You implement effective processes to improve their skills to increase customer satisfaction, and to make them as efficient as they can be. But you still need to know how they feel about a variety of critical issues. To gather their feedback another critical process is needed. Methods such as employee surveys, round tables, and complaint letters have been around for a long time. Historically sales personnel have not been shy about using these, either. However, continuous polling of employees is rarer than you might think and yet it is crucial to any appreciation of how the firm is going.

There are several common approaches to gathering employee feedback. Their purposes are to:

- assess employee morale.
- determine how well they understand company strategy.
- determine the extent to which they buy in and understand the philosophy of total quality improvement.
- learn what they think of their managers and of management in general.
- assess how customer-oriented they think the firm is.

- determine to what extent products and services meet customer desires.
- understand what they think of the tools and practices of the company.
- see how well they are being treated, paid, and rewarded.
- determine the extent of their capabilities to serve customers.
- learn their views on specific company issues and strategies.
- assess their morale in general.

The last point is most important because happy employees work well with customers; poor morale is reflected in declining customer service.

Features of Good Surveys

Effective surveys increasingly are done on-line although paper surveys still exist. The best practices for employee surveys include but are not limited to the following characteristics:

- *absolutely* confidential
- given once or twice yearly
- mandatory
- results reported to all employees within 60 days
- management to implement plans to improve morale and other problems in a spirit of continuous improvement
- progress on their issues reported to employees
- data gathered statistically over many years to show trends
- basic questions asked year in and year out to track trends
- write-in comments allowed; not just yes/no or multiple-choice answers

A growing number of such systems today also develop a morale index: usually a statistical average of a half dozen questions asked each year to provide a "sniff" test for management. The questions usually relate to how employees like their jobs, and to what extent they think the company is successful, they are paid fairly, they have opportunity for advancement, and they are treated well.

   The confidentiality issue is very important. If you cannot absolutely guarantee confidentiality, you will never get truthful answers. This feature of any employee feedback process is the single most important one to ensure is in place on day one. The best way to ensure confidentiality is to use a computer-based on-line survey, report results by organizations no smaller than seven people (otherwise withhold the data), and have the personnel department or a third party "sanitize" write-in comments to make it impossible to determine who specifically wrote the remarks.

When surveying sales personnel, you can elicit additional feedback on the quality of products and services, terms and conditions, how the company deals with customers, and how competitive its pay and benefits are. Salespeople are close to what happens outside the company, and their usually good knowledge of your products, services, support, customers, and marketplace can be a major advantage for senior management. The data customer-contact employees provide is timely and realistic. On the other hand, they know little about product development, pricing and profit practices, and too little about product liability and contract administration; therefore, surveying them on such issues is not as fruitful an exercise.

Share Findings with Employees and Seek Their Feedback

In addition to the annual employee opinion survey, a feedback system to inform survey takers is essential. The senior manager at a sales office or district owns the responsibility for ensuring employees get the opportunity to see statistical results of the past survey, discuss the issues it raises, and then see local plans for fixing problems. Employees should be incorporated into the improvement process itself rather than leaving it just to management to improve whatever came up in the survey. I have also seen situations in which sales units have set targets for themselves on how much they want to improve their satisfaction by the next survey and have built plans to improve their own lot in life.

In general written comments in surveys need to be kept from employees because it might be possible to detect who wrote such comments. Again, to repeat sound advice, in the spirit of confidentiality, someone (e.g., a personnel specialist, or the senior manager at a location) should read these to distill their messages and also to make sure that no immediate action has to be taken (e.g., helping an employee complaining about sexual harassment or stopping ongoing criminal activity).

On the other hand, sample comments from the survey provide life for the statistical data. Use the surveys to ask questions about how much employees buy in on the quality movement, what they think has been the progress so far, what needs to happen next, and so forth, and use the comments to flush out details of their opinions. Often written comments are not only very blunt but also have suggestions for improvements.

A second method commonly used to elicit employee feedback is the round table. Six to twelve employees gather around a table to meet with a manager or executive to talk about preestablished topics or whatever is on their minds. Effective sales managers find ways to get executives responsible for product development and manufacture to spend time with their employees and customers in round tables to learn about how the field or the market views products and services. Sales personnel are hardly shy in these situations, and they can effectively add to your knowledge about products and services.

The round table is also a good method for extracting lessons learned from teams that have been effective in implementing a new process. Since teams working on a particular process may stay together for several years, their continuing learning about a process can be extremely valuable. For instance, a local team that developed a suggestion process—two years ahead of the company creating a national process—can provide significant insight on how best to develop a companywide suggestion system based on their own experiences and benchmarking. However, most teams do not go out of their way to offer advice. That is why a proactive method has to be in place, such as Xerox's team rallies or Milliken's sharing rallies, in which people are brought together to tell their stories.

The Role of Management

This is not the book in which to wax eloquent about the role of managers in the late twentieth century. But there are several points to make concerning the role of sales and marketing managers in a quality-driven organization.

1. *Managers have to take the initiative in making sure there are links between customer-contact employees and those in the firm who design, build, and ship products.* It is not enough for factories to take on that assignment. Sales and marketing managers have to build alliances with their suppliers so that both are doing what is best for the customer and the firm in an organized manner. Adopt-a-plant programs are popular, hosting customer and factory round tables and councils works well, initiating surveys and sharing results of customer experiences with internal organizations work, but these exist only if management initiates them.

2. *Managers generally own responsibility for sheltering sales personnel from company politics and bureaucracy so that these employees can spend as much time as possible in front of their customers, serving them.* That means management must listen to the needs of employees and judge how best to satisfy these while being cost-effective and profitable. Ultimately managers are responsible for creating the environment in which employees can work without fear, with a reasonable level of

urgency always present in the selling world, and with utmost efficiency and effectiveness.

3. *Managers owe it to their employees to teach and preach continuous improvement, to back up that gospel with good quality process work, ongoing education, and rewards that signal clearly that customers really do come first.* The values of quality must be continuously burning issues:

- cycle time reduction
- customer focus
- work simplification
- excellence in what is done
- efficiency
- effectiveness

How You Must Change Your Role

These are different responsibilities than a manager would have had ten years ago. Back then a good salesperson would have been made a sales manager or a good sales manager a branch manager because of their effectiveness in the previous job and their ability to control others doing the same kind of work. In the worst case, they could always step in and do the jobs of their employees. Today they are being asked to relinquish much oversight responsibility while delegating authority to people who know more than they do about specific offerings and what customers want. Instead of making decisions for employees, they have to teach employees how to make decisions.

Instead of just answering customer complaints and criticizing employees for causing problems, managers have to spend their time training, coaching, and fostering improvements in the company. Suggestions become very important to sales managers playing this new role. In addition clear and frequent communications with their employees represent important tasks. In management literature, these functions are frequently called leadership skills. Management bashing is very popular today; however, true leadership is always fashionable and there is never enough of it. The world of quality in a sales organization calls for more of it than ever before because sales managers have to function as leaders:

- setting visions and selling them to employees.
- preserving high standards of quality.
- modeling the way to customer focus.
- strengthening the heart by supporting teaming, employee initiatives, and individual improvements.

- fostering a world of continuous improvement.

Instead of just reviewing losses when a sale goes to a competitor, managers need to review wins too to learn how to repeat success. Instead of just appraising employees, they have to teach them to do that among themselves. Instead of being the keyholes through which their organizations are run, they are becoming doorways for employee initiative.

Increasingly these kinds of activities are called for in new ways. As marketing organizations expand the number of partnerships and alliances with other vendors to service a customer, the need to persuade and lead becomes greater. It is not uncommon for a vendor today to have to work with several others to close an important sale. That involves multiple firms. It is also very normal to have secretarial support provided by another company, service on your products by a third, and customers uncertain as to whom to call for help. Ensuring that continuous improvement in services exists requires that sales and marketing managers communicate and negotiate well, understand statistical measurements, initiate process reengineering techniques, and be willing to learn at the same time as they delegate.

References

Byham, William C., and Cox, Jeff. *ZAPP: The Lightning of Empowerment; How to Improve Productivity, Quality and Employee Satisfaction*. New York: Fawcett Columbine, 1988.

Carder, Brooks and Clarke, James D. "The Theory and Practice of Employee Recognition," *Quality Progress* Vol. 25, No. 12 (December 1992) pp. 25–30.

Kopelman, R. E. *Managing Productivity in Organizations: A Practical, People-Oriented Perspective*. New York: McGraw-Hill, 1986.

Larson, Carl E., and LaFasto, Frank M. *TeamWork: What Must Go Right/What Can Go Wrong*. Newbury Park, Calif.: Sage Publications, 1989.

Scholtes, Peter R. *Performance Appraisal: New Directions*. Madison, Wis.: Joiner Associates, April 19, 1991.

Osburn, Jack D., Moran, Linda, Musselwhite, Ed, and Zenger, John H. *Self-Directed Work Teams: The New American Challenge*. Homewood, Ill.: Business One/Irwin, 1990.

Ryan, Kathleen D., and Oestreich, Daniel K. *Driving Fear out of the Workplace: How to Overcome the Invisible Barriers to Quality, Productivity, and Innovation*. San Francisco: Jossey-Bass, 1991.

7

Computers
and Quality

*Man is a tool-using animal...Without tools he
is nothing, with tools he is all.*
THOMAS CARLYLE, 1834

This chapter defines the role information systems and staff can play
in facilitating the implementation of quality processes in marketing
and sales. Suggestions are made about how sales and information
systems can work together.

It is impossible today to imagine implementing quality-based processes
without relying on computer technology to help. As organizations improve the way they do business, they increasingly have turned to information technology, finding new uses for computers while revamping
old applications. While computer experts in the 1980s were still writing
and lecturing on the need to use computers to gain competitive advantage, quality-focused marketing and sales firms were discovering that it
was impossible to improve performance without new approaches to
computer use.

The objectives of this chapter are to:

- explain why information technology is critical to any successful implementation of quality programs.

- show a model of how to link information technology to process improvements within the context of a business plan.

- define the role information processing professionals and sales and marketing should play together to apply information technology.

The overriding concerns are to ensure that information technology does not get in the way of a sales organization's transformation, that it supports new objectives with systems, and that such uses create timely competitive advantage by allowing you to lead with quality as a selling edge. Properly done, you are given sustainable competitive advantages much along the lines proposed by Michael Porter and other experts on competition and marketing.

Why Information Technology Is Critical

Throughout this book you have seen examples of computers being used in support roles for various processes: order entry systems using telephone ordering, telephone systems' performance tracked by software, electronic mail with which to communicate with employees, and data bases for skills, sales opportunities, and financial performance.

Computers can do three things well for a quality-driven organization. *First,* they can do "in process" monitoring. That is to say, as a process is being used, computers can track its effectiveness, generating data that allows a process owner to improve the process itself. For example, telephone systems can tell how many rings it takes before a phone is answered or how many suggestions were responded to by management by when.

Second, computers can store information useful in executing tasks or processes important to a customer in data bases. For instance, having on-line access to information on your products and their availability makes it possible to explain immediately to a customer the features of your products and when they can get them. My favorite examples of this kind of usage are airline reservation systems and those used by mail order firms like Land's End and L. L. Bean.

Third, they can shorten lines of communication and speed up how things are done, buying you cycle time reduction. Electronic mail systems (all computer-managed) allow people to communicate instantaneously across the enterprise regardless of organization, bringing together (if you want) product designers, manufacturers, marketers, and sales personnel. These systems can also be linked to customers. Oscar Meyer communicates regularly with vendors such as IBM through electronic mail. Where does IBM end and Oscar Meyer begin in such an arrangement? The two organizations become dependent on and supportive of each other. Orders placed by a customer can be transmitted immediately to a factory and a delivery schedule committed on the spot. That is what a customer would call quality service.

Computers have long been used to improve efficiencies, reduce costs, and beginning in the late 1960s, improve decision making by providing larger quantities of data and analysis with which to make decisions. By the mid-1980s, companies began employing computers to market products, thus finding new strategic and tactical uses for such equipment. That use sometimes supported growth in market share and greater sales, not just more efficient use of existing resources.

How Information Technology Is Used in Service Organizations

By the late 1980s, however, it had become very clear that as companies became more committed to being service-focused, adding value to otherwise increasingly commodity-oriented products, the role of computers was changing. Service organizations found that computers could enhance the quality of services provided, not just increase the efficiency of what was done. There is growing evidence as well that computer systems, when combined with tools, documentation, equipment (e.g., fax machines), and better working environments, also improve sales employee morale and well-being with direct implications for better customer service.

Progressive service organizations rely almost entirely on computers for supporting sales and, indeed, they are central to their operations. For instance, can you imagine buying or selling an airplane ticket without computers? Every nationally recognized mail order company has an army of telemarketers attached to telephones linked to large data centers through which orders are taken and dispatched.

But manufacturing companies committed to quality and effectiveness are also finding computers to be of great use. A good example is Motorola, an early winner of the Baldrige Award and a leading manufacturer of portable telephones, telecommunication products, and computer chips. After applying Total Quality Management principles in manufacturing, Motorola moved next into marketing, reengineering sales processes to focus on doing things correctly and on enhancing value for customers. Since it decided that a defect is when a customer does not like a product, it tied customer satisfaction/complaint systems back into design and manufacturing more closely than it had in the early 1980s. In 1990 it consolidated nearly a dozen offices responsible for customer support in its land-mobile product sector into one office. This move allowed Motorola to focus on improving one process, not twelve, much of it dependent on information processing.

In 1991 Motorola began to benefit from a vast amount of information captured by computers from its customer 800-number response center. This in-process computing gave the company better understanding of complaints, customer interests, and concerns. In this case computers consolidated a great deal of data from Motorola's various listening posts, which could be shared with any part of the enterprise that needed to see it.

Seven Benefits You Enjoy Using Computers in Sales

The benefits of using computers to improve the quality of performance in sales and marketing can be summarized quickly.

1. *Computers shorten lines of communication.* Electronic mail and report generation are two obvious examples. More important, computers eliminate geographic distance within your enterprise; it does not matter where people are as long as you have telephone links and access to computers.

2. *Computer-based applications can be designed to make sure the right information is at the right place at the right time.* These features support customer-contact employees performing well during their "moments of truth." The benefits include cycle time reduction (your view) and faster service (customer's view).

3. *Computers can gather data on transactions and also on how processes are doing (effectiveness), then do basic statistical analysis for you.* They can also merge processes to provide new insight into your business. (Recall the example of opportunity identification and skills data bases merged to provide continuous insight on how well one organization "covers" its opportunities.)

4. *Computers help make you better aware of your environment.* An early and still expanding use of computers is to do competitive analysis to determine what your rivals are doing, identify their products and services quickly, and tap into data bases maintained by other firms (e.g., financial institutions) to learn more about your customers.

5. *Computers make it possible to provide new or additional services.* New services are how you achieve competitive advantage using technology. Providing data bases that inventory the repair history of products, dispatch service personnel, or integrate multiple sources on a customer for a salesperson's use are well-understood applications. Linking your

computer to a bank's so that customers can pay for goods and services is another. Increasingly, alliances between companies have been formed largely by merging applications. The ability to order stereo equipment from a gasoline company by means of an advertisement in your last bill is an example. Travel agencies with 24-hour hot lines staffed with personnel who can access your file and airline reservation systems, and those of hotels, rental cars, and credit cards are others. At the moment imagination seems to be the only limiting factor slowing adoption of technology aimed at offering more services to customers.

6. *Computers can give you a fuller view of customers.* As a company builds interactive computer systems that have growing data bases, it becomes increasingly possible either to merge these data bases or to provide links leading to more complete views of customers.

For example, look at customer master records. The first on-line data base records were typically customer name, customer number, address, and accounts receivable files. Then came on-order files, maintenance records, and purchase history. By the late 1980s some companies had figured out that they could take Dunn and Bradstreet data, information from news clipping services, add information gathered by sales personnel and from other commercially available data bases, and bring them all together. With the capability today of splitting screens on terminals into four windows, and with microcomputers having nearly a dozen open files available on a screen, an employee working with a customer can know immediately what is on order, the accounts receivable situation, background data on the customer and on his or her firm, and so forth. Getting that kind of information into the hands of a salesperson on-line over the weekend for a more effective customer call Monday morning is also possible. In fact, some of your competitors are probably doing that today.

These kinds of applications are so attractive as competitive weapons that it is very difficult to find public references much less get companies to discuss their applications. Such uses of computers make any salesperson far more effective. However, this approach builds a series of applications into larger ones that must be disciplined through quality process management.

7. *Computers improve efficiency of services and operations.* Repair services today are increasingly being tracked and managed via computer. IBM's Retain System, for example, monitors the repair history of every IBM mainframe and its associated peripherals. This gives service personnel insight on how to deal with any specific machine, while a by-product is trend data that influences service level goals, staffing of repair offices, design points for next generation equipment, and preventive maintenance

strategies. This is an example of a traditional application (repairing products) that manufacturing firms face. With repair history information, preventive maintenance can be done before a machine breaks, leading customers to believe the product is of superior quality, making it easier for sales to market additional quantities of products.

Having systems that customer-contact personnel can use to enter questions or complaints about products facilitates the service process as well. Building data bases with answers to the most frequently asked questions of customers provides your people with fast answers less expensively than if they went back to the office, went through manuals, called friends, and took days to respond to their customers.

Dangers to Avoid

While more will be said below about how information technology should be managed to support sales, two widespread dangers to avoid are:

1. automating bad processes.

2. allowing existing computer-based applications to block your employees from improving existing processes. These are real dangers and so common that one can reasonably expect your firm to have experienced them already.

There is a third, more rare flaw in the application of computers in what otherwise is an organization that is driving toward continuous improvement. The flaw typically appears as a statement in the strategic plan that declares the firm will constantly review what its competitors are doing with technology and then decide whether or not to adopt the same applications. This approach is more than stupid, it is fatal. By the time you hear of a competitor using a technology in a particular way, that rival can reasonably be expected to be already on to the next generation of use. So at best you are a Johnny-come-lately with a "me too" strategy. Given the rapidity of change today, by definition you can never catch up.

One of the main reasons for process reengineering, benchmarking, and continuous improvement is to lead to breakthrough thinking resulting in new levels of quality service to your customers that leave your competition in the dust. That strategy cannot be implemented if you have a plan that says "let's see what others do first before we do it." Reinventing the wheel has always been a poor strategy; yours should be to invent it in the first place.

The World of Your
Information Processing
Community

Before I discuss the role information technology must play to support marketing and sales, and before you march down the hallway to tell the computer people what to do, you should understand something about their environment in business terms because it profoundly affects how the information systems (IS) community responds to you. While your competition has attacked you and turned all your markets into niches that are tough to understand, let alone identify, the same has happened in the world of computers. The information processing industry has experienced as many profound changes in its structure in the past five years as it has ever seen. In fact, one needs to drop back either to the mid-1950s or to the 1880s and 1890s to find a comparable period of change.

Users are moving away from just applying computers to increase efficiency; they are looking at value-generating applications. They want more open systems that reduce their dependence on one or few vendors. Many executives are questioning the enormous investment they have been making in IS over the past 15 years and so are slowing their continued support until they either see results or are shown how computing can be more effective. Hardware prices are dropping rapidly, and IS organizations are demanding more services from their vendors.

The IS director who, five years ago, could confidently rely on one architecture or technology platform finds that his or her options are greater and hence more confusing. That manager knows from experience that picking the wrong technology wave is deadly to both career and technical effectiveness. So market fragmentation and many more options spell risk and danger and not opportunity and flexibility. Niche players, particularly in software, are offering tens of thousands of options. IBM publicly states it has 50,000 competitors; your IS director has 50,001 options.

A variety of factors is playing havoc with IS organizations at the same time. With so many options and combinations of technologies possible— all with richer functions than years ago—your computer community continues to find IS growing in complexity, not becoming easier as they are for end users. There are never enough of the right kind of technical skills available to apply new technologies because the learning curve often is greater than the rate at which new technologies and products appear in the market. With hardware costs dropping at rates of 20 to 40 percent each year (depending on what devices you look at), the risk of making bad financial decisions also is rising. But the story gets worse.

We now have coming into the senior ranks of management a generation of executives more knowledgeable about the potential strategic value of computers; some are even computer literate and can write programs! The point is, they are not afraid of this technology and are asking some tough questions, all designed to extract the most out of information technology as part of the business. They want to employ IS as a strategic tool to enhance services and grow market share. And they are in a hurry, too.

What Computer Managers Are Doing

Enlightened IS managers understand that the ground is shifting beneath their feet; those that do not, I would worry about. But those who understand are developing priorities and strategies that, while compatible with your needs, are defined in uniquely IS terms. Common elements of an IS director's requirements and experiences today include:

- more open systems (especially for telecommunications and in operating systems).

- incorporating end users in the process of deciding what IS applications and hardware to acquire.

- greater integration of IS technologies so that various components and applications work together.

- growing reliance on applications development tools and techniques.

- distributing computing power to the desktop.

- outsourcing everything from specific applications to whole data centers.

- growth pressures on budgets as they shift expenditures away from hardware to software, with the latter growing each year by over 15 percent (an expense), while hardware (a capital expenditure) is generally slowing except for acquisition of microcomputers and terminals.

There is growing evidence that IS directors concur that their operations are crucial to the kinds of transformation I have talked about in this book. For example, in a survey of North American firms with sales of $250 million or more, conducted by *CIO* magazine in late 1991, IS executives shared common interests. Their biggest problem for 1992 was to continue the process of aligning their resources with the demands of end users and the business at large. The second most important challenge they face is reengineering both their processes and those of the business as a whole, suggesting that such executives are ready to ally with you. Third on their list was the creation of technology architectures that are effective in supporting the corporation's business plan.

About 45 percent of the surveyed IS executives had significant process reengineering under way, which obviously leaves enormous room for improvement. Apparently there is still a great deal of lip service being paid to quality by IS (55 percent said they did not have major process reengineering projects under way but they anticipated that they would by 1994). They appear not to have the sense of urgency I have emphasized as crucial throughout this book.

It used to be that IS departments acquired and installed all computer hardware and software. That no longer is true today. Beginning in the early 1980s end users began to acquire millions of microcomputers largely in response to the IS community's inability to provide quick, low-cost solutions. By the start of the 1990s, therefore, there were many organizations acquiring information technology, creating additional fragmentation of responsibility within the enterprise. Couple that development with the fragmentation of offerings in the IS industry and you begin to sense the difficulty of applying computer technology in some organized and strategic way.

Today there are few absolute information technology lords in any organization although large concentrations, of course, still exist. So we have various groups picking out mainframes, minis, micros, and terminals on the hardware side. Others are buying applications software that is either industry-specific or generic. Operating systems (software to manage computers) vary today and have cult followers. The same is true with telecommunications. Services are coming from computer vendors, traditional accounting firms, software houses, lone wolves doing applications development, consultants, professors, and systems integrators.

IS directors used to be able to go to one or two computer vendors to help them sort out the best uses of technology, and for decades that worked well. But some of those vendors are not around anymore or are called something different or are in trouble. Burroughs and Sperry blurred as they became Unisys; Wang (a leader in office systems in the 1970s) suffered severe crisis in its senior management ranks in the late 1980s, while the new up-and-coming firms in the industry today (like Lotus and Microsoft in software and AST and Sun in hardware) were never heard of 10 or 15 years ago.

The purpose of this long discussion is to point out the tension that IS organizations are experiencing today. It is no longer merely a question of tight budgets and a reluctance to invest in major, high-risk applications that possibly lead to competitive advantage. This means that IS organizations, like yours, are looking for ways to improve productivity, win friends, and make a contribution. These circumstances also mean that you would get a friendly hearing for your ideas about how IS can help your organization.

The Role Information Technology Must Play

One of the central themes introduced early in this book is that no one part of a company can totally embrace quality initiatives alone. The most effective management teams come to realize that all segments of the company need to play the quality game for any part of the firm to enjoy the full results of process reengineering, customer focus, and improved business results. Since one of the objectives is to reduce the time and tasks involved in conceiving, building and designing, and marketing and selling goods and services, anything that facilitates this effort should be encouraged. Despite the fundamental changes and churning evident in the IS world, information processing is one of the critical leverage points in an organization.

Little work has been done by academics or computer experts to define the role information technology should play in the quality movement. However, what is emerging is the important notion that information processing should be a facilitator of change. Put in negative terms, one of the top three to five reasons organizations cannot change quickly or effectively is usually because their information processing systems are too inflexible. You hear things like "the system won't allow us to do that." Or you go to the IS community and they say it will take one to two years to rewrite an application.

Begin by Forming an Alliance with IS

The effective approach for marketing and sales to take regarding their colleagues in IS is to encourage and support them, becoming facilitators of change and providing the data underpinnings so vital to any refurbished process. In other words, as you increasingly move to business practices that require activities needing greater amounts of data, you want IS to be able to respond quickly to your needs. In short, IS has to subscribe to the practices of continuous improvement and cycle time reduction no less than you.

To hit at the same point harder, if you decide to use telemarketing correctly within 90 days, you would need on-line access to customer files linked to a telephone system so that you could merge human telephone operators, IS and telephone technologies, and good old-fashioned selling. If IS is not playing with you, telemarketing cannot be implemented by your firm. You would have to go outside your company to a vendor or drop telemarketing as a strategic initiative.

The bottom line is that marketing and sales has an enormous stake today in IS and therefore cannot leave the technical community alone. You have to form an alliance with that organization; encourage, demand, and support the practices of quality within that sector of the business; and most important, cajole, persuade, or force IS to be facilitators of your changes.

What You Need from IS

In the simplest terms, sales and marketing wants data from IS, a telecommunications utility to get that data around the organization fast, and the ability to write new IS applications quickly. As an end user of IS, these are the things you really want. To get these you must support IS management in embracing quality as well as in acquiring certain tools and adopting some specific strategies that directly help sales.

Data. Information in computers has been made increasingly available to non-IS workers through terminals over the past 15 years. The phrase typically used is *on-line access to data bases* (DBs). Essentially information in machine-readable form is stored in a computer and end users write brief commands at their terminals or microcomputers to get copies of that information from data bases. The more data bases you have and the more access you offer, the more flexible IS can be in supporting your operations. Since approximately 60 percent of all end user needs are simple queries about existing files in the computer, as an end user you should be very concerned about how easily and quickly your people can get to such information. So your conversations with IS quickly center around data bases.

Invest in Relational Data Bases. The current trend, and the one you should support IS in implementing, is the concept of relational data bases. *A relational data base* is a collection of files (e.g., customer address files, purchasing history files, accounts receivable files, etc.) that can be linked together to answer a specific query. There are software packages that collect from different data base files the information you need and present it as an integrated answer to your question. Twenty years ago, when relational data bases did not exist, you would have queried an accounts receivable file, then a purchase file, and so forth, independently of each other.

But with relational data bases, the main data center or large computer in your organization becomes a huge electronic public library, but one in which the book you get is unique: one copy containing exactly the information you want. The benefits are obvious:

- faster integration of data for new insight
- new uses of IS, particularly for sales personnel
- consolidation of multiple sources of information

All lead to quicker and different uses of information processing. If you have to pick two or three things you want IS to invest in, one of them is a state-of-the-art relational data base. You also want that relational data base to be used in all future applications development by IS so that you can organically change the information your end users receive from their standard applications. Figures 5-7 and 6-1 illustrate processes that are, for all intents and purposes, a collection of easily accessible data bases.

Along with providing internal data bases, IS should be required to play a leadership role in making available access to noncompany data bases. There are thousands of these wonderful data bases ranging from Standard & Poor's type of business profiles to unique marketing niche files. Access to these is typically rented or a fee is charged when they are used. But you need to have IS support use of these systems in a number of practical ways:

- finding and letting you know of these data bases
- providing technical support to get them (e.g., terminals and telecommunications)
- protecting you from computer viruses that can wipe out your files
- educating your staff on their use

Telecommunications. *Telecommunications* is the transmission of information from one part of an organization to another or between organizations. This can be accomplished through the use of telephone lines, microwave, or radio communications. These are all managed today by computer-based technologies and usually are under the jurisdiction of the IS community.

You want two facilitative requirements met. First, you absolutely must have a strategy for and implementation of internal telecommunications within your enterprise. Second, IS must provide telecommunications with others outside your firm. Both facilitate dialogue among all company employees (hence shortening the length of the chain from design to delivery) and with your suppliers and customers.

Internal communication involves a number of requirements. First, there is the obvious need to have a telephone system that provides the kinds of capabilities I talked about in Chapter 4.

Second, as employees acquire microcomputers at their desks, they want to share information from terminal to terminal, and that requires what is known as a *local area network* (LAN). That is, simply put, a wire run among all the microcomputers that wish to share information, linked to one microcomputer that manages the traffic and even stores data, and which may also be linked to the big mainframe computer to get to other data bases.

Third, today electronic mail is absolutely an essential tool for any organization with more than a couple dozen employees. Given the fact that 80 percent of your mail is internal and takes as long as a week to travel from one end of the enterprise to the other, you can save expense and time by transmitting these messages electronically. E-mail systems, as they are called, are easy to use and have extensive functions.

External communications with suppliers and customers must also be facilitated by IS. These can be various. For example, you can extend your internal E-mail system to customers and suppliers alike, making them, for all practical purposes, look to your employees as if they were members of their own enterprise. I like E-mail with customers because they become dependent on you for goods and services.

A quick illustration makes the point. Going to a customer and offering them access to a variety of applications resident in your computer through a telecommunications network is a common strategy today. Thus, for instance, a customer could be given the capability of placing orders directly within your order entry system (saving you the cost of doing that) while you are managing electronically the backorder and inventory files for your customers. Giving them query capability to see what they owe and what is on order, to define options of things to buy, and to receive information (e.g., electronic newsletters) shortens sell cycles and creates true dependencies on you—marketing heaven!

Manufacturing has found that telecommunications improves the quality of its parts and speeds up production while lowering costs by requiring fewer suppliers. To make that work, however, they have to ensure easy communication between supplier and manufacturer, between manufacturer and deliverer, and all have to have access to commonly shared data bases. It works and is outrageously successful. So why not marketing and sales?

Require a Well-Thought Out Telecommunications Strategy. The long and the short of it is that IS can facilitate your ability to improve marketing by having a clearly thought out telecommunications plan which it is constantly enhancing. You want to make sure it touches all your employees along with everyone else in the enterprise, that it is state-of-the-art and allows access to data bases and other software tools.

As part of conversing about telecommunications with IS, you may get pulled into a discussion concerning "open systems." It happens so frequently that I should define it for you. For decades there have been collections of telecommunications and data base technologies that are unique to particular computer vendors. IBM has one, Wang another, Xerox had one for a while, and AT&T has yet another. For the most part they were mutually exclusive in the 1960s and 1970s. That is, if you had one, you could not use another one or have them "talk to each other." In the 1980s IS organizations and end users started calling for *open systems,* or systems that would enable them to get to any other part of the enterprise or data, crossing these various families of technologies. They wanted to get to IBM software, Wang software, AT&T software, using telecommunications as if they were all one. Increasingly, therefore, in response to these requests, telecommunications disciplines have been changing dramatically over the past five years to accommodate this need.

The reason you need to know about open systems is that some IS shops are wedded to a particular approach (because of what they know) and may be reluctant to change, or they want to change but require considerable amounts of additional funding to make that happen and hence need political muscle around the enterprise. That is where you have to play a role. The pros and cons of open systems versus closed systems are not so obvious and thus you may have to form an opinion after some education on your part. But the bottom line on this issue is that you want the corporatewide telecommunications system that best supports your ability to market and sell and to change your mind about strategies and tactics. Telecommunications has to be able to accommodate you quickly.

One other aspect of telecommunications you need to be aware of, because of the effect it will have on marketing in the 1990s, involves a huge revolution in capacity. We are rapidly increasing computer processing speed and also transmission speed. These changes are not at 20 percent a year but involve quantum leaps. The amount of storage and just plain horsepower in computers are also growing that fast and at competitive costs. What this means is that the amount and type of information you can transmit are changing. For example, in 1988, if you subscribed to an on-line encyclopedia and you looked up Martin Luther King, Jr., you saw text on your screen describing his famous "I have a dream" speech. With the extra capacity now available, you still get the text but also can receive video and voice of him actually delivering the speech.

Another illustration: ten years ago you could put up a nice wooden pamphlet stand in a shopping center with brochures describing your products. Today you can put up a kiosk with a microcomputer linked to your main computer in which a potential customer can touch the screen, calling up video, still pictures, and sound describing your products and services. In fact, you can take an order right on the spot with a credit card passed through a slot, check for creditworthiness, and confirm the order, all in a minute! Imagine the effect on your sales of a TV-like commercial on demand instead of a brochure. It is impossible to pull off such an effective use of technology unless IS facilitates your access to state-of-the-art telecommunications, data bases, and related technologies such as those which allow you to store and manipulate images like forms and photos.

Applications Development. Applications are uses to which we put computers. You and I think of these as collections of software that do things such as order entry and accounts receivable. Over the years these applications have become more integrated, so that they share information from one to another, and most recently, appear simultaneously on split screens. But these have all been either independent software packages that were bought, modified, and integrated with earlier systems or written from scratch by your IS organization. Development in this handcrafted approach is why you always heard IS tell you that your request would take months or years to provide. In the world we live in, you could be in an entirely different situation by the time IS develops systems you define today.

Therefore, if IS is to facilitate your flexibility, applications development must stop being a black art and a handcrafted profession and must become a mass production process to reduce cycle time. Today, tools exist to facilitate rapid applications development, and it is to your advantage to make very sure that IS is using them.

The term used to describe these tools is *CASE,* which stands for computer-aided software engineering. The concept is very simple: you provide programmers with a "workbench" of tools that reduce the amount of time it takes to write a new application. For instance these tools have chunks of prewritten software that perform basic functions such as moving data around and providing access to existing data bases. To put it another way, these CASE tools are like prehung doors. If you are building a house, you can make doors from a pile of lumber, or you can save time and improve quality by buying prehung doors you just plug into holes you cut in your walls and which you then paint whatever color you want. Other CASE functions are like prefabricated walls, which offer the same choice: build from scratch or just plug in the prefabricated option.

Many data centers today are beginning to use CASE tools (and there are many good collections of such software aids today) but many still are not. Outside the IS department some CASE tools are finding their way into the hands of more technically skilled employees. For example, packages that allow people to write queries against existing data bases were the first CASE tools. Now you see other CASE tools that flowchart processes. This tool is particularly useful. Ten years ago a programmer would sit at his or her desk with funny-looking paper and lay out in little blocks all the steps an application would perform before programming it. If you still see that happening as you walk through the IS shop, then you know CASE tools are probably not being used, because with the new software, manual flowcharting is virtually eliminated. The programmer or end user describes in modified English prose functions they want an application to perform, and the tools translate this into chunks of software.

Figure 7-1 illustrates a model of how data bases, telecommunications, and CASE tools come together to give you more rapid access to information and new applications faster. In this new world, IS's costs of producing new applications are reduced, while their ability to respond to changing market conditions is quicker and of better quality. The downside is that such a strategic use of software and computers can be a profound cultural change for IS staffs and may threaten the political position of groups of IS employees.

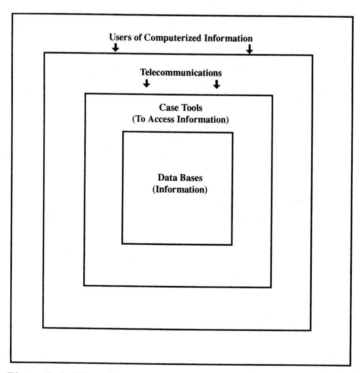

Figure 7-1. IS model.

End User Tools and Support. Another way that IS has to support you is by providing a rational plan for putting productivity tools in the hands of your employees. (The word *tools* is used in technical circles to refer to software applications, CASE tools, and programming languages.) Everyone seems to have a microcomputer today and that means they also have a variety of software packages to provide word processing, spreadsheets, graphics for presentations, and so forth. These tools are useful, expensive, and hardly used effectively. Most acquisitions are made ad hoc, one by one, and there is little or no training, much less sharing of such software. In short, in most organizations it is a mess.

How this happened need not detain us here. However, the size of the problem should. It is not uncommon to have the total computer horsepower sitting on desks today equal to what is installed in the data center. It is also not uncommon to have microcomputers used only for a few hours daily and even then only as dumb terminals or very expensive word processors. If it is the latter, it is costing three to four times what a typewriter would. Yet we all know that these tools are powerful and are profoundly changing the culture and structure of organizations and the speed and nature of our response to customers. So we have to approach these tools with the same discipline that we use with any other set of tools and processes.

Have IS Develop and Implement a Well-Thought Out End User Support Plan. IS can and must help you by developing a support plan for these tools that takes into account how:

- data is shared.
- tools are acquired and shared.
- training is done.
- user questions are answered.
- problems are resolved.
- data is protected from improper use.
- these tools can be used to sell and support.

We are past the point of trying to stop proliferation of the use of such tools; they are too valuable. But you must work with IS to develop plans for the rational acquisition of tools so that ideally they are similar across your enterprise. Then you can share information and have a common set of skills known by all employees. You can save money by buying software in quantity as well. Figure 7-2 illustrates a computer-oriented value chain involving end users applying tools that can serve as a model.

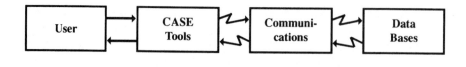

Figure 7-2. Computerized value chain.

You also need IS to develop a support mechanism that increases the speed with which tools are installed and used effectively. Such support, when done correctly, involves IS having either help desks or personnel in each building who can install hardware, answer questions about how to use specific pieces of software, and train employees on their use. Realistically that requires standardizing on certain tools because no IS shop can support all the thousands of variations available. Thus, for instance, the firm should pick the word processor it will support. The same applies to spreadsheet packages, graphics, and of course, E-mail. Other packages are okay to have, but it should be understood that IS will support these only on a "best effort" basis or not at all.

The support role that IS plays with end users is a process, not a program. Just as your staff must look at applying quality methods for ensuring effective deployment of its responsibilities through clusters of processes, so too must IS. End user support is a perfect example of a process that can be structured, measured, and improved upon to provide the benefits of any reengineering process:

- cycle time reduction
- increases in effectiveness
- better return on investment
- better responsiveness to big C and little c customers
- effective tie-in of technology, processes, and marketing efforts

To summarize quickly, what you need from IS is facilitation of the proper and fast use of computer technology in the following areas:

- data bases
- telecommunications
- applications development
- end user tools and support

Your interests are best served when IS and you are talking about access to information, quick modification of existing services, and how best to link IS to the marketing and sales plans.

The dialogue that takes place between IS and marketing and sales should itself be an ongoing process. If you are to improve the value chain of activities from design to delivery with customer focus, the technology base which supports all these activities is largely IS. If you look at the Baldrige model described in Appendix A you quickly will conclude that IS has to be a routine part of the continuous improvement process. That means IS has to participate and be supported in the overall discussions about how marketing and sales are done. IS must also be avid practitioners of the principles of continuous improvement as outlined by Deming, Juran, Crosby, and others. Shared values and a common vision of what the enterprise is all about effectively drive the application of technology in the direction you need. However, the dark side is that IS communities have been as late as sales and marketing in applying total quality management principles. That means IS too will take one to three years to see results. However, by focusing on the elements listed above (e.g., telecommunications, data bases, etc.), you can discern immediate improvements in less than a year.

A Strategy for Using Computers

Typically, discussions on how to use computers to support businesses are the preserve of information technology experts writing computer books or business school professors focusing on marketing, manufacturing, or organizational issues. The literature on quality and service enterprises is only just now beginning to focus on computer technology as a critical component of continuous improvement. I like to think of computers as offering more than just continuous improvement; you should demand blockbuster improvements. Just as you can get to blockbuster activities by having bolder visions, looking for dramatically new ways of doing things through benchmarking, so too quality principles can be applied to find dramatic new uses of computing.

The trap you can fall into is to ask IS to automate bad processes or just to improve existing ones incrementally. In fact, I submit you will not be able to avoid this sin; however, there is nothing wrong with incrementally improving an existing process as long as you understand the benefits of so doing and the costs of avoiding migration to a radically new approach. It is an issue of tradeoffs judged on a case-by-case basis.

But why look at IS the same way you view other collections of processes? Why ask, How can computers help us get to a new level of competitiveness where the rules of marketing are changed, where new levels of service are offered, and where return on investment increases? Half the battle in getting to blockbuster applications is simply to want them. Whole bookshelves of war stories illustrate this process at work; some of the better ones are listed at the end of this chapter. Also, you can refer to Appendix B on benchmarking for additional ideas.

But the point is, expect dramatically more effective uses of IS to support customers and then build the implementation plans. The approach below is commonly used in IS to determine what sales and marketing applications to acquire or develop. It can be used as a basis for a joint marketing-IS process for defining what to invest in for the organization.

Apply a Portfolio Strategy

Well-proven approaches frequently look at applications much the same way a stockbroker views portfolios of stocks. Uses of computers (we call them applications) have various values and costs. Applications also vary in complexity and time to develop or replace. They also rely on different technological platforms which in themselves are of differing ages. Different technologies can be modified or replaced with differing levels of complexity, flexibility, and cost. In short, the environment of applications development and use is messy, not any cleaner than managing a stock portfolio, hence the value of treating applications like stocks.

Figure 7-3 illustrates a simple model to characterize existing or proposed computer applications. The greater the value to customers (big C, little c) of a particular application, the higher up on the vertical axis you would plot. The risk of not implementing the application properly is plotted on the horizontal axis. Obviously the ideal application is one that delights the customer and represents minimal risk of failure—upper lefthand quadrant—and the worst is of no value to customers and has high risk of failure—in the lower righthand corner.

Some IS shops keep such a quadrant analysis of existing and proposed applications based on technical difficulty, age of applications, data-base versus non-data-base dependent, and so forth. You can do the same for existing and proposed processes in your organization to determine what is most important to work on; the process is the same. Because it is a widely used approach, the odds are in your favor that as marketing and IS sit down to talk about applications you will be using an approach that reduces the risk of miscommunication about needs and wants.

Stockbrokers believe that an ideal portfolio contains investments that would be plotted in more than one quadrant, depending on the objec-

High

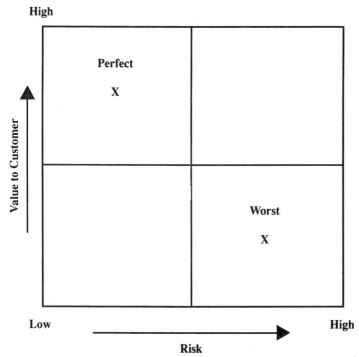

Figure 7-3. On picking processes to implement.

tives of the portfolio. The analogy works well with applications. Healthy IS applications inventories inevitably have old and young applications (e.g., more than ten years old, such as payroll, and less than one-year-old tools), large and small (e.g., companywide E-mail and a sales tool), expensive and cheap applications, old and new technologies, difficult-to-maintain to no-maintenance systems, efficient and inefficient end users and IS staff, high quality and poor quality functions, and adaptive to modification and "hard wired" in its inflexibility.

You can chart uses of computers that affect your operations in a similar way, providing a portfolio of future developments that range broadly from low to high risk, low to high customer satisfaction, and other factors. The approach should be to:

1. identify the critical processes you need to run your business.

2. set priorities on their importance.

3. have IS work with your process owners to see who can use IS most effectively to least effectively.

4. plot that on a quadrant to define which ones to work on in the next (or for some firms, first) wave, since nobody has enough resources to go after all of them.

Once selected for replacement or redesign, applications should have built into them the measurements that allow you to determine how effective are the processes they support. Applications should rely on current technology and tools.

Ensure Quality Practices Are Used with IS Applications

To help you do a reality check on all uses of computers and the IS organization's support of quality improvement plans, question the following:

- Has the process been reengineered before reprogramming or automating? If not, do so.

- Does the new use support the corporate or business unit strategic plan in the long and short terms? If not, why bother with it?

- Have you measured where your existing application is today so that you know how effective it is? If not, do a baseline study first so you can set targets for improvements in new applications.

- On the new applications that you have decided upon, ask yourself the following seven questions. If you answer no to any, you have a problem.

  Is it faster than the previous one?

  Does it have fewer errors than the previous process?

  Is it simpler to operate, perform, or conduct?

  Does it serve the customer better?

  Does it give you sustainable competitive advantage or at least increase efficiencies?

  Does it have in-process measurements designed in?

  Is it outstanding or does it just provide incremental improvements?

- To what extent does the IS organization practice sound quality management principles? I would want that organization to demonstrate its commitment to quality through its explanation of its processes. They might even illustrate their commitment through some internal Baldrige-like self-assessment. You want to take this approach because confirmation of their commitment ensures that someone knowledgeable about information technology will be coming back to you with a relatively open mind in explaining the strengths and weaknesses of existing applications, while making a solid effort to support your organization as if you were a cash paying customer.

- Question how the IS organization is set up to support quality: its culture, structure, functions, and allocation of resources. I will address the issue of what you need to do to support quality in the next chapter; but the same applies to information processing departments.

- Ask how the IS community stays current with computer technology and what its track record is in adopting new tools. If the IS community plays a "me too" game with technology, you are exposed.

References

Cash, James I., Jr., McFarlan, F. Warren, and McKenney, James L. *Corporate Information Systems Management: The Issues Facing Senior Executives.* Homewood, Ill.: Dow Jones–Irwin, 1988.

Cortada, James W. *Strategic Data Processing: Considerations for Management.* Englewood Cliffs, N.J.: Prentice-Hall, 1984.

Editors, *Harvard Business Review. Revolution in Real Time: Managing Information Technology in the 1990s.* Boston: Harvard Business Review Books, 1990.

Rockart, J. F., and DeLong, D. W. *Executive Support Systems: The Emergence of Top Management Computer Use.* Homewood, Ill.: Dow Jones–Irwin, 1988.

Tapscott, Don, and Caston, Art. *Paradigm Shift: The New Promise of Information Technology.* New York: McGraw-Hill, 1993.

Weizer, Norman, et al. *The Arthur D. Little Forecast on Information Technology and Productivity: Making the Integrated Enterprise Work.* New York: John Wiley and Sons, 1991.

8

Starting the Implementation of Quality

There's no such thing as a free lunch.
MILTON FRIEDMAN, 1974

This chapter shows you how to assess where your firm is on the quality journey and then describes the elements of a tactical plan for continuous improvement of operations. Dangers involved are described along with proven approaches.

The purpose of this chapter is to illustrate how to move forward in implementing quality business practices and values in sales or marketing. As in previous chapters, I cite examples but am not definitive because no two organizations do things quite the same way. However, I will document some of the obvious and basic moves you would want to make. For those already on the journey to quality, the issue is what to do next. Some pitfalls commonly seen a year or two into the process are also presented.

Determining Where You Are Today

Just as you would not want a doctor to prescribe medicines or surgery until he or she had thoroughly examined you and had convinced you of what was wrong, so too you should not accept the advice of any quality adviser without first understanding the health of quality in the enterprise. The process begins with assessing the portion of the organization you control, then extends to evaluating the company as a whole. A useful technique I illustrate below is to take the Baldrige Award criteria and do an initial "sniff test." As you implement changes, you then can write a formal annual report card on progress while identifying those areas that require additional focus. Then you develop plans for improvement as a by-product of the assessment. However, before we go through the process, it would be helpful to understand typical phases of evolution organizations undergo as they implement Total Quality Management principles. Your firm is somewhere on the bandwidth and each part of the enterprise is in different phases.

The Five Stages of Transformation

Figure 8-1 illustrates in general terms five stages evident in firms that have transformed themselves into high-quality enterprises. From start to "superb" takes about a decade. Encouraging results become evident in the second, or more commonly, the third year, and by the seventh year, results are generally very good. While no two organizations travel down the continuous improvement path at the same speed, the model is applicable.

In Stage 1 there is a beginning of awareness, without integration across functions, although some pockets have attempted to apply these principles. There are as yet no results and little evidence that continuous improvement is making a difference. The organization is probably not obsessed with customer satisfaction, although it may be doing well financially (so far), and the management style is very much the old "command and control."

Stage 2 is characterized by growing interest and learning about quality principles. There is some support from senior management and typically a real champion has emerged. Processes are being constructively redesigned and integrated in various parts of the company, and some employee attitudes have changed. Firms claim some success in important areas although they cannot always say for sure that the quality approach caused them. Employees begin to be empowered with responsi-

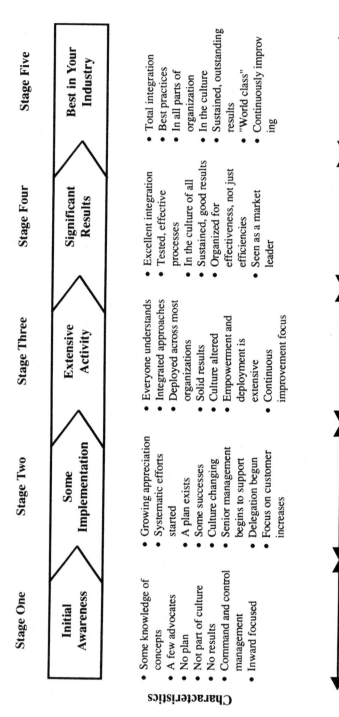

Stage One	Stage Two	Stage Three	Stage Four	Stage Five
Initial Awareness	**Some Implementation**	**Extensive Activity**	**Significant Results**	**Best in Your Industry**
• Some knowledge of concepts • A few advocates • No plan • Not part of culture • No results • Command and control management • Inward focused	• Growing appreciation • Systematic efforts started • A plan exists • Some successes • Culture changing • Senior management begins to support • Delegation begun • Focus on customer increases	• Everyone understands • Integrated approaches • Deployed across most organizations • Solid results • Culture altered • Empowerment and deployment is extensive • Continuous improvement focus	• Excellent integration • Tested, effective processes • In the culture of all • Sustained, good results • Organized for effectiveness, not just efficiencies • Seen as a market leader	• Total integration • Best practices • In all parts of organization • In the culture • Sustained, outstanding results • "World class" • Continuously improving
1 - 2 years	2 - 3 years	1 - 2 years	1 - 2 years	Ongoing

Characteristics

Figure 8-1. The five stages of transformation.

180

bilities and decision making. This is an important stage because during this period, if management lacks constancy of purpose, previous gains can be lost. It is a vulnerable time because the firm has yet to see important results to confirm the wisdom of the kinds of profound changes called for in this book. Management has to stick with it for two to three years as it builds up a head of steam.

A particularly dangerous situation exists at this juncture if, for example, a senior management change occurs, such as a new district manager or a new senior vice president coming into power. What happens is that the employees as a group pause from the new quality efforts, waiting to see if new management supports it. Since many employees at this point are barely converted to quality processes, lack of immediate and focused reaffirmation of the quality vision by the new manager along with no tangible evidence of support (e.g., personal time invested in quality initiatives), results in the word going out to return to old habits. It can happen in less than a month! If it does, it can take years to crawl out of that situation and back onto the quality path. It may even require changing the new manager, who does not even realize that he or she has lost all credibility in the situation. By Stage 3 the risk declines because a particular manager, regardless of where placed in the organization, is outnumbered by quality proponents already deeply immersed in renovations.

In Stage 3 the head of steam is clearly evident all over the enterprise. There are effective, well-documented plans for improvement, evidence of systematic approaches to business, and all important areas are being worked on. The culture and its values have undergone important changes and few parts of the enterprise remain unaffected. Employees are making many decisions and the attitude of continuous improvement is healthy and very evident. By now solid results are evident, with positive trends that people are beginning to prove are a consequence of new ways of doing business. In short, they are "living" the Baldrige approach.

Stage 4 is the beginning of a golden age in a company's history. By now all the major business journals are beginning to feature articles about the firm because results are excellent and sustained. You are gaining important competitive advantage, increasing market share and profits, and evidence is mounting that your approach to and deployment of quality principles brought in the good news. Processes are well-integrated, tested, and innovative across the majority of the enterprise. You are organized more for effectiveness and customer service rather for simply improving efficiency and ROI. Employee surveys show very high buy-in for the company approach (above 80-percent approval) and customers are applauding with approval ratings of above 90 percent. You got to Stage 4 because your firm sustained its faith and patiently paid its dues in Stage 3.

In Stage 5 people are now writing books about your firm, your CEO is on the lecture circuit at quality conferences, and you win the Baldrige Award. How you do business (processes) is considered unique and innovative. At this time how you do business is often called "world class" or "best of breed." Your approach is systematic and continuously measured and refined. Your efforts are deployed across 100 percent of the enterprise and you now have a culture that espouses continuous improvement and customer service. Management expects, and regularly gets, outstanding results. You are the best in your industry and continuously outperform competition. Results are clearly due to approach and deployment.

Is it possible to move backward through these stages? Yes, and it happens all the time. The greatest movement back and forth occurs in Stage 2 firms; backsliding decreases as one moves forward. However, since a test of how well you are doing involves the degree to which you gain and sustain market share, revenues, and profits, if you lose any of these then you have proof that the firm is sliding backward. So far we have evidence of at least one Baldrige winner, possibly two, that have slipped backward. Because there are no guarantees of continued success, all the quality gurus argue the case for continuous improvement *forever* as the way to keep a firm in the game. This approach is made even more urgent by the fact that as customers come to expect higher levels of quality in goods and services, the bar continues to rise.

How to Assess Where You Are

Where are you on the spectrum? Using the Baldrige criteria, you can quickly answer the question. Figure 8-2 is a modified list of the Baldrige criteria in a worksheet and Figure 8-3 has guidelines. You can get your staff around a table, give them a copy of each, and have them fill out Figure 8-2. Using Figure 8-3 (which gives them guidelines for judging how well your organization is doing at each stage), they can judge what percent to assign each item and calculate the points earned. You want to do this because some of your activities will be more advanced than others and you want to know more than simply at what stage you are at as a whole.

It is possible for a particular category that your approach would be valued more than deployment or results. In determining what percentage to assign a category I would balance approach, deployment, and results equally. Thus, if I thought approach on a topic was worth 30 percent, but deployment only 20 percent, and results only 10 percent, I would judge that category to be worth 20 percent. Using category 1.1 on senior leadership, if our CEO had a good plan (30 percent), but had only just started to implement it (20 percent), and had no evidence that he or

Self-Assessment Worksheet

Category	Max. Points Possible	% Achieved	Points Earned
1.0 Leadership			
1.1 Senior Executive Leadership	45	_____	_____
1.2 Management for Quality	25	_____	_____
1.3 Public Responsibility	25	_____	_____
2.0 Information and Analysis			
2.1 Scope and Management of Quality Data and Information	15	_____	_____
2.2 Competitive Comparison and Benchmark	20	_____	_____
2.3 Analysis and Use of Data	40	_____	_____
3.0 Strategic Quality Planning			
3.1 Strategic Quality Planning Process	35	_____	_____
3.2 Quality and Performance Plan	25	_____	_____
4.0 Human Resources			
4.1 Human Resource Management	20	_____	_____
4.2 Employee Involvement	40	_____	_____
4.3 Employee Education and Training	40	_____	_____
4.4 Employee Performance and Recognition	25	_____	_____
4.5 Employee Well-Being and Morale	25	_____	_____
5.0 Management of Process Quality			
5.1 Design and Introduction of Quality Services	40	_____	_____
5.2 Process Management—Services and Delivery	35	_____	_____
5.3 Process Management—Business Process and Services	30	_____	_____

Figure 8-2. Self-assessment worksheet.   *(Continued)*

Self-Assessment Worksheet

Category	Max. Points Possible	% Achieved	Points Earned
5.4 Supplier Quality	20	_____	_____
5.5 Quality Assessment	15	_____	_____
6.0 Quality and Operational Results			
6.1 Product and Service Quality Results	75	_____	_____
6.2 Business Results	45	_____	_____
6.3 Business Process and Support Service Results	25	_____	_____
6.4 Supplier Quality Results	35	_____	_____
7.0 Customer Focus and Satisfaction			
7.1 Customer Expectations	35	_____	_____
7.2 Customer Relationship Management	65	_____	_____
7.3 Commitment to Customer	15	_____	_____
7.4 Customer Satisfaction Determination	30	_____	_____
7.5 Customer Satisfaction Results	85	_____	_____
7.6 Customer Satisfaction Comparison	70	_____	_____
Total Assessed Values		_____	_____

Figure 8-2 (*Continued*)

she had yet made a difference (10 percent), I would conclude that under his or her leadership so far, we were exhibiting Stage 1 behavior.

As to the mechanics of filling out the worksheet, let us use, for example, the same item 1.1 in the self-assessment, which is leadership of the senior executive. Based on what we have said in this book, you go to Figure 8-3 and find the words that best describe leadership today on quality. You determine that there is some beginning of awareness on the part of your senior manager but no quality results of that leadership. That means you can assign only 20 percent of the 45 points on the work-

Quality Self-Assessment Guidelines

	Approach	Deployment	Results	% Achieved
Stage 1	■ Beginning of awareness ■ No integration across functions	■ Beginning in some parts of organization ■ Not part of culture	■ Few or no results ■ Little or no evidence that any results are caused by approach	20% 10%
Stage 2	■ Beginning of sound, systematic efforts, not all aspects addressed ■ Some integration	■ Begun in many parts of organization ■ Evident in culture of some parts of organization	■ Some successes in major areas ■ Not much evidence they are caused by approach	40% 30%
Stage 3	■ Well-planned, documented, sound, systematic; all aspects addressed ■ Good integration	■ In most of organization ■ Evident in culture of most parts of organization	■ Solid, with positive trends in most areas ■ Some evidence that they are caused by approach	60% 50%

Figure 8-3. Guidelines for self-assessment.

Quality Self-Assessment Guidelines

	Approach	Deployment	Results	% Achieved
Stage 4	■ Well-developed and tested ■ Excellent integration ■ Innovative	■ In almost all of organization and functions ■ Evident in culture of all groups	■ Excellent, sustained in all areas with improving competitive advantage ■ Much evidence that they are caused by approach	80% 70%
Stage 5	■ World-class approach: sound, systematic, effective, continuously evaluated, refined, and improved ■ Total integration across all parts of organization ■ Proven innovation	■ Fully in all of organization ■ Ingrained in culture	■ Exceptional, world-class, superior to all competition ■ Sustained, clearly caused by approach	100% 90%

Figure 8-3 (*Continued*)

sheet to that question. You fill in 20 percent in the Percent Achieved column and 9 points in the Points Earned column of Figure 8-2. Go through that exercise for all the items and tabulate the point totals at the bottom. Collect the worksheets from everyone and come up with an average for each of the seven major categories (not the subcategories) and a bottom line point value. That data will tell you where you think you are in the seven categories and as a whole. Figure 8-4 gives a rough indication of how many points you should have for each of the five stages.

Look at where your points fit to see at what stage you are. For example, if you have 198 points, you are still in Stage 1, and if you have 600 points, you are in Stage 4. Warning: the worse you are, the more inaccurate is your self-assessment. Also, those who know more about quality management principles tend to grade themselves harder than those who do not. Reading Appendix A will help refresh memories about what to value in this exercise. Some managers go the extra step and give each participant an actual copy of the Baldrige Award brochure published by the American Society for Quality Control (ASQC), which is short and easy reading.

Evaluating categories takes up most of the time in this exercise. You should look for the extent to which plans exist to improve operations continuously and then the extent to which a system exists for accurately measuring those improvements. Look for benchmarking to compare performance with that of other enterprises, close links with your suppliers (e.g., your manufacturing plants), and to what degree the organization understands customers by use of such processes as surveys and other fact-finding exercises. To what extent are relations with customers transitory (e.g., one transaction at a time) as opposed to ongoing? Finally, to what extent are you committed to preventing mistakes rather

Baldrige Assessments Compared to Stages

Points	Stage	Comments
0 - 200	Stage 1	Slight attention to quality
201 - 400	Stage 2	Some evidence, limited efforts
401 - 600	Stage 3	Fair; but good prevention-based processes
601 - 800	Stage 4	Good to excellent; yet more improvements needed
801 - 1,000	Stage 5	Superb in all categories

Figure 8-4. Baldrige stages correlated to points received.

than just correcting them? Is your approach a focus or a wish? A commitment to quality must run from the top of the house to the bottom.

Organizations that do self-assessments have found it useful to draw up sets of questions to ask themselves as part of the process of evaluating each function (in Baldrige these are grouped into seven chapters). All the handbooks on Baldrige provide useful questions. Each enterprise that develops an internal Baldrige-like assessment package also develops questions. These are typically written in language familiar to employees.

An example from the Baldrige assessment illustrates the process. Using leadership (Chapter 1), section 1.1 calls for the assesser to describe the senior executive's leadership, personal involvement, and visibility in maintaining a customer focus and quality in all that gets done. A perfect score is 45 points. Questions that might be asked to determine whether or not certain activities were present are:

- What evidence is there that the senior executive is involved in the quality effort?

- How many hours did the executive spend last year on quality-related activities?

- What is the breadth of quality-related activities in which executives are involved?

- How much training did this executive receive in quality?

- How much time did this individual spend with customers discussing quality issues?

- What percent of the budget or other resources was devoted to quality improvement efforts?

Over time, these kinds of questions become clearer and more relevant to the enterprise. For example, in Baldrige Chapter 5, Process Quality, section 5.1 focuses on design and introduction of products and services. Typically sales personnel look at this section and say it affects manufacturing, not them. In reality it affects both. However, in 1990, IBM's internal version of the document asked sales personnel to focus on their "leadership of goods and services based primarily upon process design and control, including control of procured materials, parts, and services." Two years later, the topic included language concerning "service-related requirements" and "use." IBM wanted to know about processes associated with the introduction (read "sale") of products to customers—making the language more relevant to a field organization.

For section 1.1 on executive leadership, the questions cited above were paraphrased from IBM's self-assessment for 1992. In 1990 the assessment had no questions, just statements of what needed to be addressed. For example, "Areas to address: (b.) senior executives' approach to building market-driven quality values into their leadership process and the organization's culture." While helpful, feedback from employees led to development of the laundry list of questions for 1992.

Assess Your Approach to Improvement

As they think about results, it is not unusual for managers to realize that their organizations are not as well run as they might be. Guiding subsequent discussions around the three aspects of approach, deployment, and results is very consistent with how marketing and sales managers normally do their jobs. The issues are very basic.

- Is there a management system and defined, repeatable processes focused on customers? If they answer yes, Are these approaches prevention-based rather than designed to detect problems and then react to them?

- Is the approach grounded on quantitative data that is reliable and objective? If not, the approach is faulty.

- Does the approach to quality include such elements as evaluation and feedback, and encourage continuous improvement? Related to that is the whole issue of what tools are available and to what extent they are used effectively to support the evaluation process.

Deploying Your Quality Efforts

Deployment issues focus on the extent to which actions are taken to support customers. They involve the extent to which quality initiatives are embedded in business transactions and interactions with customers, suppliers, and the community at large. Looking at processes, are quality features evident in all internal activities and operations, products and services? To a large extent the debate is over the extent of quality deployment in these areas.

Finally, there is the question of results. In the world of quality, results that happen by accident do not count. Results that occur because you applied an approach that was effectively deployed and could be measured do count. In other words, what you planned to do, then did, caused specific, measurable results. Questions often asked about results and quality include:

- Was there a defined base line?
- Was there relative improvement?
- To what extent were achievements sustained as gains?
- How much benchmarking takes place against the best, or how much competition takes place?
- How are results linked back to approach?

Answers to these questions form the basis for the desire to build or improve quality strategies in any organization. Armed with the kind of insight gained from your exercise (although it was not as rigorous as a formal Baldrige-like assessment which Stage 3 through Stage 5 firms usually perform at least annually), you can begin to lay down plans for what to do next.

What the Assessment Teaches You

While Figure 8-3 tells roughly at what stage you are, you can next appreciate in more detail where you are on your journey to a transformed enterprise. Using the Baldrige point system helps.

- If you have 125 points or less, you should conclude that there is no evidence of effort in any of the seven categories and that hardly any attention is given to quality, even as a concept.
- If you have between 126 and 250 points, you would be given some credit for slight evidence in some categories. Quality is probably still a very low priority as a disciplined approach to running the business.
- At the range of 251 to 400 points, some evidence exists of efforts under way in a few categories, but none of the efforts is outstanding. In this range you would expect to see limited integration of efforts. People are still reacting to problems, not preventing them in the first place.
- Between 401 and 600 points the first important corner on quality has been turned. You see evidence of effective efforts in a number of the Baldrige categories. By now prevention-based process redesign is under way, although many new procedures are still young and being stabilized. You would recommend at this stage that additional deployment of quality principles is required, and you should be looking for continuity in the application of new processes.
- Between 601 and 750 points, you can feel good about where the organization is on quality because there is considerable evidence of effectiveness in each of the seven categories and typically, outstanding

performance in a number of them. There is good deployment and lots of results. Pockets of improvement become very obvious while some processes remain too immature to show significant results.

- A 751- to 875-point assessment indicates an outstanding commitment to quality, excellence in approach and deployment, and significant results tied back to approaches. In short, wonderful things are happening in all seven categories with industry leadership in some.

- Above 876 points your firm is breathing pure oxygen! Hallmarks at this point are effective integration, sustained results in all facets of the business, and recognition as either national or world leaders in your industry.

Elements of a Tactical Approach

The discussion below is targeted primarily toward those in early stages of implementing quality because the majority of marketing and sales organizations has only just started to deal with the issue. Those further along would instinctively want to know how others are approaching quality and thus would find the ideas below useful because they are based on experiences from industry.

Quality begins with leadership. The individual who introduces quality into an organization has to do the same things other leaders have done elsewhere.

1. *The senior manager establishes a vision of what quality is in that organization by explaining that it is a companywide initiative, that it is supported by the top of the house, and that it will implement well-known business practices.* The vision should be tied to corporate values that cherish customer service, employment involvement, and dignity in a world of continuous improvement.

2. *Leaders work within their organizations to document and establish challenging objectives for the transformation that lead to better understanding and fulfillment of customer requirements.* This is typically a good stage to demand documentation of existing processes and then start using benchmarking methods to find better ideas.

3. *A master plan developed.* We saw these illustrated in the case studies of IBM and the ASQC.

4. *Tools with which to practice quality are provided to employees.* The primary tool is education on quality practices, training, and practice in

deploying such skills as teaming and statistical measurements. Associated with the deployment of training is the early establishment of teams to gain experience working on processes.

5. *Leaders find they need to create an environment conducive to improvements.* The four critical elements here are quality plans, progress reviews of those plans, recognition for achievement of quality improvements, and then appropriate rewards. That is why many of the sample processes described earlier in this book were chosen—to give you examples of these important activities.

6. *Leaders must "walk the talk," leading through example.* Beyond making presentations, leaders must also go to classes on quality, insist on quality reviews at staff meetings, be team leaders on important processes, and approach problems as opportunities to learn and to improve. Leaders who spend 15 to 25 percent of their time on quality-related activities are probably in Stages 2 to 4.

How Sales Management Should Perform

The management structure surrounding quality initiatives can either support the early education and process reengineering efforts or hurt them. Successful approaches typically involve the senior manager (i.e., district sales manager, vice president of sales, CEO) treating his or her immediate direct reports as the quality board of directors of their enterprise. In such a scenario, each staff member would own a critical process (e.g., customer feedback, order fulfillment, etc.), would be expected to report progress at staff meetings, and would be held accountable for improvements. Ideally, a process owner would also be given authority to spend resources of the organization to deploy his or her process plan. Staff meetings in such a world begin with quality reviews, which take between 20 and 100 percent of staff meeting time.

In the beginning, work would be done to identify critical processes, lay plans in place, and deploy. By Stage 3, process owners and their senior executives would be spending time reviewing results, tuning plans, and ensuring that focus remained on customer service and continuous improvement. Much of the discussion would involve skills and activities of employees focused on processes.

The key point is that the line managers, reporting to the senior manager or executive, own quality; they are process owners and dedicate considerable portions of their time to continuous improvement as a process of planning, executing, inspecting, replanning, and redoing.

It is also a common strategy to implement at each level of the organization a similar structure in which every manager who has employees is responsible for processes. Each staff member focuses time continuously on quality improvement. At each level of the enterprise a quality plan is documented and inspected.

How to Use Quality Councils

Also useful is the concept of establishing quality councils populated with individuals from multiple organizations and backgrounds but all bound together by better-than-average understanding of Total Quality Management principles. Councils serve as "technical" advisers to line management on quality and may have several levels of employees (managers and nonmanagers). They act as the quality conscience of the organization, often do quality audits (e.g., conduct Baldrige-like assessments), may be given responsibility for training employees on quality, and serve as advisers to process teams. There is no right answer on how best to deploy such councils. Stage 2 firms typically create them. Figure 8-5 illustrates an organizational structure with a quality council.

Stage 3 organizations have gone the extra step of having cross-functional teams look at processes in very broad terms. For example, a common type of cross-functional team, made up of sales, administration, manufacturing, and design people, focuses on development of a new product line. Another is made up of customers and employees working on a particular process, product, or service. In each case the teams are improving the goods or services at hand.

But the quality councils remain at the heart of successful management processes, providing line managers have already assumed responsibility for being the primary facilitators of quality improvement. This is a serious point, particularly in sales organizations where initial resistance on the part of sales managers to the responsibility of quality improvement is often the case. It is easy for them to push quality off to some quality council. Senior management runs an enormous risk of failure if this problem is not addressed quickly. But assuming that managers have become process owners, that they see themselves as a unified team attempting to make the entire organization more effective, then quality councils serve a good role.

Members of quality councils should have more training on quality methods of management than the average employee and should be given the opportunity to advise senior line management on what processes are most broken or in need of reengineering. They should help those managers determine which are the most critical processes. This is a good orga-

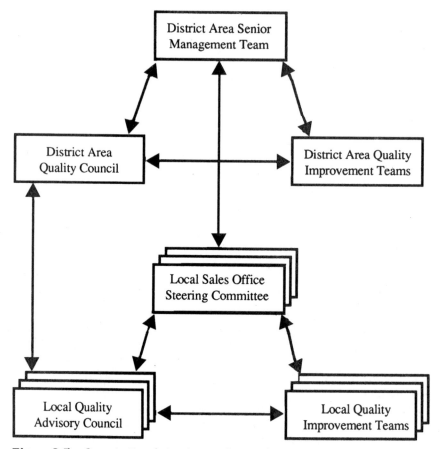

Figure 8-5. Organizational structure with a quality council.

nization to charge with responsibility for training employees, providing you give them the time to do so. Since training in Stage 2 and 3 companies is extensive, you may have to put in place full-time instructors.

Sales organizations with fewer than 1000 employees probably can use part-time instructors, providing there are close to a dozen who can devote up to 25 percent of their time to the task over a two- to three-year period. For bigger organizations, a small full-time instructor staff works better. Full-time instructors can act as coaches to process teams to help figure out measurements, apply statistical analysis, do benchmarking, and conduct self-assessments, among other tasks.

Quality councils are teams and thus should be populated carefully. Obvious skills to look for include compatibility with each other, the ability to communicate and sell quality to the rest of the organization, commitment to and not just an interest in quality, and preparation for process reengineering. Ideally the council should represent all factions or organizations, possibly even have representatives from manufacturing and other parts of your company, and enjoy the absolute support of the senior manager. In some enterprises, the senior executive or manager is the chairperson of the council and attends all meetings.

Yet mistakes are often made in the selection of council members. Some people play politics, others are not able to devote sufficient time, and others have no experience. Common errors on the part of management include not telling the council what is expected of it or why individuals were selected to participate. Always in the beginning, the council has to work together to become a team.

The Role of Effective Quality Managers

We are beginning to see the appointment of quality managers and directors in marketing headquarters and field sales organizations. These individuals perform the same kinds of tasks their counterparts have been doing for years in manufacturing. They typically have a sales background, have run sales organizations, and report to the senior manager or executive of the organization. They are best placed in sales districts or regions reporting to district or regional managers, and if they are at headquarters, directly to the vice president of marketing or sales. They are considered senior members of the staff, may even have staff reporting to them (e.g., to educate and train, etc.), and are responsible for coordinating quality activities of the senior staff, including the quality council and organizationwide assessments. In addition, they advise all levels of management on process improvements. They also play a "booster" roll in helping the senior executive sell quality and articulate the vision of the enterprise.

The more effective ones also ensure that the quality implementation plan does not take on a life of its own, keeping it tied intimately to the business plan. They spend a considerable amount of time talking to other enterprises and customers about their quality efforts, articulating to them their own organization's efforts in the field of quality. Xerox and IBM, for example, frequently employ quality managers who grew up in marketing and sales, to perform these functions in their district sales offices.

Managing Process Reengineering Correctly

Michael Hammer, in an article entitled, "Reengineering Work: Don't Automate, Obliterate," in the *Harvard Business Review* (July/August 1990), summarized some of the more practical guiding principles that senior managers, quality councils, and quality experts find true. I find they are particularly valuable for sales organizations. Like others working on transformation of organizations, Hammer recognizes that the central cluster of activities concerns processes. But he wisely points out that "just speeding up processes with automation cannot address fundamental performance deficiencies." While he points to the information systems (IS) organization to reengineer processes and not just automate them, his lessons are true within sales organizations, regardless of computers.

Breaking away from outmoded practices and longstanding assumptions is crucial in any attempt to improve fundamentally the effectiveness of an organization. His suggested list of guiding principles is increasingly becoming evident in sales and marketing:

1. Organize people around outcomes instead of tasks.

2. Have those who use the output of a process be those people who perform the process.

3. Embed IS activities into the real work that is done which produces the information used.

4. Always treat resources which are dispersed geographically as if they were centralized.

5. Try to link parallel activities rather than integrate their results.

6. Let decisions be made where the work is done but integrate controls into the work.

7. Always capture data on what is going on, or the output of work (information) only once, and at the source.

Managers and their allies on quality (e.g., quality councils and quality managers and staffs) are charged with the fundamental responsibility for fostering organized change—difficult in the best of times, even more so in the worst of times. There is growing evidence that the transformation can be a positive one if the underlying strategy avoids programmatic changes and instead focuses on reorganizing people's roles, responsibilities, and relationships so that they concentrate on resolving specific business problems that directly affect customers.

Mounting evidence suggests that the most effective transformations, while they begin with vision at the top of the organization, ultimately succeed only if they reach and indeed, take off at the lowest levels. Initially this happens on an informal basis anyway as groups get together to solve specific business problems. Later, management institutionalizes many of these efforts for greater effect.

One common problem that occurs is that the senior executive of the organization is not committed to the quality management approach. Why this is so can take pages to explain; suffice it to say, however, that these senior executives must buy in to quality's disciplines before any serious work can be done in the enterprise. So how do you ensure this happens?

1. Have such an individual attend one or more seminars on the subject, preferably taught within their industry as part of a national annual industry show. That can start the process.
2. Even more effective is to take that executive to a peer executive who already has started to implement quality management principles, and let that individual explain to your executive the benefits and mechanics of what gets done.
3. Point out in some detail the work being done with quality by those competitors of yours whom you most respect and who are doing the best job of eating your lunch.

In almost every case that I am aware of, a combination of the three steps must be taken. In addition, it helps if your business is in economic trouble because then you almost have no choice but to try something different. What you have today obviously is not working if business is down substantially.

How to Focus on What Needs to Be Done

Three experts on organizational behavior and human resource management (Michael Beer, Russell A. Eisenstat, and Bert Spector) have identified six critical activities that emphasize focusing on the work at hand rather than on more abstract concepts such as employee participation or culture change. Their work is very relevant to both marketing and sales and is confirmed by my own experiences.

They studied six organizations for four years and concluded that in these enterprises, as well as in others, senior management incorrectly assumed that companywide programs caused transformation and that employees changed their behavior when management simply modified formal structures or systems. In reality education and attitudes alone will not do the job. Rather, people will do different things because of the organizational roles they are asked to play. In other words, to make people change, put them into new organizational contexts, as I demonstrated in Chapter 3. To do that requires coordination, commitment, and competencies all managed in an interrelated manner. Focus on the work at hand, not on some concept such as "quality" or "empowerment."

They have observed that organizations which are effective in changing culture—what Stage 1 and 2 companies have to worry about—have taken several actions. (One plan is shown in Figure 8-6.)

1. *They found specific business problems and engaged those affected by them to diagnose issues, thereby gaining commitment to change.* They changed a specific process because of a specific business problem.

2. *They had a shared vision of how one should organize and manage for competitive advantage.* A leader can get employees to reorganize "toward a task-aligned vision" which then leads to new roles and responsibilities. They can define new organizational structures, jobs, and measurements of success.

3. *Management needed to foster consensus for the new vision, which emerged as a result of attacking specific business problems* (e.g., loss of market share, declining customer satisfaction, etc.). The consensus must also extend beyond vision to define the competencies needed to implement it, and finally to develop the cohesion required to "move it along." This requires general management to provide support, tools, education, reorganization, and protection as people assume new roles. The sales executive must also maintain constancy of purpose in this phase as people buy in to the new vision at various speeds. You may have to replace some managers as you go through this conversion.

4. *They focused next on extending changes horizontally and vertically across the enterprise, but avoided a top-down approach.* Cross-functional teams, quality councils, even some "reinventing of the wheel" helps. General sales managers at this point are tempted simply to force the issue, especially in sales organizations, but must let employees sell the vision to each other to make it stick.

5. *As the revitalization process emerged, then management institutionalized changes through such traditional methods as policies, organizations, and systems.* For example, if a team is in place and has a process for accomplishing its goals, then recognize it as such on the organization chart. Over time the organization and its practices mirror a structure and tasks that are focused on what the business considers important.

6. *Taking a page out of the quality gurus, sales management measured, monitored, inspected, and then adjusted the game plan in response to problems that surfaced as the organization moved from one stage to another.* The au-

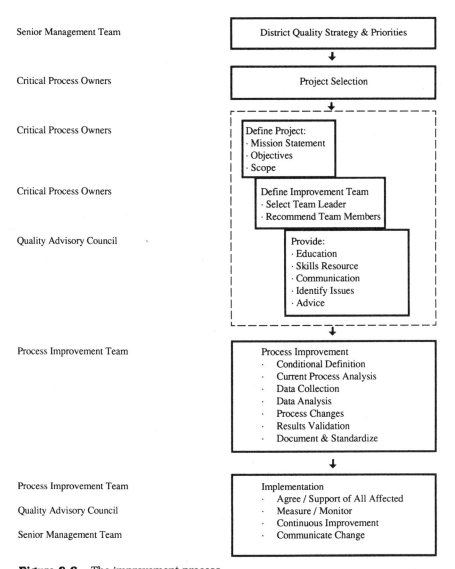

Figure 8-6. The improvement process.

thors argue that "the purpose of change is to create an asset that did not exist before—a learning organization capable of adapting to a changing competitive environment."

Their survey of general managers also turned up some other lessons. One was that effective executives created a need for change by setting very high levels of expectations and accountability. That tactic forces individuals to find better ways to get their jobs done without senior management having to articulate what methods to use. They also discovered that successful business unit organizations then proliferated around the enterprise. The most effective general managers early identified with organizations with the greatest likelihood of success in transforming or achieving new results; then they offered support and resources to speed them along. Finally, new career paths were created that fostered and rewarded leadership in transformation, not in simply managing for efficiencies. "Corporate renewal depends as much on developing effective change leaders as it does on developing effective organizations." They conclude that:

- a process focus was crucial.
- organizations change best on a unit-by-unit basis.
- programs do not cause significant change.
- persistence over time (instead of the quick fix) leads to positive results.

That is a very different type of mindset than the average sales or marketing manager in the western world has!

9

Making Quality the Way You Do Business

The genius of good leadership is to leave behind a situation which common sense, even without the grace of genius, can deal with successfully. WALTER LIPPMANN, 1945

This chapter is intended for those who have started to implement quality management principles and are beginning to move beyond Stage 2, and are for the most part in Stage 3 development. Process reeingineering, weaving Baldrige assessments into the fabric of the business, and dangers to avoid are some of the major topics discussed.

After the wild enthusiasm of the first year of discovering quality is over, after the Deming videotapes have been misplaced, and after the realization that changing your culture is an uncomfortable job, comes years of hard work. It is no surprise, therefore, that Deming's message so strongly emphasizes the gospel of "constancy of purpose" because so many firms start and never carry through their transformation. It is also no wonder that from time to time, leading business journals carry articles saying that Baldrige is flawed, that the quality movement is getting a bad name, that there are too many people doing quality for the sake of quality, not to improve the business.

The biggest problem today is that many people are in the process of reengineering their businesses and have yet to see results. A common error on the part of management is to let people work on processes for the sake of processes without demanding results. A second fundamental problem evident in almost every organization is that quality has been assigned to a quality staff, not to the people who really do the work in the enterprise. Many managers still have short-term views of the world, when in fact quality is a process that takes years, which is difficult for American and European executives to accept. In large organizations there is also the problem of bureaucracy, which focuses on improvements important to the enterprise but of little or no relevance to the customer.

The fix is obvious: keep the faith until quality has led you to more sales and profits, then you will not back off; pay attention to interim and long-term results of any process reengineering work; and do not do anything that ultimately is of no value to your stakeholders, be they customers, employees becoming effective, or stockholders.

Process Reengineering

A great deal has been said about processes in this book, and there are now hundreds of volumes published on how to design and implement them. What I intend to do here is simply offer a strategy for implementing processes appropriate to sales and marketing in the most general terms. My underlying approach is to do processes quickly and get results early. That may seem obvious; however, the reality is that depending on which stage you are in, quick implementation may not be possible. Stage 1 companies have, as a fundamental objective, to introduce concepts of quality and to defend the need for change.

Beginning in Stage 1 and continuing through Stage 2, companies must expose employees to the concept of process management, teach them how to reengineer processes, and persuade them to adopt permanently a new set of values and working principles. Therefore, the conclusion usually reached is, "Let's expose them to process reengineering, regardless of results, so that they can learn what it's all about." A shotgun approach is taken so that employees can get their proverbial feet wet. Initially this strategy works well but sometime in Stage 2, employees want to see results or they lose faith in the transformation.

Management, now worried, but also concerned about how much time teams are spending in education and in process reengineering, and also impatient for results, correctly concludes that it's time to change tactics. Now they set priorities on processes in need of reengineering, focusing resources only on these, and expecting results. Their ability to set priorities on what needs to be reengineered is a result of experiences gained in Stage 1 shotgun approaches. They are now in the market for all the techniques that consultants and authors recommend to implement new processes.

At this stage you can see approaches becoming more realistic, deployment more effective, and results more apparent. This is the stage when the disciplines discussed by quality gurus concerning how tasks and processes should be managed come into play as relevant and necessary. At this time other kinds of lessons documented by business professors and consultants also offer insight.

Apply Short-Term Tactics

While fundamental transformations of organizations take time and patience, that does not mean tactical means should not be applied. Thousands of little improvements are needed. Approaching the selection of processes to be worked on as small results-driven projects makes very good sense. This calls for management either to select, or have employees choose, functions of the business that can be assigned specific, short-term goals for improvement. Then they apply quality reengineering techniques.

For example, asking an administration manager to restructure the order entry process to cut in half the time it takes to book an order, and to accomplish this in the next 60 days, is specific and focused. A team can learn whatever skills it needs to accomplish the task, knows when it has achieved it, and experiences success early, not a year or two later. Doing this many times empowers employees, incrementally driving confidence up since many little reinforcing successes are achieved, and generating results that make sense to the organization.

Think of this approach as just-in-time quality improvement. Whatever needs to be improved the most gets worked on first, with tools and resources applied in exchange for specific results. As a little victory occurs, treat it as an empirical exercise by learning what worked or did not, then apply the lessons to the next process reengineering. That approach also leads to continuous learning on the part of individuals and the organization at large, and always with some rewards and results earlier rather than later.

Focus on Specifics

By making sure that the quality movement in your organization is tied to a business plan, it becomes easier to select the processes to work on first and to know what to expect of them. One company, for instance, found that it took weeks, sometimes months, to negotiate a price on its products. Using such a tactical approach, it documented the existing process in two days, identified what caused the delays, then quickly set about designing a new approach that gave it pricing turnaround of a few hours. The initial result accomplished that but also led to additional areas that could be improved upon. Some of these were later improved while others were ignored simply because there were other, higher-priority items to upgrade. One of these was the merger of telemarketing, fee education programs, and outward direct selling into a new process.

Teams learn to expect short-term results. Many short-term accomplishments do add up to long-term significant improvements. You can boil the ocean; just do it in teacups. After a while many people boil water for tea, and then you have an organization boiling the equivalent of an ocean.

Process improvement or process reengineering methodologies—and every organization seems to have its own 5-step, 7-step, or 10-step approach—should include establishing early exactly what is to be accomplished and what results to expect. That forces fluff out of the process quickly. Education is focused on matters important to a specific team, processes are broken down into manageable pieces, and incremental benefits are earned. This approach works particularly well in sales organizations. Because of the short-term nature of the goals set, it is compatible with sales management's sense of urgency to accomplish things this quarter. Results seem achievable and require less of a leap of faith in quality, particularly in Stages 1 and 2; later, experience will have reinforced the notion that continuous improvement approaches are worth the time they take.

I particularly like the sense of urgency that is fostered in quality projects; it is an atmosphere that generations of marketing and sales managers have found drives business volumes. Trying to find this week a measure of customer satisfaction for a particular process that can be implemented next week, for instance, appeals more to salespeople than developing an umbrella customer-satisfaction process that will be ready a year from now.

Employees are validating that a particular approach will work by testing it first. For instance, many firms train one or two people on a process before they train the whole team, or they apply the technique for a minor issue before imposing it on an important process. Small approaches, carried out in a disciplined manner, do not require huge investments of people and tools; a little team can always find time to nail a problem or define a new way.

How to Apply Reengineering to Customer Satisfaction

A quick example of an actual customer survey process illustrates putting a short-term perspective on reengineering by using a more urgent approach, while still respecting the long-term commitment to quality improvement.

You can create a simple statement that names the process owner and defines an objective (e.g., "using a written survey, gain timely feedback from customers which will help sales personnel better understand how to delight their customer").

Next, you document the existing process as a sequence of repeatable steps. Then you compare the current activities against the stated objective. Wherever an action occurs inconsistent with the objective, it is marked for change. All is documented, including anticipated benefits. If bold goals are assigned in the beginning of the process, you may cause the entire customer satisfaction approach to change radically, but at least for good reason.

Documentation can be simple, like a flowchart of the dozen or so steps typically found in any customer feedback process. Particularly effective is listing problems with the current process. In our case, these included untimely surveys, lack of acknowledgment and feedback to both customers and sales personnel, incomplete surveys, and sometimes surveys completed by the wrong person. The current approach lacked flexibility and was poorly understood.

In this specific case, the replacement process essentially eliminated the national survey approach, substituting another in which the local sales team could trigger a survey to customers of their choice and with questions of their own making. That made the data timely, relevant, and actionable. Because the format was kept similar to that of national surveys, comparison with companywide feedback became possible.

In this customer feedback process, there were many anticipated benefits (expected because of the approach):

- improved return rates
- local account control
- surveys going to the correct customer
- more flexibility

- acknowledgment of customer participation
- actionable data in terms relevant to the local sales office

The approach, once deployed, had a positive effect on customer satisfaction because the sales force knew better how to service customers.

This particular exercise was done in a couple of meetings, followed by a three-month implementation period. The in-process measurements included percent of target customers surveyed by period (objective of 100 percent), return rate within 30 days (objective was 100 percent within one year), monthly reports, and total percent return rate of surveys mailed as a rolling total generated monthly.

The business strategy supported by this simple process was to gain ongoing customer feedback, which leads to identification of actions that would please customers immediately and in the long term, while increasing the focus on customers who rated their supplier merely satisfactory or neutral. Since we know loyal customers are less expensive to sell to, going after satisfied and neutral ones became possible and a lot less expensive than wasting time on those who were very upset.

As a by-product of the effort, sales personnel had to think through who should be surveyed and when. Some conclusions they reached on when included:

- after major competitive activity
- after a major win or sale
- before the fall planning cycle
- to coincide with national surveys
- within a year of the last survey

This is a basic "blocking and tackling" approach to process reengineering. The one previous investment made was several days of training a year earlier in quality and process redesign for all team members. Guided by two experts in process reengineering (both with sales backgrounds), the team made the process of redesigning go quickly.

Weaving the Baldrige Management System into Yours

Ultimately your transformation into a TQM sales and marketing organization will depend on having a way to weave the kinds of values and concerns raised in this book into the daily lives of all concerned. What you measure and how you reward, after all is said and done, will do more to drive the entire organization in one direction than anything else. Using a model of ideal behavior for the organization, then applying measures and inspections against that, for example, is a practical way of moving forward.

Since I have used the Baldrige model throughout this book, the process can be illustrated with it. However, there is nothing to prevent you from developing a variation of that model suitable to your firm. Many companies do that so that they wind up with a structure written in their language but very similar to the generic Baldrige model. But what you do afterward can be similar to the Baldrige approach.

Have clear objectives of why and how you want to use your management model. These normally should include:

- weaving quality practices and values into the fabric of the business.

- developing a management process based on the model's criteria.

- causing continuous evaluation of progress in fulfilling your vision, strategies, and quality objectives.

This approach moves you away from reaction to a focus that prevents problems through planning and forces closer coordination of the various parts of the business.

Assign management owners to each Baldrige chapter, or function. Take the most senior managers of your enterprise and assign each to at least one year's monitoring of a chapter. Their role for that year or more would be to look at the organization constantly through the lens of their topic and then to report problems, improvements, and suggestions. Specifically their responsibilities would be to:

- inspect performance and advise on how to improve.

- advise and support peer organizations within the firm (e.g., other sales districts, divisions).

- perform an annual assessment with other chapter counterparts.

- report results of that assessment to the entire sales organization.

- become experts on their subjects by dint of working on them in their organizations, by attending seminars and reading, and by benchmarking.

Each of these chapter or topic owners should form a miniteam to help them track and respond all year long, and each should be able to train and support a replacement should he or she move on.

By making the senior managers of the sales organization the chapter owners, you have collected into one group those who have sufficient power to modify measurement systems to conform to the requirements of their chapter and who have the capability to reward or punish. So ownership should not be delegated to lower staff; only the data-gathering activities associated with the responsibility should be delegated.

Define a simple process for the flow of activities that occur during the course of a year. A simple flowchart would do the trick. More important is deciding what gets done.

For example, one sales organization that I am familiar with determined that each fall it would write a formal self-assessment along the Baldrige lines. Therefore, it appointed next year's chapter owners in the summer, conducted its first written assessment in the fall, and reported conclusions to senior management and to the entire sales organization in December. Then once a month over the next seven months, a chapter owner would present a detailed analysis of his or her topic at the monthly senior staff meeting. These discussions included analysis of problems, anticipation of future changes, processes that needed improvements, and ultimately what such changes would mean to future assessments. Each chapter owner was required to develop a Baldrige forecast that said, "If we do such and such, our Baldrige assessment next year would go up by so many points." By spring, the organization was able to forecast next year's Baldrige assessment in points much as sales management forecasts business, based on the probability of certain changes or recommendations taking place. Those approved for action were then tracked just like a sales lead until they were completed.

The miniteams assigned to each chapter meanwhile began gathering data all year long for the next assessment, while tracking trends over multiple years. By the time of the second assessment, the actual annual writing event was relatively easy in comparison to the first year because the data was there, the teams understood the issues, and they were linked to each other through the ongoing dialogue of the previous year. This approach alone can buy you hundreds of Baldrige points over a period of two or three years.

Have your chapter owners network with other chapter owners in your enterprise or in other companies. If you are part of a large corporation this process may be forced on you by necessity. For instance, if a number of sales districts each followed the process described above, and the vice president of sales was also preparing an annual self-assessment, all the customer feedback owners would be comparing notes and then feeding observations up to whoever was watching that chapter for the vice president. Thus they would be learning from each other and getting ideas about how to improve the enterprise at the district and national levels.

The same can be done by finding similar counterparts in other companies. What a wonderful way to get closer to some of your better-run customer enterprises!

Once you have this initial chapter owner process up and running, you can then move to a second phase in which a set of "top sheet" measurements can be implemented along the lines described throughout this book. Each chapter owner can monthly or quarterly report to all the one or few measurements most relevant to their topic, just as financial data is presented.

Baldrige Certification Process

Finally you can move to the third phase becoming evident in Stage 3, 4, and 5 companies—certification of a sales organization. Such a process would allow a company to measure and compare one sales office or sales district to another in Baldrige terms. This approach is more important in large organizations that have multiple sales offices or districts. There is no evidence available yet to establish if the approach would work at the individual or marketing manager level.

The typical objectives for a certification process include:

- establishing minimum actions and activities that an organization must take (defined in Baldrige terms).
- tying local and national goals and activities together.
- providing a vehicle for recognizing and rewarding approved behavior.

Minimum expectations by chapter can be set nationally and, when met, can result in, for example, more budget dollars invested in certified organizations for education and business expansion. Let us illustrate an example using customer satisfaction. You do national surveys and conclude that next year you want every certified sales district to have customers, on average, happy with you 91 percent of the time. Organizations that meet or exceed that percent would obtain *x* number of points toward the following year's certification; if they missed, they would receive fewer or no points in this category. You can do this for all chapters, add them up, and if an organization is not at a minimum, it receives no certification. Each year the bar can be raised. So, for example, if in year one minimum certification is 400 points, the next year it could be 450, the following year 500, and so forth. Your highest point earners serve as the benchmarks of "best of breed," telling you how fast you can increase the points each year.

Certification should first begin with the senior manager of the sales organization. Just as the first chapter of Baldrige calls for transformation to a quality-driven organization to begin with the personal leadership of the local executive, so too should the certification process. Only when that individual is personally performing well in Baldrige terms can the rest of the enterprise be expected to follow suit. Using the issues listed under Baldrige Chapter One (leadership) in Appendix A, you can quickly draw up the criteria of expected behavior of your sales leaders.

Have the sales executive do an annual self-assessment followed by an outside audit of the assessment. Using the same process that accountants in companies employ, have the executive or manager subject to certification prepare a self-assessment (the Baldrige assessment of their organization) and submit it to whoever does the certification (probably the vice president of sales or president of the company). That senior executive then must have the assessment audited to validate its contents and to make observations about how to improve processes. That assessment can be done by peer managers from other parts of the organization or by Baldrige-trained examiners.

Broaden what you measure to determine success. As you move toward a process of certification, traditional measurements of success (such as revenue generation, growth in market share, and so forth) become only parts of a large mosaic of measurements, rather than the most critical ones. Ultimately, you end up with a Baldrige-like score that is a statement of how the entire sales organization functioned as a team and focused on customers, within the context of the seven major Baldrige categories. Many types of success are required in order to meet minimum goals, ranging from skills development to improved billing and telephone handling, to growth in revenue and customer satisfaction.

But what about the commonly raised objection that people would take their eye off the revenue ball? That focus on revenue would be diluted? In fact, what happens is that a large number of activities that experience dictates do generate revenue is forced on the organization: improved efficiencies, doing what customers want, improving customer satisfaction, driving your costs down, doing things better and faster—all things you and I know ultimately improve revenue and market share. The firms surveyed in Chapter 2 that grew revenue, profits, and market share would argue that Baldrige quality-related activities all were the revenue drivers, not just good sales calls or cheap pricing

Some Concluding Advice

To a large extent everything talked about in this book represents common sense and longstanding good business practice. For instance, focusing first on customers made IBM successful in the 1920s. Focusing on fact-based management—by collecting data and improving incrementally—could be seen at Ford Motors in the 1940s. Focusing on services and support has been the hallmark of any company that has operated for many decades.

William B. Given, president of a shoe company, in his book, *Bottoms-Up Management*, argued the case for delegating authority down through the ranks to those closest to problems and customers. He argued that people were central to the business and that what each did should be practical and effective. "Experience has demonstrated that the combined judgment, initiative, enterprise and creativeness of a business organization produce a better end-result in terms of progress and profits than does the autocratic administration of a single individual." One other fact you should know: he published his book in 1949! What is new is that methods employed in the past are more articulated today.

If yours is a service company, customer focus is probably quite high although your methods of servicing them are too labor-intensive. The challenge is to improve all the backroom activities that support sales. If your firm is a manufacturer, the challenge is to become more of a service company and to shorten lines of communication and coordination among sales, manufacturing, distribution, and design.

Five Barriers to Overcome

Transformation of companies by revitalizing organizations, energizing employees, and continuously improving before competition gets ahead, is hard work and many will resist it. There is growing evidence documenting barriers to success that you should be aware of as you move to effective service management.

1. *Excellent service and effective processes are often blocked, if not destroyed, by outmoded organizational structures.* That is why reorganization was selected as an early project to work on in Chapter 3.

2. *Internal regulations, outmoded computer systems, and ineffective processes always prevent employees from doing what their instincts tell them to: to serve customers better.* Your infrastructure has to change; you cannot just educate and empower employees. That is why Chapters 2, 3, and 6 focused on internal issues.

3. *How sales management treats employees reflects how employees treat customers.* Management needs to be part of the change process, being close to customers, and treating their staffs with the same respect and enthusiasm they do customers. Ford, Disney, Xerox, Motorola, and almost any Japanese company you can think of, all believe this

point. That is why we spent time discussing personnel and processes in Chapters 1, 4, and 5.

4. *Poorly defined strategies, weak visions, and bad communication all combine to confuse decision making and focus throughout the enterprise.* Service levels have to be easily understood, clearly measured, and focused to avoid chaos and frustration. That largely is why so many companies concentrate on vision and leadership as key roles for management, and let the management of activities move to employees within the context of structured processes. That is why we focused on strategies in Chapters 2, 3, and 4.

5. *The inability of an organization to take good quality practices (such as statistical analysis), and make decisions based on facts with courage and vision acted upon, is a fifth barrier to success.* In fact, it may be a greater problem than the first four. Poor management will always stop an organization dead in its tracks.

As you think about how to apply the concepts described in this book, remember that these five barriers never quite go away, but their effect can be mitigated. The bottom line on all that you do is to get your sales and marketing organizations to lead with continuously improving quality and services, not just with price and availability.

References

Beer, Michael, Eisenstat, Russell A., and Spector, Bert. "Why Change Programs Don't Produce Change," *Harvard Business Review* (November–December 1990): pp. 158–166 (Reprint No. 90601).

Champy, James A. "Mission: Critical," *CIO*, Vol. 6, No. 15 (January 1992): p. 18.

Davis, Stan, and Davidson, Bill. *2020 Vision: Transform Your Business Today to Succeed in Tomorrow's Economy.* New York: Simon and Schuster, 1991.

Given, William B., Jr. *Bottoms-Up Management: People Working Together.* New York: Harper and Brothers, 1949.

Hammer, Michael. "Reengineering Work: Don't Automate, Obliterate," *Harvard Business Review* (July–August 1990): pp. 104–112.

Schaffer, Robert H., and Thomson, Harvey A. "Successful Change Programs Begin with Results," *Harvard Business Review* (January–February 1992): pp. 80–89 (Reprint No. 92108).

10

And if You Remember Nothing Else

Those of you who have read this book to this page I congratulate, because you are exhibiting one fundamental characteristic of a quality-oriented manager: you are willing to invest time in learning more about your trade. To those of you who read this chapter first, I know you are busy and want to get my silver bullets quickly. So what does the whole quality movement boil down to? What does it say to management in sales and marketing?

If you remember nothing else, just do the following and you will participate fully in the profound reengineering going on in businesses around the world.

Think of all activities as clusters of tasks called processes. Measure and understand how they work, especially as you improve them. Focus on customer and employee satisfaction as if you were a religious fanatic (see Figure 10-1). Because you are closest to customers, you must represent their interests, like a good defense lawyer, within your enterprise. That means more than anyone else, you must be the champion of disciplined quality performance.

Next, my five most critical things to work on in applying your zeal for customers and employees are:

- customer satisfaction and feedback.
- customer and employee complaints.
- employee feedback and suggestions.

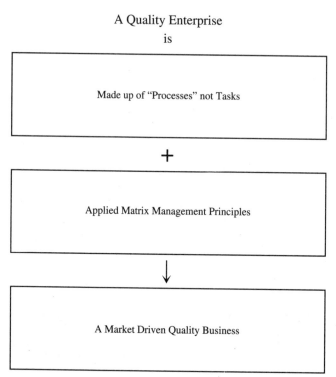

Figure 10-1. The quality formula in brief.

- compensation, rewards, and performance evaluations.
- benchmarking.

Work on these five in an environment in which there is forgiveness for errors, where all employees learn new skills and experiment with new ways, and in which customers can get to you easily. What needs to get done will then become obvious. What does get done then should dictate the structure of your organization. In exchange, you will perform, grow market share and sales, and gain repeat customers. It really works!

Malcolm Baldrige National Quality Award

The Baldrige Award promotes "awareness of quality as an increasingly important element in competitiveness, understanding of the requirements for quality excellence, and sharing of information on successful quality strategies and the benefits derived from implementation of these strategies." Awards are given in three categories: manufacturing companies, service companies, and small businesses. Nominations are by the companies themselves submitting an application. Finalists are also judged on site visits to confirm the contents of the nominations. Award criteria purposes are "to help elevate quality standards and expectations; to facilitate communication and sharing among and within organizations of all types based upon common understanding of key quality requirements; and to serve as a working tool for planning, training, assessment, and other uses."

The award has as its core values and concepts:

- customer-driven quality
- leadership
- continuous improvement
- full participation
- fast response
- design quality and prevention

- long-range outlook
- management by fact
- partnership development
- public responsibility

The seven categories (think of them as chapters) share common themes. The criteria are designed to produce results ranging from customer satisfaction to cycle time reduction to increased market share, and to contributions to national and community well-being. Trends, current levels, benchmarks, and evaluations are important. The criteria avoid prescriptions in the belief that each organization has to travel a different path to quality improvements. Processes must be linked to results; successes by accident do not carry weight in this assessment. It calls for a diagnostic system in any organization that focuses first on requirements (e.g., those of a customer) and on those factors that should be employed to assess strengths and areas for improvement across an enterprise. The criteria are intended to be comprehensive, covering all departments, divisions, organizations, processes, and work units.

Feedback and learning based on experience defined by facts provide a closed loop of continuous improvement. "These cycles of learning, adaptation, and improvement are explicit and implicit in every part of the Criteria." They have stages: planning, design of processes, selection of indicators, and their deployment; their execution; assessment of results and progress; revisions to take into account progress, learning, and new information gained in the cycle. Finally the criteria emphasize cycles of improvement to occur at all levels and across all parts of the organization. Overall aims and purposes have to be consistent so that nobody is working at cross-purposes.

The Baldrige approach places emphasis on "incremental and breakthrough improvements" with concentration more on what needs to be enhanced. Financial performance is crucial via results that lead to superior market performance, lower operating costs due to process improvements and better use of assets, and "support for business strategy development" and decisions. Invention, innovation, and creativity are recognized as "important aspects of delivering ever-improving value to customers and maximizing productivity." The seven chapters, or categories, are:

1. *Leadership.* This category focuses on the role senior executives play personally "in creating and sustaining a customer focus and clear visible quality values."

2. *Information and analysis.*   This category focuses on the "scope, validity, analysis, management, and use" of information to improve quality and competitiveness.

3. *Strategic quality planning.*   This category focuses on a company's planning process and "how all key quality requirements are integrated into overall business planning."

4. *Human resources development and management.*   This category focuses on how the firm realizes the full potential of its employees in the pursuit of the organization's quality and performance objectives.

5. *Management of process quality.*   This category focuses on the "systematic processes" used to seek ever higher quality and performance.

6. *Quality and operational results.*   This category focuses on quality levels, improvement trends in quality, operations, and suppliers.

7. *Customer focus and satisfaction.*   This category focuses on a company's relationship with customers, knowledge of their requirements, and factors determining marketplace competitiveness. Emphasis is on results.

In each chapter assessments are done on approach taken, deployment, and results achieved. Many companies do internal self-assessments each year using these criteria without necessarily submitting a nomination for the award, because the process is a useful way of taking a snapshot of internal operations. At IBM, for example, there is a Market Driven Quality (MDQ) self-assessment process in which all major business units write an annual assessment that looks much like a Baldrige nomination. The company recognizes outstanding results by presenting three classes of awards to business units when they achieve certain levels of performance as measured by the Baldrige point system. The chapters have fixed point values which are summarized in Table A-1.

Table A-1. Baldrige Award Criteria

1993 Examination Categories/Items		Point Values
1.0	Leadership		95
1.1	Senior Executive Leadership	45	
1.2	Management for Quality	25	
1.3	Public Responsibility and Corporate Citizenship	25	
2.0	Information and Analysis		75
2.1	Scope and Management of Quality and Performance Data and Information	15	
2.2	Competitive Comparisons and Benchmarking	20	
2.3	Analysis and Uses of Company-Level Data	40	
3.0	Strategic Quality Planning		60
3.1	Strategic Quality and Company Performance Planning Process	35	
3.2	Quality and Performance Plans	25	
4.0	Human Resource Development and Management		150
4.1	Human Resource Planning and Management	20	
4.2	Employee Involvement	40	
4.3	Employee Education and Training	40	
4.4	Employee Performance and Recognition	25	
4.5	Employee Well-Being and Satisfaction	25	
5.0	Management of Process Quality		140
5.1	Design and Introduction of Quality Products and Services	40	
5.2	Process Management: Product and Service Production and Delivery Processes	35	
5.3	Process Management: Business Processes and Support Services	30	
5.4	Supplier Quality	20	
5.5	Quality Assessment	15	
6.0	Quality and Operational Results		180
6.1	Product and Service Quality Results	70	
6.2	Company Operational Results	50	
6.3	Business Process and Support Service Results	25	
6.4	Supplier Quality Results	35	
7.0	Customer Focus and Satisfaction		300
7.1	Customer Expectations: Current and Future	35	
7.2	Customer Relationship Management	65	
7.3	Commitment to Customers	15	
7.4	Customer Satisfaction Determination	30	
7.5	Customer Satisfaction Results	85	
7.6	Customer Satisfaction Comparison	70	
	Total Points		1000

How to Do
Benchmarking

Benchmarking is a method for finding how to improve processes quickly by learning from others dealing with similar issues. It is a critical tactic used by organizations interested in continuous improvement. It involves sharing ideas and descriptions of processes. Benchmarking is done between organizations within an enterprise, and also between firms. The latter approach frequently is the most productive since no two firms seem to approach processes quite the same way. David T. Kearns, former CEO at Xerox, called benchmarking "the continuous process of measuring products, services and practices against the toughest competitors or those companies recognized as industry leaders." His is a good definition, coming from an individual who has spent his whole life in sales and marketing. IBM's formal definition is "the continuous process of analyzing the best practices in the world for the purpose of establishing and validating process goals and objectives leading to world-class levels of achievement."

Either definition, however, leads to some clear objectives. It allows you to set process improvement goals that exceed those of the best as measured quantitatively. Such an approach increases your confidence that the best approach is continuously being developed and shared across the enterprise. Another appropriate goal is to ensure that benchmarking becomes part and parcel of all management systems. These are goals widely shared. Today nearly half the Fortune 500 companies do benchmarking, with Xerox the acknowledged leader today in its methodologies.

In addition to using the approach to see how your processes are doing compared to those of acknowledged leaders, you can benchmark for other purposes. Benchmarking lends itself to objective assessments of the strengths and weaknesses of existing processes. It stimulates thinking and acceptance of new ideas and approaches. Benchmarking frequently helps justify changes either in quantitative or qualitative ways, even pushing aside internal resistance to change by legitimizing new ideas.

In its simplest form, benchmarking is not a difficult process. First you define the process to be benchmarked. You measure how you are doing it today, documenting the process. Then select benchmark partners who also have documented a similar process and you compare notes, once or on a regular basis over time. Discussions center around how to improve each other's processes and share what you are learning, and then on experimenting with improvements. Assessments are fact-based and rely on measurable results. Findings become the basis for changes in your process as you continuously improve its effectiveness. This is time-consuming, so most firms pick the most critical processes for benchmarking.

Benchmarking can be as simple as reading an article about a process and comparing it to your own. Another approach is to hire a consultant to conduct the benchmarking activity. Often the process owners of two or more organizations will personally lead the benchmarking activities, complete with joint meetings, site visits, and sharing of process documentation. Benchmarking can be done with peer organizations within your company (e.g., how one sales district does against another). Comparing common processes across multiple firms in different industries is useful (e.g., how customer feedback is handled in insurance versus industrial manufacturers). A third approach is to compare your performance against competitors, which is absolutely critical anyway to all marketing and sales operations.

Experience suggests some basic rules for effective benchmarking.

1. Train people in the process of benchmarking to ensure effectiveness.

2. Make sure company secrets that could damage your firm are not at risk.

3. Coordinate benchmarking with other parts of your enterprise so you avoid two or more groups benchmarking on the same process (a real problem in large organizations enthusiastic about the application of TQM principles).

4. Share benchmarking results widely within your enterprise for the same reasons as in item 3.

5. Document all benchmarking results in detail so that processes can be improved and lessons learned along the way are not lost.

From a tactical point of view workable approaches include setting up an internal clearinghouse or benchmarking competency team, designating benchmarking coordinators in each organization (e.g., in each sales district or branch office), establishing focal points for dealing with outside companies, and developing a process for documenting and communicating benchmarking activities. At IBM, for example, there is an electronic bulletin board with a data base of such projects. Benchmarking education becomes a real necessity once an organization has gone down the TQM path for a year or more and is deeply involved in process reengineering, so offer it to employees as needed. The best practice is to look at benchmarking as a process in itself too, subject to continuous improvement. Figure B-1 is a model of the process used at IBM, but which also incorporates the approach taken at both Xerox and at AT&T.

Since the primary purpose of benchmarking is to accelerate the process of improving business practices, it can be employed early in the development of a new process to get ideas on which way to go before investing a lot of time reinventing the wheel, or in the worst case, just slightly improving existing practices. Looking at other processes early definitely gets your teams thinking in bolder, more effective terms because there is always somebody who has developed a process far better than yours. The fastest way to get these ideas is to go to the American Productivity and Quality Center (APQC), which has been building a data base for benchmarking for many years. If you are a member of their organization, they will do research on how other people do a process and get you articles, names, and telephone numbers. They work fast and are effective. Process teams find them very useful. Their address:

American Productivity and Quality Center
123 N. Post Oak Lane, Suite 300
Houston, TX 77024-7797
Telephone 800-324-4673; fax 713-681-5321

The APQC is one of the best things to come along to help those wanting to do process reengineering. They will tell you that over half of the Fortune 500 companies do benchmarking, including many of your competitors. They also can show you that companies that routinely benchmark have more profitable performance—on average, a third better than those who do not.

By benchmarking you learn who does billing most effectively (American Express), has the best product pricing practices (IBM), management practices (Xerox), and so forth. APQC has a particular expertise in competitive benchmarking since many of their requests concern marketing issues and involve processes such as market research, customer satisfaction measurements, complaints, mystery shopping, and product positioning.

Good benchmarking practices follow classical process reengineering stratagems of plan, do, check, and act by planning studies, collecting data, analyzing it, and then adopting improvements on a continuous basis.

Benchmarking, while effective with all processes, tends to be best when applied to key business processes, areas causing customer dissatisfaction, applications subject to rapid changes in technology, areas

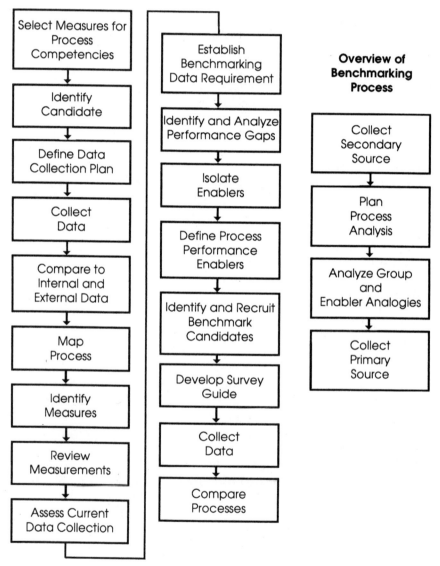

Figure B-1. The benchmarking process.

causing employee dissatisfaction, and of course, for the sake of efficiency, with processes that cost more than the benefits they generate.

The common benefits currently being achieved by benchmarking are based on surveys done on those who have applied this approach. Benchmarking:

- leads to stretching objectives.

- makes goals realistic and actionable.

- encourages pursuit of excellence and breakthrough thinking.

- forces study of competition and other firms.

- focuses attention on customer needs.

- represents one of the most effective ways to energize process teams.

- illustrates the need for change and how to achieve it in manageable and precise terms.

Benchmarking is in itself a process to be learned, not a single event or a tool. Continuous benchmarking is built into good process management.

For additional details on benchmarking, see Robert C. Camp, *Benchmarking: The Search for Industry Best Practices that Lead to Superior Performance* (Milwaukee: ASQC Quality Press, 1989).

Since Appendix A concerned the Baldrige criteria, it should be noted that benchmarking is specifically mentioned in criteria 2.0 (Information and Analysis), 3.0 (Strategic Quality Planning), 5.0 (Quality Assurance of Products and Services), and 6.0 (Quality Results).

Appendix C

How to Learn More About Quality

The purpose of this appendix is to provide tips on how to learn more about the topics discussed in this book. The field of quality is growing. Books, seminars, and knowledge about processes are in themselves a growth industry. Have you checked your junk mail lately? Everyone is offering seminars, tapes, and yes, even books!

For Those New to Quality

For those honest enough to admit they have everything yet to learn, I would begin by reading one or two general books on the topic, then follow up by attending one or more conferences. There is nothing like attending a conference in which people who make more money and are more successful than you, are preaching the gospel of quality to get you fired up!

Quality or Else, by Lloyd Dobyns and Clare Crawford-Mason (Boston: Houghton Mifflin, 1991), is an excellent introduction that addresses the changing nature of the world economy, the quality movement, and its basic tenets. It has lots of war stories and is easy to read. Follow that book with Carl Sewell's *Customers for Life* (New York: Doubleday, 1990). In this book you see quality practiced in a marketing and sales environment. Once you have read those two books, the short bibliographies at the end of each chapter of this book list other useful materials. These have been carefully selected to reflect the interests of sales management, not manufacturing or engineering. The most useful introduction to process reengineering is *Business Process Improvement* by H. James Harrington (New York: McGraw-Hill, 1991).

I would invest in membership in the American Society for Quality Control (ASQC). This used to be just for engineering and manufacturing people wanting to apply statistical measures, and so forth, but it has evolved into the leading organization providing literature and education on all aspects of quality, including for the service industries. They produce a monthly magazine, *Quality Progress*, that contains short case studies in easy-to-read formats, keeps you up-to-date on seminars and shows, and advertises and reviews books on quality. The address for ASQC is:

American Society for Quality Control, Inc.
611 E. Wisconsin Avenue
P.O. Box 3005
Milwaukee, WI 53201-3005
Telephone 414-272-8575

When you join ASQC, you will wind up on everyone's mailing list, so expect a lot of junk mail on quality from all quarters of the economy. At least you will learn about what is available. Both the ASQC and every other major management society in both the United States and Europe have been developing local chapters specializing in topics relevant to their membership. In the United States, for example, in every state there are local quality councils in which you can meet others interested in quality, where local managers make presentations on their work, and which hold conferences and workshops. These tend to be worthwhile.

The American Productivity and Quality Center (APQC) is another source of quality information. Like ASQC, it sells all the major books on quality and presents seminars. APQC is also the major source of benchmarking information. APQC is an association of companies and so is very focused on "how to" education and strategies. It has a wealth of information on applying quality in services and sales. You can find APCQ's address on page 222.

In addition to the seminars and publications offered by these two organizations (and today almost every other professional management association), there are other useful sources. One of my favorites is the seminars taught by community colleges aimed at the business community. So these should be checked out, along with those being offered today by just about every business school. The most outstanding examples of local education that I have seen are the courses taught by the Quality

Academy at Fox Valley Technical College in Appleton, Wisconsin. It has been offering the usual short seminars on the basics of quality and how to apply its principles, and it provides consulting. The Quality Academy has been operating for nearly a decade and therefore has a mature program. But it is not alone in such offerings; you may find equally good offerings in your area.

A recent development is the creation of consulting services by major corporations that offer to transfer their best quality practices to clients. Almost every Baldrige winner, for example, provides these kinds of services. These are valuable for specific topics in which they specialize because of the experience already gained in actually implementing the programs. So, for example, if you need help in developing a new customer satisfaction feedback process, you might go to IBM, or if you want a reservation system, to one of the major hotel chains or airlines. These pockets of real competence are developing rapidly, and you see them emerging by way of the various quality conferences and articles in *Quality Progress*. They are also tracked by the APQC.

For Those Already Familiar with Quality

If you are familiar with quality, your needs are probably very specific. Membership in ASQC is just as important, along with organizations in your industry. However, there are several books I would recommend that go beyond the basics. You should first read Christian Grönroos's *Service Management and Marketing: Managing the Moments of Truth in Service Competition* (Lexington, Mass: Lexington Books, 1990). It is a serious academic study that brings you up to date on what the business school community has learned about services during the late 1980s, and as such it is a practical reference book. Next, read Kenneth and Edward Primozic's *Strategic Choices* (New York: McGraw-Hill, 1991). This is a hands-on, no-nonsense guide to strategic marketing planning in the world of changing technologies and global competition. Its value is the linkage it offers between basic marketing principles and the realities of a more quality-focused global economy. You will find it short, to the point, and streetwise. The third book then would be Mary Walton's *The Deming Management Method* (New York: Putnam, 1986), which summarizes Deming's ideas in a short book. You will find this to be more theoretical, but if you are in a Stage 3 company, you are ready for it. Deming's own book on the subject, *Out of the Crisis* (published by MIT Press), I find impossible—it is more than 600 pages long and ponderous.

Walton can get you where you need to be very quickly. If you are at Stage 1 or 2, you may think of Deming and some of the other quality gurus as unrealistic for a sales environment; by Stage 3 you understand from experience how to translate many of their useful insights into sales and marketing realities.

You would also benefit from establishing linkages in your community and across the nation with like-minded sales managers and executives to compare notes on quality activities. In many cities, professional associations have started to form round tables and other forums to facilitate dialogue. I find most of these not very effective because they are not focused specifically on sales and marketing. Therefore, I suggest you find a dozen other peers in various local companies, all in sales and marketing, and form your own round table. Meet once a quarter for a half day either to review quality programs at each others' firms or to discuss in depth a specific issue (e.g., customer surveys, employee training, compensation, and so forth). Take turns putting the agenda together and hosting the event. These councils invariably get wonderful reviews and are easy to launch. One other suggestion: populate the council with marketing and sales management from many industries so you avoid the problem of sharing information with a competitor; you can get data on rivals in other ways.

The last suggestion is that you "pitch" quality at local and national meetings and even write on the subject, because those exercises will force you to clarify your thinking and reflect on your successes and failures. Such activities rapidly spur your education on quality.

Index

About the Author

James W. Cortada is one of IBM's leading experts in developing tactical TQM solutions for sales and marketing processes. He is currently a management consultant on market-driven quality for IBM Wisconsin, where he has created and implemented a Deming-based TQM program that serves as a model for many other IBM marketing organizations across the United States. He is the author of more than twenty books, including three on management topics. He holds a Ph.D. in history from Florida State University.